The Piano Shop on the Left Bank

The Piano Shop on the Left Bank

The hidden world of a Paris atelier

T. E. CARHART

McArthur & Company

Toronto

Published by McArthur & Company 2000

2 4 6 8 10 9 7 5 3 1

First published in Canada in 2000 by
McArthur & Company
322 King St. West/Suite 402
Toronto, On.
M5V 1J2

Canadian Cataloguing in Publication Data
Carhart, T. E. (Thad E.)
   The piano shop on the left bank
ISBN 1-55278-171-2
1. Piano—History.   I. Title.
ML650.C37 2000   786.2'19'09   C00-931316-8

ISBN 1-55278-171-2

Typeset in Bembo by SX Composing DTP, Rayleigh, Essex
Printed and bound in Great Britain by Biddles Ltd, Guildford

for Simo

ACKNOWLEDGEMENTS

Many people helped me as I wrote this book, but two were indispensable. Alberto Manguel first encouraged me to tell this story and then generously shared his ideas as I worked. Marion Abbott tirelessly reviewed my drafts, and her good sense supplied me with imaginative suggestions and saved me many times from the dangers of muddy prose. To them both go my heartfelt thanks.

I am grateful to all those who read parts of the manuscript and offered suggestions and comments, including Simo Neri, Grazia Peduzzi, Joni Beemsterboer, Norman Packard, Edith Sorel, Ronnie Scharfman, Craig Stephenson, Claire Miquel, Lorna Lyons, Ronald Chase, Judith Hooper, and Alev Croutier.

A good number of pianists, piano teachers, historians, and technicians spent time talking over with me the challenges and rewards of their chosen instrument, among them Andreas Staier, Laurent de Wilde, Peter Feuchtwanger, Masaru Tsumita, Alfred Neumark, Yoheved Kaplinsky, Jean Haury, Laurence Libin, Jimmy McKissin, Christine Laloue, Jean-Claude Battault, David Dubal, the late Daniel Magne, and the late György Sebök. While much of this material lies outside the narrative of this book, these interviews were invaluable to me in understanding the work of those whose lives revolve around the piano.

For their constant encouragement and support I'd like to thank Robert Wallace, Stéphane Jardin, Lisiane Droal, C. J. Maupin, and my parents, May and Tom Carhart. I'm also grateful to the staff of the American Library and of the *Centre de Documentation du Musée de la Musique* in Paris for helping me track down source materials.

My two editors, Rebecca Carter at Chatto & Windus in London and Courtney Hodell at Random House in New York, pooled their extraordinary talents and managed to bring forth the book that I discovered I was writing only as I worked with them. I am indebted to them both for their painstaking help and pithy advice. I'd also like to thank my agent, Bruce Westwood, and Kim McArthur of McArthur & Company for believing in this book from the outset.

I disappeared from the daily rhythm of family life so many times while writing this book that it must have seemed as if a ghost filled the role of husband and father in our house. My wife, Simo, and my children, Sara and Nicolas, were always there to remind me that I had not sunk below a far horizon, and I am forever grateful for their patience and support.

Finally, I'd like to thank all of the people who appear in this book. They are all real, but I have changed some names and a few identifying details. Please don't try to find Luc or Mathilde or any of the others; they are not waiting to be discovered. They share that peculiarly French respect for what is called *pudeur*. 'Privacy' is not an adequate translation, since the French has about it an important element of modesty and of basic decency. As a childhood friend once said to me, solemnly and without rancor, when I tried to impinge on his spaceman fantasy, 'Go find your own astronauts!' In the same spirit, let me say to the reader, 'Go find your own Luc!' Knock on doors, ask questions, be patient and Paris may yield forth some other of its inestimable pleasures.

CONTENTS

1

LUC

Along a narrow street in the Paris neighborhood where I live sits a little store front with a simple sign stencilled on the window: '*Desforges Pianos: outillage, fournitures*'. On a small, red felt-covered shelf in the window are displayed the tools and instruments of piano repair: tightening wrenches, tuning pins, piano wire, several swatches of felt and various small pieces of hardware from the innards of a piano. Behind the shelf the interior of the shop is hidden by a curtain of heavy white gauze. The entire facade has a sleepy, nineteenth-century charm about it, the window frame and the narrow door painted a dark green.

Not so many years ago when our children were in kindergarten, this shop lay along their route to school, and I passed it on foot several times on the days when it was my turn to take them to school and to pick them up. On the way to their classes in the morning there was never time to stop. The way back was another matter. After exchanging a few words with other parents, I would often take an extra ten minutes to retrace my steps, savoring the sense of promise and early morning calm that at this hour envelops Paris.

The quiet street was still out-of-the-way and narrow enough to be paved with the cobblestones that on larger avenues in the city have been covered with macadam. In the early morning a fresh stream of water invariably ran high in the gutters, the daily tide set forth by the street sweepers who, rain or shine, open special valves set into the curb and then channel the flow of jetsam with rolled-up scraps of carpet as they swish it along with green plastic brooms. The smell from *la boulangerie du coin*, the local bakery, always greeted me as I turned the corner, the essence of freshly baked bread never failing to fill me with desire and expectation. I would buy a baguette for lunch and, if I could spare ten minutes before getting to work, treat myself to a second cup of coffee at the café across the street from the piano shop.

In these moments, stopping in front of the strange little store front, I would consider the assortment of objects haphazardly displayed there. Something seemed out of place about this specialty store in our quiet *quartier*, far from the conservatories or concert halls and their related music stores that sprinkle a select few neighborhoods. Was it possible that an entire business was maintained selling piano parts and repair tools? Often a small truck was pulled up at the curb with pianos being loaded or unloaded and trundled into the shop on a handcart. Did pianos need to be brought to the shop to be repaired? Elsewhere I had always known repairs to be done on site; the bother and expense of moving pianos was prohibitive, to say nothing of the problem of storing them.

Once I saw it as a riddle, it filled the few minutes left to me on those quiet mornings when I would walk past the shop, alone and wondering. After all, this was but one more highly specialized store in a city known for its specialties and refinements. Surely there were enough pianos in Paris to sustain a trade in their parts. But still my doubt edged into curiosity; I saw myself opening the door to the shop and finding something new and unexpected each time, like a band of smugglers or an eccentric music school. And then I decided to find out for myself.

I had avoided going into the shop for many weeks for the simple reason that I did not have a piano. What pretext could I have in a piano furnisher's when I didn't even own the instrument they repaired? Should I tell them of my lifelong love of pianos, of how I hoped to play again after many vagabond years when owning a piano was as impractical as keeping a large dog or a collection of orchids? That's where I saw my opening: more settled now, I had been toying with the idea of buying a piano. What better source for suggestions as to where I might find a good used instrument than this dusty little neighborhood parts store? It was at least a plausible reason for knocking.

And so I found myself in front of Desforges one sunny morning in late April, after dropping off the children down the street. I knocked and waited; finally I tried the old wooden handle and found that the latch was not secured. As I pushed the door inwards it shook a small bell secured to the top of the jamb; a delicate chime rang out unevenly, breaking the silence as I swung the door closed behind me. Before me lay a long, narrow room, a counter running its length on one side and along the facing wall a row of shelves laden with bolts of crimson and bone-white felt. Between the counter and the shelves a cramped aisle led back through the windowless dark to a small glass door; through it a suffused light shone dimly into the front of the shop. As the bell stopped ringing and I blinked to adjust my eyes, the door at the back opened narrowly and a man appeared, taking care to move sideways around the partly opened door so that the view to the back room was blocked.

'*Entrez! Entrez, Monsieur!*' He greeted me loudly, as if he had been expecting my visit; he looked me up and down as he made his way slowly to the front of his shop. He was a squarely built older man, probably in his sixties, with a broad forehead and a massive jaw that was fixed in a wide grin; the eyes, however, did not correspond to the mouth. His regard was intense, curious and wholly without emotion. I realized that the smile was no more than his face in repose, a somewhat disquieting rictus that spoke of neither joy nor social convention. Over his white shirt and tie he was wearing a long-sleeved black smock that hung loosely to his knees and gave him a formal yet almost jaunty appearance, like an undertaker on vacation. This was clearly the *chef d'atelier*, wearing a more sober version of the deep-blue cotton smocks that are the staple of craftsmen and manual laborers throughout the country.

We shook hands, the obligatory prelude to any dealings with another human being in France, and he asked how he could be of help. I explained that I was looking to buy a used piano and wondered if he ever came across such things. A slight wrinkling of his brow suggested that my question surprised him; the smile never varied, but I thought I detected a glint in his eyes. No, he was sorry, it was not as common as one might think; of course, once in a great while there was something and if I wanted to check back no one could say that with a stroke of luck a client might not have a used piano for sale. Both disappointed and puzzled, I couldn't think of how to keep the conversation going. I thanked him for his consideration and turned to leave, casting a last glance at the ceiling-high shelves behind the counter stuffed with wooden dowels, wrenches, and coils of wire. As I pulled the door behind me he turned and headed towards the back room once again.

I returned two, perhaps three times in the next month and always the reaction was the same: a look of perplexity that I might consider his business a source of used pianos, followed by murmured assurances that if ever anything were to present itself he would be delighted to let me know. I was familiar enough with the banality of formal closure in French rhetoric to recognize this for what it was: the brush-off. Still I persisted, stopping by every few weeks out of sheer doggedness and curiosity. I was just about to give up hope when a development changed the equation, however slightly.

On this occasion, as before, my entry set off the little bell and the door at the back of the shop opened a few moments later. But instead of the black-smocked *patron* there appeared a younger man – in his late thirties, I guessed – wearing jeans and a sweat-soaked T-shirt. His face was open and smiling, and ringed by a slightly scruffy beard that gave him the look of a French architect. More surprising than the new face was the fact that he left open the door to the back room; as he walked towards me I peered over his shoulder for a glimpse of what had so long intrigued me.

The room beyond was quite long and wider than the shop, and it was swimming in light pouring down from a glass roof. It had the peculiar but magical air of being larger on the inside than the outside. This was one of the classic nineteenth-century workshops that are still to be found throughout Paris behind even the most bourgeois facades of carved stone. Very often the backs of buildings were extended to cover part of the inner courtyard and the space roofed over with panels of glass, like a giant greenhouse. I took this in at a glance and then, in the few seconds left to me as he made his way along the counter, I realized that the entire atelier was covered with pianos and their parts. Uprights, spinets, grands of all sizes: a mass of cabinetry in various tones presented itself in a confusion of lacquered black, mahogany, and rich blond marquetry.

The man gestured with his two dirty hands to excuse himself and then, as is the French custom when hands are wet or grimy, he offered his right forearm for me to shake. I grasped his arm awkwardly as he moved it up and down in a parody of a shake. I explained that I had stopped in before and was looking for a good used piano. His face broke out in a smile of what seemed like recognition. 'So you're the American whose children go to the school around the corner.'

I accepted this description equably and asked how he had known. It didn't surprise me that in the close-knit neighborhood he was aware of a foreigner who daily walked down his street even though we had never met.

'My colleague told me you had been here a few times looking to buy a piano.'

'Actually, I was asking for a suggestion as to where I might find one. I didn't, in fact, expect to find one here.'

I couldn't stop my eye from wandering over his shoulder to the gold mine in the atelier and the look in his eyes told me he noticed my puzzlement. 'Of course, we only repair other people's pianos here,' he said cryptically. At this point he paused, turned his head slightly to one side and raised his eyes slowly, as if some enormously improbable and entirely original thought had just occurred to him. He continued slowly, gazing upwards as if he were a companionable schoolmaster seeking to capture the one phrase that would make things clear to a particularly problematic student. 'Now if you were to have an introduction from someone who has done business with us, it might make it easier to find the piano you're looking for.' On this last phrase he lowered his gaze and looked me straight in the eyes.

I didn't know what the game was, but I sensed that this was not the time to ask a direct question. He had made it as clear as possible that he could not be clear, that an unguessable exchange had to be played out in this oblique and baffling way.

'Someone who has done business with you,' I repeated mechanically.

'That's right, one of our customers. There are many right here in the *quartier*,' he added.

I thanked him for his help, as if everything were now perfectly clear. As I turned to go I was presented once more with the magical image of the atelier bathed in a golden light, an El Dorado of used pianos that glowed tantalizingly at the end of a close and musty little cave of stacked felt.

I was puzzled by the odd necessity of finding a customer before I could become one and I didn't know how to go about it. I no longer believed that this out-of-the-way shop was merely what it proclaimed on its sign, a piano parts store. Fueled by the younger man's air of

6

intrigue, my curiosity took on a different aspect, as if I had been unwittingly sucked into some subterranean drug deal or obscure quest with enigmatic personalities, cryptic directions, uncertain rewards.

For the next few weeks, whenever I had dealings in the *quartier*, I made a point of asking as offhandedly as possible if anyone had done business with the piano repair shop on our street. Most often people had not even noticed it or, if they had, they had never gone in. I began to resign myself to failure, to remaining an outsider in this closed world.

One afternoon I was picking up our daughter at the house of a classmate whose parents I knew only slightly from hurried conversations at the school door. When the unfamiliar door was opened to me, the rich polyphony of an early liturgical piece for chorus, perhaps a Palestrina mass, spilled out from an interior room. From another part of the apartment I could hear the laughter of the girls at play.

The mother offered me tea and showed me into the salon where a beautiful baby grand piano immediately captured my attention. A rich walnut cabinet with clean, flowing lines showed just enough carved detail to suggest art nouveau. Its music stand bore the legend 'Pleyel', subtly worked into the wooden lacework. When my hostess returned from the kitchen with our pot of tea I pounced: 'Véronique, do you play piano?'

'Not as much as I'd like, but it has always been a part of my life.'

'And has this beautiful instrument always been a part of your life?'

'No, actually, Marc and I bought that years ago when we first moved to the *quartier*. There's a wonderful little shop near your street that is full of such treasures. They're called Desforges.'

I looked up excitedly, nearly spilling my cup of tea. Véronique looked puzzled by my broad smile. 'It's a very nice piano, don't you think? It's French, you know.'

'It's absolutely exquisite.' I then described the false starts of the past month and my awkward attempts to get into the back room of the little shop on our street.

'But of course you need an introduction. You could be anybody at all unless they know you've been referred by a client.'

'And what difference does that make?' I was still baffled, but Véronique talked as if this were the most self-evident thing imaginable.

'Well, they sell used pianos, of course. Lots and lots of them. They're very well known for that. But their main business is in parts and refurbishing, and the old man, Desforges, doesn't like to sell a used piano to someone who hasn't come recommended. He says it's more trouble than it's worth and he's got plenty of customers for the pianos that come his way.'

I understood and yet I didn't. This sounded more like a hobby than a business, a kind of retail trade for a very limited public. I was still wholly ignorant as to the mechanics of the business, but at least I had found out the essential point. And I still wanted a piano. 'Véronique, can I use your name as a reference the next time I stop by?'

'Of course, they know me well.'

The next day I hurried to the shop as soon as I had dropped off the children. No morning daydreams down the narrow street, no leisurely walk home; I felt like a character in a fairy tale who has performed the difficult task and has returned to the palace to claim his reward. I paused in front of the old green door, armed with Véronique's introduction, excited at the prospect of being welcomed into the inner sanctum.

Once again the small glass door at the rear opened slowly. This time, however, it was not swung wide but only enough to let the *patron* scoot around it before he closed it firmly. I masked my disappointment with a greeting, telling him that I had come with the introduction of a former client of his and was still interested in finding

8

a used piano. His perpetual smile firmly in place, he had the patient and patronizing tone one would use to a child more dull than naughty who had made some annoying mistake. '*Monsieur* is still looking for a used piano?'

'Yes, I was hoping that you might have come across something.'

'I am afraid that we have not had that good fortune, *Monsieur*.' As he had on each of my previous visits, he told me that they rarely had such instruments but he would keep me in mind if ever he had the good luck to come across one that was available for sale.

At this I feigned confusion, insisting that his colleague had suggested that a recommendation from a former client might facilitate matters. His expression did not change, but his eyebrows twitched furiously as he looked me straight in the eyes and asked me to wait. He then disappeared into the back room and I heard his sharp voice bark '*Luc!*' as he stood behind the door, visible to me only in profile through the glass.

There ensued a lively discussion between the two men, whose silhouettes bobbed and weaved before me like some bizarre shadow play, the leonine head of the *patron* inclining towards his younger assistant, whose arms waved wildly as he argued. For it was clear that it was an argument and, although I couldn't make out the phrases, I knew that I was the subject. This went on for two or three minutes until the assistant yelled, 'Enough! Trust me on this one!' The two shadows faced each other for a long moment, utterly motionless and silent. Then the massive head of the *patron* moved slowly away as he muttered something in his gravelly voice. There was another pause, this one briefer; the hands of the remaining figure moved up and stroked the beard, and then smoothed the head of scraggly hair as the open mouth let out a deep sigh. An instant later the door opened wide and the young man beckoned me: '*Entrez, Monsieur. Entrez.*'

I moved uncertainly from the darkness of the shop towards the brightness of the back room, unsure whether I dared to venture into this forbidden territory, but the assistant motioned me in through the narrow door. Before me were arrayed forty, perhaps fifty pianos of every make and model, and in various stages of dismantling. On my left, legless grand pianos, of which there were at least fifteen, lay in a row on their flat side, the undulating curves of their cabinets a series of receding waves. Uprights clustered on the other side of the workshop, pushed up against one another as one would store two dozen chests of drawers in a spacious attic. At the back stood a group of very old instruments, delicate little nineteenth-century square pianos with complicated marquetry worked into their cabinets. Nearby, on top of a well-organized work bench, sprawled the insides of several instruments: disassembled keyboards, hammers and dampers, pedal mechanisms.

Around the edges of the room, behind and around and even under the pianos, in every available corner, lay scattered parts and pieces that had been removed from them. The legs of the grand pianos lay alongside, an anthology of furniture styles stacked high in a pile. Music stands, pedal housings, fall boards were all similarly grouped together, each one reflecting a different era and style. The tops of the grand pianos leaned precariously against the adjacent wall, a kind of two-dimensional hillscape of sensuous curves and precious woods. Pairs of candelabra were heaped in the corner, gleams of brass and silver catching the light. Around the upper edge of the atelier ran a narrow gallery and upon this were massed more pieces still: music stands with delicate scroll work spelling 'Gaveau', benches and stools, tuning pins and strings, even a pile of old metronomes, their blunt little pyramids a mass of wooden stalagmites. And at the center of the cluttered room, partly obscured from my view, lay a clearing, a magic glade hidden in a forest. In it stood three pianos in a loose circle, polished, completely assembled and ready to be played, their keyboards open and benches drawn up.

The silence was broken by the assistant, Luc, who now introduced himself to me by name and invited me to have a look around. I explained that I was a friend of Véronique and he nodded in approval. Without a trace of irony or embarrassment he told me that all of the pianos were indeed for sale and that I was free to roam about and ask any questions I liked. Together we wandered around the room and looked at six or seven pianos. Occasionally Luc would roll back the fall board of a piano and play a few chords. The grand pianos were impressive, even when stored on their sides, but they were unplayable, like ships in dry dock that have temporarily lost the essential element that is their *raison d'être*. I saw several Steinways, a number of Pleyels, many makes I had never heard of, and even a magnificent Bechstein concert grand whose gleaming black mass of cabinetry was fully twice as long as the Gaveau baby grand alongside which it was stored.

We walked among the uprights: European makes, both well-known and obscure, American and Japanese pianos, even a nearly new Chinese instrument, almost comical in the brassy shine that glared off every square inch of its black lacquered surface, like a miniature hearse in a quirky used-car lot. I looked at Luc with what must have been an air of surprise on my face and I asked how a Chinese piano had come to his shop.

'I had to take it; it was a favor for a friend.' He paused and then added, almost apologetically, 'It's actually well made, but this one is a mediocre piano.' It was clear from his manner that being well made was only a part of the whole for this man whose passion was pianos, but what were the other elements? Their design? Materials, finish, reputation? What makes one piano good and another mediocre, even if well made? The answer hinged on more than their physical attributes, that much seemed clear, as if a piano could have a temperament of its own that draws us to it. Luc's attitude made me feel as if I were looking at pianos for the first time.

Towards the end of the row of uprights we approached a piano quite a bit larger than the others, with a strange blond cabinet worked in what looked like stripes of shiny wood grain. On its cabinet was a name in Cyrillic script, done in a streamlined chrome typeface, as if it were a car from the fifties.

'Russian?' I asked doubtfully.

'Worse: Ukrainian.' Luc's tone was doleful. 'Let's just say that they learned half the craft from the Germans and for the rest' – he trilled on an imaginary keyboard – 'they improvised.'

Throughout our tour I had eagerly anticipated a visit to the back of the room where I had spied the oldest pianos standing daintily, curious little boxes on slender legs inset with half-keyboards almost as if their potential for making music were an afterthought to their appearance as symmetrical pieces of furniture. When we reached them, I ran my hand over their cabinets. The precious woods showed deep whorls and burls, their keyboards yellowed ivory with worn edges set in a slightly uneven line. 'Paris', 'Amsterdam', 'Vienna': the gold script on their fall boards was an elaborate suite of serifs and curves, the masterful and self-assured flow of nineteenth-century handwriting.

'These are exquisite,' I said to Luc.

'Yes, they're very beautiful. The oldest was built in 1837.' He looked at them with a mix of tenderness and disdain. 'But they belong in a museum, not here. They're part of the history of the instrument; in some sense they're dead. What interests me is pianos that live.' He smiled at his own sudden enthusiasm and motioned me to the small clearing in the middle of the maze we had just negotiated. 'Now these pianos are very definitely alive.' Luc sat on the bench of a Steinway grand with its top open. He paused for a moment, immobile and pensive, then his hands descended on the keyboard and a Bach three-part invention filled the space, its delicate melodies and counterpoint enveloping and somehow expanding the sunny volume beneath the glass roof. He stopped abruptly in the middle of a trill and the notes lingered in a lasting resonance. The sharp thrill of music in the quiet workshop changed the atmosphere entirely, as if a carillon of bells had suddenly rung out in a sleepy town square. These instruments did have a kind of life and their breath was a music that still sounded in the air around us.

'This is a magnificent instrument, built in Hamburg in the twenties. It belonged to a conductor who brought it with him to Paris.' Luc rose from the keyboard and ran his hand delicately along the curved side. 'I completely rebuilt it; and now, of course, I don't want to see it go to just anyone.'

'No, of course not.' I was quick to agree because I had already forgotten what I had come for, a piano for myself. The sheer number of pianos, their beauty, the suggestiveness of their various origins had cast a spell on me; it was only a conscious effort that brought me back to the dusty atelier.

And yet there was something in Luc's attitude that told me that this was not a business like any other. He had drawn the distinction between pianos that were alive and were to be played, and those that were museum pieces. This made immediate sense in his workshop, surrounded as we were by examples of both. I sensed that he was not a sentimentalist, but I also saw an abiding respect for all these complex, ungainly, and gloriously impractical instruments, as well as a fascination with what came forth when the ones in good condition were played.

To be in a workshop where the mechanics of such witchcraft were attended to was, I realized, infinitely more exciting than to be in a dealer's showroom surrounded by fifty brand-new pianos, however great and costly they might be. I felt I was looking at the physical evidence of a demographic ebb and flow that had coursed through Europe for the better part of this century, a flux that had Paris as a point of departure, a destination, and a way station for all these people with their beloved pianos so inconveniently in tow.

I had in mind to buy a small upright that I could tuck away in a corner of our small apartment. Like most Parisians, I was concerned with the amount of floor space, 'the footprint', of any sizeable object that I introduced into our home. While our apartment was not dark and cramped like so many of the nineteenth-century spaces that make up the majority of Paris's housing – we had converted an old work-shop – the total surface area was still minuscule by American standards. I calculated that even a baby grand would require four square meters, while an upright would take less than two. But after looking at the splendor of these instruments the last thing I wanted to do was to 'tuck away' a piano. I wanted it to be visible, useful, beautiful as an object in itself, placed so it would be played daily. Practicality and reason-ableness had deserted me; perhaps thrift, too.

Luc gently interrupted my reverie by asking what I thought of the pianos and whether I saw something that might suit my needs. I blurted out that I wanted them all and he answered wryly, 'You're welcome to the whole business.' I asked the prices of some of the instruments that sat before us and immediately his manner changed: he wasn't the tough businessman moving in for the sale, but neither was he the smiling repairman he had at first seemed. This was clearly an area that concerned him deeply and he proceeded to talk about the 'value' of particular pianos with price mentioned almost as an after-thought. He shared with me his personal feel for this landscape of pianos and his evaluations were original, sometimes quirky, and fascinating. I learned much that morning about used pianos, about the market in Paris, and – not least – about Luc himself.

The French have a preference for things French: automobiles and wine, clothes and bicycles, food and movies. So, too, with pianos. This attitude had been considerably complicated in recent years by the fact that the once great French makers, Erard and Pleyel, were no longer independent companies and their new pianos were generally recognized as inferior to the very finest makes or, for that matter, to their own predecessors. So new Erards and Pleyels were not prized, but this only made their antecedents, refurbished and gleaming, all the more desirable and costly.

Steinways were felt to be very fine pianos, but they were not necessarily revered as they were outside France. Old Steinways were sought after for the quality of the craftsmanship and their renowned singing tone; Luc allowed that the biggest competition for brand-new Steinways from the fancy dealers, at least for those of means who were buying an instrument and not a bauble, was a reconditioned Steinway from the twenties and thirties, the 'Golden Age'. German-made Bechsteins, with their clear, bright attack in the upper registers, were at least equally respected by many of his customers, and Luc described Bösendorfers as 'the aristocrat of pianos'. It wasn't clear whether he considered this to be altogether a good thing, but it was a trait, with its overtones of the Vienna of Mozart and the Hapsburgs, that seemed to have a particular resonance with the French. A long tradition of fine workmanship is still accorded a special status in France.

But of all the things that I learned on that brief morning visit, there was one practical detail I would never have suspected. Because of the relatively small size of most Paris apartments, Luc said, uprights were in far greater demand than grands and they commanded a corresponding premium. This surprised me greatly. Put another way, a used grand piano – with the exception of the very top-of-the-line models whose prices were no lower than new Bechsteins or Steinways – was not likely to be snapped up the way uprights were. They could, with some questionable logic, be regarded as bargains, a new and tempting idea for me.

We talked a bit about what kind of piano I was interested in and what might be affordable. I reluctantly came back to the idea of an upright, small and unobtrusive, but in truth my eye and my mind were constantly drawn to the big pianos arrayed along the floor like enormous suitcases ready for a voyage. A niggling voice began to introduce itself into my mind – 'Why not?' – and I should have recognized then that the shape of my desires and the place of music in my life were changing rapidly. But I was still unaware of the powerful seduction conjured by this workshop. It had pulled me in. When I thought I was merely a browser delighting in the improbable number and variety of old pianos, in fact I had succumbed to a voluptuous fantasy before I could guard against it.

2

FINDING MY PIANO

Summer set in early and the sidewalks in the *quartier* came alive after hours. In a city where few apartments are air-conditioned, the terraces of cafés and restaurants become the common refuge from a withering heat in the evening. The long light of June and July encouraged those gathered at the outdoor tables to linger well into the night, while swallows threaded the air with their shrill whistles. Before the August dispersion, everyone in the neighborhood seemed to revel in the slower pace that the heat imposed.

As the weather grew warmer, I stopped by the shop several times to talk to Luc and to see what new treasures he had gathered. I had recently made a career change, leaving the corporate job that had originally brought us to Paris and setting up as an independent writer. While my hours were as long as before, my work schedule was far more flexible and I took advantage of the new arrangement to indulge myself in these brief visits. Increasingly, it felt like a good time to change my daily rhythms and to open myself again to the pleasures of music.

Even when Luc was busy and could not talk he always made me welcome and allowed me to wander around the inner sanctum of the back room on my own. When things were quieter, he seemed glad of the company and would tell me about the pianos that had just arrived. Our talks made real for me one of his fundamental beliefs, that each and every piano had completely individual characteristics, even if of the same manufacturer and age.

Sometimes he knew all the details, had even met the owners and talked about their instrument with them and knew intimately how they had treated it. Other times he knew nothing beyond what he could see, feel, or hear. Most often pianos came to him from auctions and charity sales, their history anonymous. But even then, like an expert in artifacts, he could deduce a great deal: whether a piano had been played much or little, whether it had been in an environment with the proper level of humidity (one of his cardinal rules), whether there had been children in the household, even whether it had recently been transported by ship. ('The worst thing you can possibly do to a piano,' he told me more than once.) At these moments he was part detective, part archaeologist, part social critic.

His attitude about how people treated their pianos seemed to mirror his philosophy of life. While regretting the depredations worked by children on keyboards and strings, he regarded them as tolerable because the piano was at least used and, as he put it, *'au sein de la famille'* ('at the heart of the family'). It was more than just any piece of furniture, but it was that, too, and if drinks were spilled and stains bit into shiny finishes, it was the price one paid for initiating the young to a joy that should stem from familiarity rather than reverence.

Those who preserved their piano as an altar upon which the art of music was to be worshiped irritated Luc, but he was deeply respectful of serious musicians who used and depended upon their instrument for their livelihood. Without ever saying so explicitly, he made me understand there were a vast number of pianos that were owned and rarely played, the vestiges of a certain bourgeois sensibility, where a piano was as indispensable in the family quarters as a television or a stereo would be today. He didn't regard this as a tragedy, but it always gave him pleasure when a piano that was highly polished but little played came to him. 'Now it can stop being a piece of furniture and start to live,' he would say with his half-smile and I would get the feeling that there was something of the orphanage director about him, an unsentimental hope for his charges as he waited for them to be adopted.

Luc's greatest scorn was reserved for those who used great instruments merely to display their wealth and, more loathsome yet, their musical pretensions. These pianos rarely ended up in his atelier, although he often saw this situation since he had a reputation, I soon learned, as a gifted piano tuner.

'They might as well park a Mercedes at the end of their *grands salons*,' he would rail, 'for all they know of music! Today I tuned a Steinway concert grand in an apartment that was at least four hundred square meters and I swear it hasn't been played in years. The owner told me it made him feel good just to see it in the morning, and there it sits with the cover open as if Horowitz himself were about to enter and play. He might as well look at his Swiss bank book or his stock certificates!'

His contempt was accompanied by a kind of sadness for the piano itself whose fate was to remain unplayed. 'It's like a great conversationalist who is put in solitary confinement,' he once told me and I better understood how for him a piano could suffer a kind of death, even though it was wholly intact and technically maintained.

In time, I began to look more closely at the pianos I might own. My initial enchantment was still there, but I had developed an appraising eye and a practical inquisitiveness.

The first hurdle was price. Many of the pianos, by no means only the renowned makes, were far beyond my budget. Unavoidably, size was also an important consideration, so I had gradually reconciled myself to owning an upright even though Luc repeatedly reminded me that they were not as good value for the money. And I wanted something with a simple cabinet, nothing adorned with candelabra and carved details that would look foolish among our modern sticks of furniture.

Luc let me play any of the uprights that were not buried deep within the atelier; not all were in perfect tune, but all were playable. It had been over twenty years since I had practiced with any regularity, and I was both thrilled with the opportunity to try out different pianos and embarrassed to reveal the level of my playing to Luc. My hesitant rendition of the first prelude from Bach's *The Well-Tempered Clavier* sounded thin and dry to me, but the atelier's workshop atmosphere and Luc's discussion of the pianos' various tone qualities put the focus more clearly on the instruments than on the person at the keyboard. I played a little Sauter, a German brand; it had a lovely bell-like tone and the feel of the keys was wonderfully fluid, but the price was more than I could afford. Another time Luc set up a Gaveau baby grand in the center of the atelier and invited me to try it. The keyboard was a bit stiff to the touch, but the tone was rich and round, and thoroughly captivating.

He nodded his head approvingly as the echo of my little dash of Mozart filled the quiet room. 'Beautiful, isn't it? That's the magic of the French tone in late nineteenth-century instruments.' And then he added with a frown, 'But you might as well buy a piano tuner to go with this instrument; it's completely impractical.' He explained that French pianos maintained wooden pin blocks – the massive slabs of wood in which the tuning pins are seated – that were only partially braced with iron until the beginning of the twentieth century, although the German manufacturers had long since switched to full cast-iron braces to hold the tuning pins firm. A question of aesthetics was involved – the French regarded the uncovered wooden board as more beautiful than the painted metal plate that covers it – but the force of tradition was the principal obstacle to change. Eventually, though, practical considerations carried the day. Pianos with full metal braces hold their tune far longer, I discovered, while wooden pin blocks that are only partially braced make a piano almost as fickle and labor-intensive as a harpsichord. I regretfully forgot the Gaveau.

A month later, on my fourth or fifth visit, Luc greeted me at the door with an enigmatic look. 'There's a piano that's just come to me that I think would be right for you. Come see.'

Luc always used an oblique phrase to describe how he acquired his pianos. It was never 'I bought' or 'I traded' or 'I bid at an auction'; he said a piano 'has come to me' or 'has arrived', as if it were an angel that had appeared on his doorstep. It kept his dealings secret, of course, and hiding the provenance of his instruments seemed to be important to him. But I sensed that that was only part of the picture. The way he referred to their 'arrival' really did correspond to how he felt: they were so many spirits who came to live with him for a while and for whom he would care until they departed.

Now he was telling me that a piano that was right for me had arrived. What did he mean? Over the course of the last few months I had come to know Luc through our agreeable banter when I stopped by the shop and he had listened carefully as I described what I was looking for: something small, inexpensive, in reasonably good condition, and suitable for me and for our two young children. Never once had he suggested that I buy anything at all, still less had he insisted that I buy a particular piano.

His approach consisted of pointing out certain attributes in pianos we looked at together and then in asking simply if I found the piano pleasing. More than once I observed him with other customers who were in the atelier when I visited and his manner was always the same: an invitation to play, to touch, to look at the instruments that appealed and then to decide for oneself, as if the piano should help to determine who its next owner would be.

As I followed him to the back room I wondered what I would find. I had a fleeting image of a little upright, black lacquer with a few scuffs, mechanically perfect and magically inexpensive. I realized later that this was the pipe dream of every parent who hopes to find a good used piano for his children, but it didn't occur to me how unrealistic it was as I hastened to the atelier, excited by what for Luc amounted to a bold declaration.

He led me past the ranks of uprights, though, straight to the back of the room where perhaps twenty grand pianos lay against one another on their sides. Squeezing between two of them, he turned to the one on his right, its strings and soundboard exposed, and gestured grandly with his arm. 'I think this would make a good piano for you.'

I looked at him warily, not at first sure if he was teasing me, but he eagerly nodded his head. I took in the dust-covered black lacquer cabinet and the glint of silver strings over a pale wooden soundboard. It was indistinguishable to my eyes from the other grand pianos that flanked it, all angled on the floor in the same direction with their tops removed. How could this one be mine? 'But Luc, this is a grand and I'm sure I can't afford it. And I've told you, I don't have room for an instrument this size.'

'It's a *baby* grand,' he corrected, 'and both its size and its price are smaller than you think.' He then proceeded to tell me what he knew about the piano or, rather, as much as he wanted me to know. It was in fine condition, manufactured in Vienna by Stingl, a house that no longer existed. Its serial number showed that it had been made in the mid-thirties, 'a very good era for piano building in Austria', an assertion that sounded at once poetic and questionable and which, in any event, I was powerless either to credit or to refute. It had come to him 'after a very long time in storage' and by this time I knew there was no point in asking for more information.

I told him that it was hard to tell what I was looking at since all of the dismantled pianos looked alike to the untrained eye. This was true, but it was also true that I was buying time, trying to find a graceful way out. I was suddenly afraid of commitment, aware that things were moving faster than I had expected.

'Of course, it's impossible to tell anything in this sad state. Come back in a few days and I'll have it set up on its legs. Then you can play it and see what I mean.'

'But Luc, I really don't want you to go to the trouble when I'm not at all serious about a grand piano.'

'Yes, yes, of course. But I'll be assembling this one anyway. Just come and play it and then we'll talk.'

I knew better than to decline, although I intended to hold out for an inexpensive upright. Also, I was intrigued to see what transformation would be worked on this heap of wood, metal, and ivory at my feet by the mere process of attaching its legs and pedals, adjusting the action, and cleaning it.

Three days later I returned and Luc greeted me in the front with a look of mock concern. 'Did you bring sheet music?'

He led me to the back room and into the clearing where four pianos now stood, one of them the Stingl. It flanked a massive Bechstein grand twice its size. Luc had cleaned it thoroughly. All of its parts gleamed: the exterior lacquer, the open keyboard, the interior brightwork. Yet it was clearly not brand-new; a soft patina to the black lacquer made it less a mirror than the misted surface of a pool, with traces of matte where the finish was worn. The keyboard was of real ivory, a prohibited material for new pianos since the 1980s, and the keys had yellowed over the years, some of them considerably. Its strings, although far from rusty, had the steel-grey luster of worn metal and the red felt dampers showed a softer tone of purple than the vivid scarlet felt of new pianos. This piano had lived, had been played.

Looking at the two pianos side by side, I was struck by how much smaller a baby grand was than a true grand. It had something of the endearing quality of a miniature and yet it was certainly no child's toy. It stood as high as the Bechstein and its keyboard was just as wide; only the size and length of the cabinet set them apart, and the volume of sound projected by the bigger piano was proportionately greater.

As I took in its diminutive size and its beautiful array of details, a word formed in my mind, a word that I at first resisted but that imposed itself nonetheless: plucky. This piano, I decided, looked plucky, a Cinderella of an instrument. Images of underdogs disenfranchised by their wicked betters, only to emerge triumphant, swam around in my head. By this reckoning the Bechstein was blandly arrogant; it had been invited to the ball through the front door. In a flash I realized that I was entirely taken by the idea that this little piano was somehow *good* and therefore right for my family. Had Luc so perfectly gauged my slowly awakening desire?

The Stingl's cabinet was simple almost to the point of severity, with straight legs and no fancy woodwork. And yet the music stand was worked with a delicate curve and pierced with a diamond motif inscribed in a circle, a single detail that gave it a *moderne* look of stylized restraint. It reminded me of the plain lines and subtle curves of Charles Rennie Mackintosh furniture, imposing but uncomplicated. The fact that I was immediately drawing such analogies set off alarm bells in my mind, but I felt myself giving in to a strange but pleasurable vertigo.

I sat on the bench and smiled at Luc. I was nervous, almost spellbound; suddenly this great impractical hulk was the gateway to a territory from which I had been absent for too long. Something said 'Yes!' before I even touched the keyboard. I trusted Luc but I realized, too, that I *wanted* to love this piano, I *wanted* to invite music back into my life. I tried a few scales, then some harmonic progressions and finally, with more certainty, some arpeggios. A thrill that I had not expected ran through me as the notes resounded. The Stingl had a good, clean action, but it took some work to move the keys. None of the vaunted silkiness of the Steinway or the velvet touch of other famous makes; no, this was a profoundly physical undertaking, almost athletic in its requirements. And yet the tone it produced was very sweet and full, a strange and wonderful combination of the robust and the delicate.

'It's a nice one, no?' Luc was beaming at my very apparent pleasure.

'It's a nice one, yes! It takes some work, but what a beautiful sound.'

'You're a big guy, you can play a piano like this properly. Not everyone could.' I wasn't sure if this was flattery or a dispassionate estimation of my capabilities. A bit of both, no doubt.

This was not just any old piano, Luc assured me. It had been made in Vienna in the thirties at a time when Vienna still had a craftsman's tradition worthy of the name (only Bösendorfer remains today) and its clear tone and solid feel suggested a solid pedigree. Never mind its pluck, this had all the marks of a rare find, a fine piano disguised as something simple and dependable. I could imagine it surviving the assaults of my young children, to say nothing of my own.

I laughed inwardly at all these musings; the combination of my vanity and artistic longings, together with the ungainly beauty of the piano itself, struck me as funny and vaguely absurd. I imagined myself flawlessly playing Chopin's Heroic Polonaise in A-flat at the keyboard of this unassuming instrument, an impossibility that nonetheless appealed to my sense of fantasy. One of the most difficult compositions for the piano, it would never be within my grasp, but the daydream itself was strangely satisfying. What would a visitor from another century think of this notion of personal fulfillment that sought a pedigree in the past? My expression must have reflected the deep sense of irony I was feeling because Luc asked me why I was looking puzzled.

'It's just occurred to me how much of ourselves we project on to a piano when we consider what we're going to buy.'

'Ah, but of course, that's the beauty of a piano. It's not just another instrument like a flute or a violin that you put away in the closet. You live with it and it with you. It's big and impossible to ignore, like a member of the family. It's got to be the right one!'

25

'And if one were interested, how much would this piano cost?'

'Fifteen thousand francs,' was his unhurried response. 'Of course, that includes delivery and tuning.'

I made noises about having to measure my apartment to be sure, but I think that we both knew I was going to buy it. Actually, I think he knew well before me and it puzzles me still to consider how he made that assessment after our brief encounters. But then, we reveal far more of ourselves than we suspect when we enter the bedizened world of our passions and our longings.

I returned two days later, having measured my apartment carefully.

My wife was surprised to hear that all my practical arguments in favor of an upright – the cost, the size, the children – had vanished virtually overnight. 'What happened to the idea of a small piano?'

I listed all my points in favor of a grand, babbling with enthusiasm as I recited the litany.

She listened silently, gave me a long look that mixed skepticism and understanding, then responded to my fervor with the practical point: 'Well, we'd better figure out where your new baby is going to live.'

Together we found a corner between the window and the book-case that formed an acute angle where the Stingl could be wedged in our apartment's main room. We adjusted our budget for the price Luc quoted. It was a lot of money, particularly since I was just setting out on a new career path as a freelance writer, but my wife encouraged me to indulge my newfound sense of freedom: 'Think of it as an investment in personal expression.'

This time at the atelier I did bring sheet music and Luc nodded approvingly when he saw me set it on the music stand. I've never been comfortable playing in front of others, but somehow this was different; his presence seemed encouraging as we listened together to the particular voice of this instrument among so many other pianos. I played for perhaps ten minutes, pieces I knew reasonably well and could listen to while I sight-read: some Beethoven bagatelles, a few of Schumann's pieces for children, an early Mozart fantasy. I was not disappointed. The Stingl's resonance filled the room with tones at once clear and robust, and a sharp sense of pride welled up at the prospect of owning this distinctive piano, of seeing and playing it daily, of living with it. Good God, I thought, this is a kind of love; and, as in love, my senses amplified and enhanced the love object, all with an insouciance and willing enthusiasm.

I finished playing and turned to Luc with what must have been a delighted look on my face.

'I would say that you have found your piano.' His eyes sparkled, the successful matchmaker rejoicing in his skill.

'And I would say that you were right.'

Luc and I then set about the practical arrangements for having the piano delivered and assembled in our apartment. When Luc explained payment I was a bit taken aback. 'You must pay the delivery man, in cash. No large bills, please, and make sure the sum is in an envelope when you give it to him. Separately you may give him three hundred francs as a tip.'

'But I can come back here tomorrow with cash if you like.'

'No. You pay the delivery man as I have described. That is the way we do business.'

Not for the first time at Luc's I was puzzled by an alien practice, but by now I knew not to insist or even to question. I remembered my first weeks of confusion and curiosity, trying to find a way into the back room, and now here I was, buying a piano from a man I had come to trust absolutely, even to admire. 'Very well, Luc. I'm very pleased with this transaction.' I extended my hand and he shook it warmly.

'You will not be disappointed, I can assure you.'

3

THE STINGL ARRIVES

Less than a week later a knock sounded on our door at the appointed time, loud and insistent, as if someone could not be bothered to use the bell. When I opened the door there stood before me an older man of about my height but with fully twice my mass in his upper body. His torso was the size and shape of a bass drum; he seemed to be all chest. Behind him, almost hidden by his bulk, lurked a slender young man with a narrow moustache and a nervous look on his face. The large man addressed me in a gruff voice. 'You're expecting a piano.'

'That's right.'

'Where do you want me to put it?'

'Please come in and I'll show you.'

We live on what in France is called the *premier étage*, one up from ground level. Our front door opens from a small, plant-filled court-yard on to a straight staircase that leads directly up to our apartment. He took this in as we ascended and he grunted approvingly: 'No spiral staircase, that's good.'

I thought of all the tiny twisting staircases that are so common in Paris and wondered what contortions must sometimes be necessary to deliver pianos. When I indicated the corner of the main room where I wanted the piano, he nodded. 'No interior doors or hallways; this will be quick.'

'Will you and your crew need anything special for the assembly?'

I assumed that there were at least three or four other men in a truck at the curb, waiting with the piano.

'What crew?'

'I mean . . . Well, how will you get the piano up here? Do you put a ramp on the staircase or something?'

'We'll bring it up the same way we always do. Trust me; we've done this before.'

With that, he and the skinny young man marched down the stairs, leaving the front door wide open. Less than two minutes later I heard a chuffing noise out in the courtyard. I looked out the window and saw a huge black mass – our legless piano – making its way across the cobblestones, borne sideways on the shoulder of the barrel-chested man. The assistant trailed behind, his hand on the tail of the piano but apparently bearing none of its enormous weight.

At the open front door they paused and set the back tip of the piano on the doormat. I raced down the stairs, utterly amazed at what I had just seen and unsure how they proposed to come up the staircase. The older man stood before me, the piano strapped to his back with wide brown leather straps blackened and shiny from years of sweat. They ran diagonally over his shoulders and under his arms and looped around the piano so that the side curve of the cabinet hooked across his right shoulder, its snub tail resting on the ground. He was breathing heavily.

'Surely it's not just the two of you! Can I help somehow?'

'*Monsieur,*' he stammered as he gasped for air, 'I'll tell you what I tell all our clients. Just stand clear and let us do our work.'

I ran up the stairs, baffled by how such a huge weight and massive bulk could be moved up the staircase by these two. Suddenly from below came a hoarse and rhythmic shout: '*Un, deux, trois: allez!*'

The older man leaned into his straps and tilted forward so the full weight of the piano – nearly six hundred pounds – rested once again on his back. He then headed up the stairs, slowly but methodically. I watched, horrified but fascinated, powerless to help. The piano bowed him low and the straps disappeared into his flesh, pressing deep furrows through his shirt into the muscle and bone below. The younger man followed behind, carrying nothing but holding the tip of the piano and pushing it forward. I thought of the dragging tail wheel on an old airplane whose sole function is to stabilize.

About a third of the way up the stairs the man paused and stood partly up from his stoop. There was a precarious wobble as the mass of the piano swayed lightly and I had a vision of a singular disaster on our staircase; if the piano went, this man went, too. He was literally strapped to his load.

He exhaled hugely, like a draft animal at maximum exertion, and straightened a little. Then, with a quick intake of air through his clenched teeth, he leaned back into the straps and continued up the steps. This pause was repeated once more before the top, all the more terrifying for being higher on the staircase. The young man's position was almost comically dangerous, like a cartoon; if the piano slipped he would be crushed instantly.

At last the summit was achieved and the tail of the piano set down once again. The man before me had been transfigured into a red-faced mass of sweating muscle and bulging veins. As if to pause too long would break some strange spell that gave him power, after only a few seconds he once again hefted the entire cabinet and crossed the room, each footstep shaking the apartment mightily. He set it down in the corner on its side. At once the younger man attached two of the legs to the exposed underside. Then the older man lifted the piano to the horizontal while his assistant scurried underneath and attached the third leg.

The whole undertaking from the bottom of the stairs had taken perhaps three minutes, but I felt as if we had shared some major life experience. I had just witnessed the single most extraordinary feat of human strength that I could imagine.

This Atlas was once again a normal human being. His face was no longer flushed and he was breathing normally. I looked at him more closely now, as if to discover some hidden sinews or unnoticed muscles that would account for what I had just seen, but he stood before me in a relaxed, unremarkable stance, the same barrel-chested man who had appeared at my door less than ten minutes earlier. 'Is this where you want the piano?'

'Why yes, that's perfect.'

'Then we'll be going.' He stood before me expectantly.

'Here, let me pay you.' I handed him the envelope full of money and he took it without a glance at its contents. 'And here is something for your trouble.' I handed him three hundred francs, a sum that now seemed ludicrously inadequate in light of what I had just watched him do, but his face lit up with genuine pleasure.

'Thank you, *Monsieur*, that is most generous of you.'

Better than paying for your funerals, I thought to myself as we shook hands. I saw them to the front door and, as I shut it behind them, I let out a long sigh. I was exhausted in the mid-morning calm and I could hardly find the strength to walk back up the stairs. *I'll always see this staircase differently*, I pondered. *There'll always be a man with a piano strapped to his back teetering on the edge of eternity*. I sat down and breathed deeply, and as I looked up I saw for the first time this object that changed the entire room.

Here we are, alone at last, I thought, in a spoof of Hollywood's big romantic scenes. But in fact it was as if I had not seen this piano before, and now I indulged myself in the luxury of examining it closely and at leisure, glad to have survived a potential disaster in the process of gaining my heart's desire. Now I could relax and look at what had, as Luc put it, arrived in my life. I felt I had not sought it out; it had come to me.

What a remarkable instrument: the sheer black bulk of it, perched on skinny legs like a spider. The voluptuous curve of the cabinet top, both subtle and extravagant when closed. But, ah! the thrill when I opened the top and revealed a jewel box of gold, red felt, and silver strings, an improbable and wonderful combination of the mechanical and the sensuous. And the forty-five-degree angle of the top, propped up by the slender stick, reiterated the tension created by the massive cabinet on the narrow legs: weight and heft held up by graceful struts, a vaguely menacing suggestion of disaster if gravity were to prevail, made all the more intriguing by the sureness of the structure. Tops don't slam down, pianos don't collapse in the usual course of things, but it's easy to see how they could.

The emblem stamped on the wooden soundboard inside the cabinet was a wonder in itself. The intricate lacework decoration around the edges, conventional in its busyness, suggested a tradition that went back to the nineteenth century, yet there was something curiously deco about the racy, minimal lettering of the builders' name at the center: 'Gebrüder Stingl, Klavierfabriken'. Below that, the magic word, 'Wien', spoke volumes about the place that means music, evoking the spirit of everyone from Mozart to Mahler. And at the back of the cabinet, cast in the metal frame, the purest paradox of sweetness and kitsch for a baby grand piano that ended up in Paris, its model name: '*Mignon*'. Little One indeed, yet not without character. And all of these inner secrets were reflected, ever so finely, in the inclined and lacquered cover.

Opening the fall board was a more intimate delight. From a plain black horizontal, a deft and simple roll of the board revealed an ordered expanse of white and black. The regularity of the spacing was nevertheless not symmetrical, and the 2–3–2 pattern of the black keys spoke of the mysteries of the chromatic scale. In the middle of the fall board was the manufacturer's name and, centered underneath this in a smaller brass inlay, the word 'original'. Was there another claimant to the Stingl legacy, a dark cousin?

To the left, again in small brass inlay, the letters 'L.A.'. Was this some private affectation, a somewhat vulgar indulgence that proclaimed status and power? Or perhaps, I thought, it was the dealer's filigreed attempt to please a favored client. Speculation about its meaning has since become a kind of parlor game in our household. A French friend postulates that Elsa Triolet bought the Stingl for Louis Aragon and had it lovingly inscribed. An American insists that Louis Armstrong used it as his practice piano on his European tours. The wildest imaginative flight contended that homesick movie people had the abbreviation for Los Angeles placed on a piano that they used on location shoots in the fifties.

The other inlay, dimly visible at the far right of the fall board, suggested another, more mercantile vanity: 'Tagrin-Axelerat & Co. in Braila'. It had since been painted over, hinting that a subsequent owner had preferred to keep the fall board plain – or hide its origins. This one sent me to the atlas of Europe to search for 'Braila'. After some looking I found it in Romania on the Danube, a medium-sized port near the Black Sea. Another, richer layer: built in Vienna before World War Two, sold by a dealer in Romania, ending up in Paris. Had it descended the river in the hold of a freighter, threading the Bosporus and crossing the Mediterranean on one of Luc's dreaded sea voyages? Or had it hopscotched around Europe by truck, one step ahead of political turmoil and war before arriving in the tenuous calm of Paris? Perhaps it had just been shipped here by train, plain and simple, by a traveler who couldn't bear to leave it behind. I would never know, but I needed to wonder, to imagine a past for this creature whose life would now be entwined with my own.

As promised, Luc came to the house to tune the piano just after it was delivered. It would need, he had explained, a breaking-in period during which it would acclimate itself to its new environment. The different level of humidity in our house and what he referred to as the shock of the move had to be taken into account; it was normal that it should go out of tune fairly quickly.

Between the delivery and Luc's second visit I played the Stingl several times a day. Sometimes I'd put some sheet music on the music stand – Bach or Bartók, it didn't matter – and play easy pieces slowly just to listen to the intoxicating resonance in our apartment that filled the main room with a surprisingly full, rich tone, especially in the bass registers. Often, though, in those first couple of weeks, I'd set the top fully open on the prop stick and let loose with anything at all – jazz, rock, classical. The sheer volume of sound was thrilling; it was like driving a convertible with torrents of wind in my face, the exuberance of the moment drowning out all other sensations but that of music's delicious momentum. My wife and children were tolerant if not entirely understanding of my adolescent excitement and only gradually did I realize that in order to play without an audience I'd have to wait for them to leave the apartment; with our open-plan space there was no hope of privacy when anyone else was home. Once my seven-year-old daughter, Sara, caught me looking at the piano from across the room. 'It looks nice there, Daddy,' she offered as I nodded dreamily. 'But it doesn't sound good any more.' She was right on both counts. It looked spectacular in our large main room, but what Luc called the 'shock of the move' had begun to tell and it was quickly untuning itself. Certain keys gave forth a dissonant twang that set my teeth on edge; it rapidly became unbearable as the simplest harmony sounded strange and twisted.

When Luc arrived he had the air of a doctor making the rounds of a very special ward, at once diagnosing and prescribing for a well-loved patient. He even carried a bulging black leather handbag, but instead of stethoscopes and thermometers his contained tuning forks and pin wrenches, and the sundry tools of his trade. I welcomed him warmly and showed him his old charge. I had not, I realized, stopped by the shop since the Stingl had arrived; my fascination with the variety of pianos at Desforges's shop had been concentrated on a single one.

Luc was initially concerned about the placement. The one corner available was near both a radiator and a window. 'Drafts are not good, but direct heat is death,' was his saturnine observation. I assured him that the window was permanently locked and that the radiator had been turned off for good. Hearing this, he relaxed a bit, but his parental air remained, a mixture of concern and hope. He gave me a reproachful look when he saw a vase of flowers on the piano, but I showed him that they were in fact dried blooms with no water in the container. With this he smiled and set down his bag. 'You know, it is really very hard to let them go.'

There was a moment of silence when we both reflected on this, and on the delicate bond that existed between these big-souled instruments and the man who gave them a kind of life.

'Yes. And this piano has already brought fun and music to this room, to this whole house.'

'Well, then, I'd better make sure that it's in tune.'

Luc opened his bag and set to tuning the piano. When he had finished he explained that the process of acclimatization would likely go on for some months until the various woods and fittings breathed together. He did not regard pianos as delicate or even fickle, but as complex instruments whose parts had to adjust to any major change. Only then could they work together to give forth the alchemy of music.

At the door he gave me a few final pieces of advice, insisting that I call him if there were strange noises or sticky keys, or if the piano went seriously out of tune. With that it was time for him to leave and we both knew it.

'Don't be a stranger at the atelier just because you've now got your piano at home.' He smiled lightly and added, 'And remember, you're now a client, too, so you can send me your trusted friends.'

4

MADAME GAILLARD

Stopping by the atelier as I now did regularly was, I began to realize, the fulfillment of a fantasy nurtured since childhood. Pianos have always been a source of fascination for me. My first memories of them are vague but highly colored, an uneasy combination of the real – great big pieces of shiny furniture that looked like nothing else – and the imagined. What allowed a person sitting in front of this strange giant to call forth beautiful sounds just by moving his fingers up and down? They were huge and wonderful objects from which music issued forth by some inscrutable process: I found it tremendously satisfying to press these black and white strips of wood with my fingers, or even to smash them with my fists. Something then happened 'inside' and out came strange sounds, bright and unexpected, and sometimes amazingly loud. It seemed unimaginable to me that adults would conceive of an entire contraption, at once huge and respectable, whose sole function was to make noise.

In buying a used piano in Paris, I was in a sense coming full circle. As a boy I had first felt their notes echo through me when we lived south of Paris in Fontainebleau, where my father was assigned as a staff officer at the headquarters of the Allied Forces. I was the fourth of five children and my parents had the good sense to send us all to French schools. I started at an ancient establishment known as the Institution Jeanne d'Arc and it was there that I met my first piano teacher.

Madame Gaillard was an old widow, invariably dressed in a shapeless black dress, with a shawl pulled around her shoulders in every sort of weather. She came to the school on Thursday afternoons to give lessons on the old Pleyel upright that sat in the school's salon. The only details of that piano that I remember are the double brass candelabra affixed to the front panel over the keyboard; their holders were always coated with melted wax, although I never saw them bearing candles. This model of piano has brothers I have often seen at Luc's atelier.

Walking down the long corridor that led past the salon and out to the cobbled courtyard, I would overhear Madame Gaillard's lessons. Her pupils were generally older girls – playing the piano was, even then, something that girls *de bonne famille* were expected to be reasonably familiar with if not to master, as they might also ride horses or embroider. In those days we had no school on Thursday afternoons, although we were obliged to attend on Saturday mornings, so Thursdays had a special air of freedom and play. I was five years old when I first became aware of this marvelous activity that sent music down the hall and out into the schoolyard. Occasionally I would stop at the door to the salon and listen, and it was in this attitude that Madame Gaillard came upon me unawares one day. I had thought that she must be inside, but apparently one of her students was practicing while waiting for the teacher to arrive.

'That's nice, isn't it?'

I was so startled that I couldn't speak, so I nodded dumbly, with an embarrassed smile on my face.

'Come see me in a quarter of an hour, if you like.'

I thought I was to be punished, or at least reproved for eaves-dropping, but her manner had been kindly, so I couldn't be sure what was in store. When the school bell chimed three I knocked on the door of the now-silent salon and Madame Gaillard said loudly, '*Oui, entrez!*'

The rest of this first meeting is shadowy to me. It was as if I had been hypnotized and shown into a room – a whole world, really – that held secrets both beautiful and mysterious. I remember being surprised that I was not scolded for standing outside the door; instead, Madame Gaillard invited me to sit down on the velvet-covered stool that was drawn up to the keyboard and to play a few notes. Gently she made me understand that if I wanted to learn to play the piano it would be possible, so long as my parents agreed.

From that day I had a short lesson with Madame Gaillard every Thursday at three. We began with a slim book bearing the title *Les 7 Notes* and learning the names of the various notes was as arcane, and as deeply satisfying, as deciphering a runic system might be for an archeologist. She taught me to read sheet music and, as is still practiced in France, she introduced me to what is called *solfège*, the system of syllables (do, re, mi . . .) sung to the notes of the scale. She encouraged me with smiles and surprised looks when I would master a chord or a bit of quick fingering, and her reaction to my mistakes was one of infinite patience.

'Why don't you try it this way?' she would say without a hint of censure when I had butchered a passage. She taught me not to be in a hurry. '*La frustration est notre ennemi*,' she would declare when I was exasperated, and then we would start over, more slowly.

There were no recitals or concerts, just my weekly lesson and the slow, enjoyable introduction to the symbols and signs that made up the language of music. I learned all of the words in French, of course, and ever since that has been my frame of reference for naming things musical: a quarter-note isn't a quarter-note but a '*noire*', an eighth-note is a '*croche*', a sixteenth-note a '*double croche*' and so on. And the names of the notes themselves – *les sept notes* – didn't just repeat the first seven letters of the alphabet. Instead, each had a sound associated with it – fa, so, la . . . – long before Julie Andrews codified the system for audiences worldwide in *The Sound of Music*.

My first years of piano lessons in France were hobbled by the fact that we didn't have a piano in our house. At first this didn't seem like a problem since I didn't have to practice: the weekly lessons with Madame Gaillard were self-contained, a brief and agreeable encounter with the world of music that fed my young appetite without requiring work. Gradually, though, my head couldn't hold all of the new information, delightful though it was, and Madame Gaillard asked me to bring a *cahier de musique*. This was a notebook whose spiral-bound pages were lined from top to bottom with the five lines of the musical staff; she began to fill the pages with notes and symbols and scrawled advice. She also told me that it was time for me to begin playing on my own some of what I had learned with her.

When I explained that we didn't have a piano at home, she told me that she would take up the matter with my parents. She talked to them the next week when I had finished my lesson and I recall the phrase *vente aux enchères* coming into the conversation more than once. Since it was never certain how long we would actually stay in France, my parents were unwilling to invest in a new piano that they might soon have to leave behind. Moreover, in those days moving a piano by ship was very much more perilous to the instrument's condition than would be the case today with modern sealed containers. And I was, after all, only five years old and no prodigy. As it happened, Fontainebleau had a well-known weekly auction that often featured used pianos and my parents warmed to Madame Gaillard's suggestion that we find a serviceable keyboard there.

Two weeks later my father returned from the evening auction with an upright piano loaded into the back of the family station wagon. It was black and it had the same sort of candelabra that Madame Gaillard's had above the keys. I was beside myself with delight; I couldn't imagine that we would actually have one of these extraordinary things, big as a chimney, sitting in the living room of our house. I think that even then I was at least as fascinated by the size of the piano and its exotic character as I was by its ability to spill out music at my pleasure.

The honeymoon didn't last long. At first it was a great novelty, and I had to wait my turn while my brothers and sisters played with the new toy. The others soon lost interest, however, and I had the piano to myself for longer periods of time. After two weeks something felt terribly wrong: everything I played sounded hopelessly sour. My father verified that the piano was out of tune and he had an *accordeur/réparateur* (tuner/repairer) come round and put it right, figuring that the initial heavy playing had been too much for our new charge. The tuner made noises about *acclimatation* and was on his way. After another two weeks, however, the same thing happened.

The end was swift and pitiless. The tuner came again and this time my father pressed him for particulars. '*Monsieur,*' he said, with a look that the French do better than anyone else: reproach, regret and resignation all wound into one. '*Il n'y a rien à faire.*' Even at the age of five I knew what that meant: there was nothing to be done. At my teacher's advice my parents gave away the piano. From that point on I think the word 'piano' to my parents was equated with 'problems' – who can blame them? It was as if they had given their children a puppy, only to take it away once it was discovered that it had distemper. Eventually, they arranged for me to use a neighbor's piano for my practicing. It was a nice little German upright and the woman who owned it always offered me cookies when I showed up for my half-hour, but it wasn't the same as having my own piano in my own house. That was a luxury, I learned, that was not readily available to those of us who moved often.

I continued my lessons with Madame Gaillard for the four years we lived in France and my memories of that time spent with her in the school's salon are full of the pleasure of becoming familiar with the mysteries of music. The piano became a kind of flying carpet by which I could travel to an entirely different place, and I would leave the room with the half-dazed sensibility that children sometimes show when they have discovered a new and agreeable and utterly private world of their own.

5

THE ONE THAT FITS

Our *quartier* is in a quiet part of the *Rive Gauche*, and its atmosphere is in many ways less frenetic than other parts of Paris. The Seine divides the city into roughly equal halves, north and south, and as you float down the river from east to west, the southern half is on your left: the Left Bank. This part of the city retains a quiet air, one less infused with commerce than with narrow residential streets, numerous parks, and several of the urban campuses of the University of Paris. Although much of it has been gentrified and real student poverty is as distant as Puccini's *La Bohème*, artists and artisans, craftsmen and skilled laborers still can be found in many of its neighborhoods. The building we converted into our apartment had been a carpentry shop in the nineteenth century, and its high ceilings and multiple skylights suited my wife's work as a photographer. Luc's atelier was hidden, but as I came to know the neighborhood better I realized that it wasn't really surprising that his activities should find a home in this *quartier*. The avenues with their cafés and plane trees look like much of the rest of Paris, but along the side streets the courtyards hold secrets that aren't readily found elsewhere.

Although I didn't fully realize it at the time, Luc's invitation to continue to stop by the atelier changed the face of the neighborhood for me. I was now a 'client', a member of the loose assemblage of neighbors, friends, and customers whose paths sometimes crossed in the secluded back room of his shop. It was like being asked to join a club where neither democracy nor personal influence prevailed; pianos were the thing and only Luc could let you in. We had lived nearby for almost three years, getting to know neighbors, shopkeepers, and tradesmen in the daily routine of running a household, but this was my first experience of a real *vie de quartier* from the inside, a neighborhood life that was richer and more varied than anything I had imagined.

At first I felt obliged to offer some pretext for my visits to the atelier that would justify my stopping by: a question about the humidity levels around the piano, a concern about how best to polish the cabinet. Gradually, though, my reasons became less plausible until one day Luc, no doubt sensing my hesitation, said after our greeting, 'You know, you can stop by any time just to see what's new in the back. You're always welcome.'

When I hesitated, thinking that my presence would change his work habits, he waved this away with a shrug. 'Look, it's very simple. I'm like a fisherman with his line in the water; until the fish bite, I've got all the time in the world.'

His words convinced me that I was welcome in the easy and mysterious ambiance that ruled the atelier. My visits were not necessarily more frequent, but they were very much more relaxed once the need to have a practical objective was gone. Often Luc would be on the phone, or customers would be in the shop, and I did not linger. Other times he would be alone and the pace was slow – '*C'est calme,*' he would say – and we would have relaxed conversations as I wandered around and looked at various pianos.

Luc was in the process of buying the business from the old man, Desforges. After more than thirty years of selling pianos, Desforges was ready to retire and Luc was his choice to take over the establishment. They had worked together for eight years, Luc told me, and most of what he knew about running a business came from the old man. There were to be three months of transition before he left for good, but already he was much less present. I realized that this change was probably the only reason the *patron* had given in to Luc and let me in the door to the back. When I asked Luc about that dramatic moment, he admitted that his insistence had been a test of wills that proclaimed his growing independence from Desforges. Véronique's introduction had been important, of course, but Luc was also intrigued by my difference from most of his customers. 'An American in search of a piano doesn't walk in the door every day.'

Occasionally Luc would greet me with 'Come see what has just arrived!' and his excitement would be infectious as we made our way through the dust and the clutter to his latest infatuation, like two boys hurrying to find what has been left beneath the Christmas tree. Sometimes the sheer rarity and magnificence of an instrument captivated him: a beautiful concert grand, say, or an Erard from the last century in smoked mahogany. On other occasions it was a peculiarity that held his attention: an odd-looking mini-piano with four octaves and a cabinet like a sewing chest, or a ship's piano whose cabinet was built entirely of plastic.

Once in a while he would be interested in a new arrival because of the story behind it and he would tell me a bit of how he had come to acquire it. On one occasion he enthused over a black Pleyel grand from the turn of the century; I couldn't understand exactly why he was so delighted. It was old but not especially rare and, although the cabinet was in fine shape, it was not the carved legs or the delicate fretwork of the music stand that held his imagination.

'I bought this from a fine gentleman just yesterday,' he said, standing back to admire the instrument. 'A Spaniard who's a specialist in Near Eastern languages at the Sorbonne. He used it to play very old tangos very badly.' He paused, then added, 'But it gave him a lot of pleasure.'

I soon learned that this, coming from Luc, was the supreme compliment. If someone had *beaucoup de caractère* and took pleasure in making music, no praise was too great.

After he told me a bit about this lover of old tangos and of old pianos on which to play them, I asked what for me was the inevitable question: 'Why did he sell his piano?'

'Ah, he has to move to a smaller apartment. Retirement isn't what it used to be.'

This aspect of Luc's business continually confounded me. My tendency was always to feel sad for the bad turns and sorry circumstances that obliged people to part with their pianos. Luc had an entirely different frame of reference; he refused to sentimentalize or pity those from whom he bought his instruments, but he was not without a certain plain sensitivity. Far more easily than I, he saw that selling a piano was not always a bad thing, let alone a tragedy. His pragmatism readily accepted that such instruments were valuable commodities with a cash surrender value that could considerably change their owners' circumstances. Something of the pawnshop hung about these undertakings and yet he never gave me the feeling that he was preying on dupes, nor were his purchases contingent. When he bought a piano, he bought it definitively and he usually sold it again in short order.

'Life is a river', he once told me, 'and we all have to find a boat that floats.' This was not said cynically, but rather as a simple observation of how the world works.

When I went by the shop one day, Luc was up to his ears in paperwork but he told me to go and look at something 'very special' in the atelier. Wandering into the back room, I was amazed to see how many new pianos crowded the space, and how many of the ones I had seen on my last visit of a few weeks previously had already been sold and sent off to their new owners. An exquisite black Erard grand that I had admired recently was nowhere to be seen, nor was the quirky-looking Pleyel upright with a keyboard that folded flush into the cabinet. Several new legless grands lay recumbent as odalisques.

In the chaotic confusion of new instruments, it was difficult to see how I was going to spot the one that Luc considered special. On one side of the atelier, almost buried under a pile of carved piano legs, sat two little spinets; one bore the name 'Focke, Paris', another was inscribed 'Frincken' with a specific street address on the fall board: '7, rue Guénégaud, Paris'. In a row of uprights nearby there stood a 'Lys' from Honfleur, a 'Schindler' from Lyon, and a 1.35 meter 'Kriegelstein' baby grand from Paris, all of them brands I had never heard of. Luc called the Kriegelstein *un crapaud*, a toad, the French term for a very small baby grand. 'All of them have been out of business for a while now, but they used to make good pianos,' Luc told me later. As I looked at them all bunched together, though, I couldn't figure which one held Luc's fancy.

To one side stood a dark-brown upright with straight, almost severe lines. When I opened the fall board it revealed the name of another obscure maker and a city in Holland unknown to me, all in an unadorned modernist typeface in tasteful lower case. This piano looked as if it had come out of the Bauhaus. Was this the unusual piano that Luc had referred to?

Just then he walked by. 'That's actually not a bad instrument, but its cabinet has a bit too much of the Reformation spirit,' he said as he hurried into the adjoining room.

I was beginning to understand that for him a piano had a kind of personality and all of the parts had to be considered, not just the narrow 'musical' elements, in evaluating it. Doubtless part of his perspective was related to his sense of what would, and would not, sell; he could not afford to be insensitive to the preferences of his customers.

Gradually I absorbed his philosophy by listening to what he had to say about the various pianos that arrived and soon left again. Eventually it was a way of getting to know the man, perhaps the best way since our discussions, even when far-ranging, almost always had as their common point of departure and of return our shared interest in these instruments. Things moved slowly, but that was in keeping with the essential guardedness, even formality, of the initial stages of getting to know someone in France. Being given free access to the back room was an enormous expression of trust, I now realized, like being let in to the inner circle. I sensed that this common ground imposed its own rhythms and haste was not part of it.

As I squeezed through the narrow passages I noticed that towards the back there stood one of Luc's clearings, an opening in the clutter where a piano had been set up and room was made for the bench. Even from thirty feet away I could tell that the top was clearly an exotic wood and I hurried to see what had been given pride of place.

There, bathed in the overhead glow from the skylight, stood an apparition. The cabinet was unlike anything I had yet seen: a deep reddish-brown with black stripes alternating irregularly, the contrast made even more dramatic by the fiery sheen – almost an iridescence – that seemed to come from within the wood. The curved side of the cabinet was extravagantly voluptuous, the richness of the wood heightened by the long baroque undulation of the box. The solid top, angled up on its prop stick, seemed to give off sparks from within. As I walked slowly around it I saw that the gold lacquer of the iron frame was perfectly matched to the gold tones in the wood. The wood was astonishing: at first appearance it had the stripy contrast of a zebra, but the longer I looked at it the more I realized that it contained an infinitely subtle gradation of colors, as if every conceivable tone of red, orange, yellow, and brown were present, blending ultimately into the deep black of the stripes. I almost felt that I could plunge my hand into the colors and swirl them around. At the front I read the elaborate inscription on the fall board: 'Steinway & Sons, New York and Hamburg; Patent Grand'.

As I stood staring at this apparition Luc walked up slowly and said in a low voice, 'Now this is a one-of-a-kind: a real piano and a real work of art.'

I had never heard such high praise from him before and yet his tone was subdued. 'You don't sound too enthused.'

'It's hard to be enthused when you've got to pass up such an opportunity.'

'What do you mean? Isn't this piano yours to sell?'

'Oh, yes, indeed it is. But I had hoped to keep it for myself, and' – he held the palms of his hands a foot apart – 'it needs that much more room to get into my house.'

Luc had never before expressed, or even suggested, a personal interest in any of the pianos I had seen in the atelier. He went on to tell me the whole story and the details seemed to help him to accept the reality of the situation, as if to recite its wonders were a way to caress it gently before he let it go.

It was a Steinway model C from 1896, in exquisite condition. The mechanics were essentially those you would find in a Steinway of the modern era. Sitting horizontally inside the case and anchoring the strings from the perimeter, the full iron frame was covered with patents, their raised lettering cast directly in the metal: 'overstrung scale'; 'tubular metallic action frame'; 'capo d'astro bar'. On the soundboard beneath the strings was an elaborate rendering of the Steinway logo, and above it the legend 'Piano Furnishers to'. This was flanked on both sides by a list of European monarchs and their numerous coats of arms: 'King of Prussia and Emperor of Germany', 'Queen of Spain', 'Queen of Italy', 'Queen of England', 'Prince of Wales'. The warrants were almost baroque in their ostentation and yet were proof that, at the time, Steinway was at the very pinnacle of piano building.

It was the case, however, that transformed this instrument into a rarity: solid beech with a thick veneer of Brazilian rosewood. The lines were very clean, as if even in the high Victorian era they realized that such an extravagant wood did not need any complication. The two exceptions were the music rest, an elaborate tracery of scrollwork, and the legs – ponderous neoclassic pillars with flutings, capitals and bases.

Luc pointed out how ugly the legs were and how he would have substituted something simpler 'if this piano were to be in my house'. He was far from a purist. Whereas a collector or a piano historian would never consider disposing of original elements, Luc's priorities were far more personal and far more flexible. What mattered to him was the overall feel of a piano and he didn't hesitate to consider changing something as extraneous as the legs if it would make a more pleasing whole. 'But unfortunately that won't be necessary; this instrument will go to another.'

He had anticipated having this Steinway for himself to replace 'a little Erard that has grown tired'. But when he measured and re-measured the dimensions carefully he found that there was a discrepancy of twenty-five centimeters that could not be resolved. He had even considered enlarging the front room of his house by knocking down an exterior wall and extending it, but he soon discovered that he could not obtain a permit for even a minor expansion in the tightly regulated neighborhood, a bureaucratic dead end so typical of France. And so this jewel would go to someone else. Doubtless he would make good money on the transaction – he told me he had two willing buyers already competing with each other – but the business side of the deal seemed almost irrelevant in the face of his own disappointment. I had never before seen him so discouraged, almost disconsolate. 'Well, surely you'll find another Steinway of similar quality eventually.'

'Ah, I never wait for "eventually".'

He motioned with his head to draw me away from the Steinway towards the back of the atelier. I followed him to where a small piano was set up with the top removed. At first I thought it was a harpsichord: it had the squared cabinet and delicate paneling that were conventions for that instrument. But as I looked closer I saw the name

'Pleyel, Wolff, Lyon et Cie' worked into the iron fame and I realized it was a small Pleyel grand. 'I'm restoring it for myself' – Luc's tone was eager – 'and this time I'm sure about the dimensions.'

He pointed out its unusual attributes, particularly the diminutive size and the beautiful conceit of a harpsichord case. I noticed that there were six legs rather than the usual three. 'Yes, it's very unusual in that regard. But unlike its cousin, the harpsichord' – he slapped the side soundly – 'this is a solid little bruiser. Kind of a wolf in sheep's clothing. I like that.'

But his enthusiastic tone was obviously compensating for the loss of the tiger-striped grand. He looked around the shop, at the uprights and the grands, at the august instruments and the lesser-known brands, and then he looked at me. 'Sometimes' – he shrugged his shoulders almost imperceptibly – 'you just have to take the one that fits.'

6

MISS PEMBERTON

We moved back to the United States when I was eight, living outside Washington, in northern Virginia. My parents found a piano teacher who was almost a caricature of the spinster who gives lessons in her home. Miss Pemberton was a genteel Southerner of a certain age and she lived with her mother in a dilapidated mansion set back from the road where the suburbs had encroached on what had until recently been wild.

At first I had a great deal of trouble making the transition from French to English, learning all of the names for musical notation in a different language. She was patient with me, however, and she seemed to regard my strange need to translate a specialized jargon back into English as a kind of game. Gradually, *tonalité de mi majeur* became the key of E major, *dièze* transformed itself into sharp, *accord* was turned into chord, and so forth.

We had a serviceable upright at home, a Kimball, bought second-hand from a neighbor, and I was able to practice the exercises that were so essential a part of Miss Pemberton's approach. Hanon was her Bible: *The Virtuoso Pianist in Sixty Exercises for the Piano*. Compiled in the nineteenth century by a Frenchman, C. L. Hanon, its yellow cover looked down at me reprovingly from the piano's music desk. 'Hanon will never let you down,' she would announce as I was leaving the big gray house where I had played to a metronome for the previous half-hour, as if betrayal and being 'let down' were what I most feared from the world of music. And so I practiced 'chromatic scales', 'arpeggios on the triads', 'legato thirds', and all the joyless rest of it for hours at a time. I think her sense of imminent danger for her students came from her commitment to annual recitals, a rite of passage that I had not known before and that I came to loathe.

Miss Pemberton's recitals were always held on a Thursday evening in May and for months before the announced date she would discuss with each one of us the possible choice of a piece for the concert. Its selection and subsequent study were accorded as much importance as a decision on which college one might attend, and the sense of occasion that built up made it feel like some sort of pagan ceremony in which the initiates would be made to pass a trial by fire in order to be found worthy. The order of performance was severely hierarchical, beginners first, with the finale reserved for the advanced students who would play a Chopin ballade or a Mozart sonata for the assembled parents. In between the two extremes there were many of us grouped together with less demanding pieces and I can still remember asking Miss Pemberton, plainly and naively, why I had to play my Beethoven étude for others when I had mastered it to her satisfaction and had already become tired of it.

'Music isn't music unless we share it with others,' she told me, but even then that sentiment seemed unsatisfactory to me. The kind of controlled hysteria that coursed through the bodies of her students like an electrical charge on the night of the recital surely had its usefulness in preparing one or two of our number for the experience of playing in public, but it was a high price to pay for the rest of us who had no intention of becoming professional musicians. Why couldn't we just play for our own pleasure? Part of the answer, of course, is that parents want to know that they're getting their money's worth, and their hopes and aspirations for a musical career are all too readily projected on to their children. And music can be a wonderful thing to share: in concert, with friends, for a loved one in private. But the idea that one would want to play alone, for the sheer pleasure of getting to know the music – and its composer – from the inside is regarded as a kind of blasphemy.

The night of the recital Miss Pemberton's dark wreck of a house was, for a single occasion in the year, transformed into a faded echo of a mansion. The threadbare rugs were rolled up and the hardwood floors glowed under a coat of thick wax that perfumed the air. The long windows sparkled as they had not all winter long, and they were left open to the already warm Virginia evening and the soft murmur of crickets in the surrounding woods. Every chair in the house – every couch and bench and kitchen stool – had been drawn up in a rough approximation of a church's pews, and in place of the altar the Mason & Hamlin grand stood in all its American majesty. The dark wood was polished so that it shone like a topaz, hard and brilliant, and the insides gleamed and were reflected in the angled top raised on its prop stick. Every horizontal surface around the room bore plates with paper doilies upon which were arrayed sweets and cakes and fruit gelatins rolled in sugary powders that perfectly matched the pastel colors of the girls' taffeta dresses.

The first year that I went through this ordeal – I was nine years old – I didn't suspect what was in store until I actually entered the big room that was called the parlor, dressed in a blazer, with my hair slicked down. Then and only then I experienced first-hand the controlled terror of my peers: the stiff-legged walk to the front of the room, the explosion of sound from the big piano against a soundless gathering, the smattering of applause, and the rapid repetition of the sequence with the next student. To say that I panicked is too simple a formula to describe what happened.

'Now we'll have an early Beethoven piece from Thad Carhart,' I heard Miss Pemberton say and only dimly did I connect that name with my own. My legs carried me uncertainly up the narrow aisle that threaded through the parents and siblings of my fellow students, and I sat down on the piano bench. A strange giddiness possessed me, as if I might start pounding the keyboard at random and expect it to pass for a difficult piece, and yet my own piece, the real one, was as alien to me as the dark side of the moon. *How does it go?* I asked myself. *How, at least, does it begin?* My features were frozen in a rictus of false enthusiasm and my fingers rolled into fists as if they were retractable. After many motionless seconds, Miss Pemberton came over from her place at the side and, with the pretext that the height of the bench needed to be adjusted, she screened me from the audience and hissed in my ear as she leaned over, 'It starts with a C-minor chord.' I looked at her with no hint of comprehension in my eyes, and she placed her right hand on the keyboard and played the chord softly, as if she were checking that the piano was in tune. The instant I heard those notes the spell was broken. *I know that piece*! I thought to myself and as my eyes brightened her hand patted me firmly on the back. She moved away and I attacked the keys as if they were the enemy, playing the piece straight through without a mistake. That is, I played all of the notes, but I must have taken it at double the usual tempo with no regard whatsoever for phrasing, much less interpretation. When I finished I felt the way a circus animal must feel that has just successfully performed a particularly difficult and silly trick, and my sense of disappointment was commensurate with my surprise that such a big deal was made of this strange ceremony.

I played in two more of Miss Pemberton's recitals, but each time it was like holding my breath and swimming under water until I reached the other side, the end of the piece. Hanon, I suppose it could be said, never did let me down: my fingers were nimble, my retention was good, but there was never for me a feeling of the music coming back to me. It was an ordeal that had to be tolerated so that I could then continue to learn to play music for myself.

These kinds of recitals seem to me to be based on an enormous confidence game that sets up every prospective pianist to be the next

Horowitz. Only a handful of soloists will, of course, rise to the top and make careers out of their music, but the conceit is that any talented youngster might have this capacity, this dubious and rare gift. And so there has developed over many years a system for subjecting thousands upon thousands of young musicians to the ordeal of playing repeatedly in public to see if they have the peculiar sort of talent that flourishes in front of others.

I didn't have that talent, that much was clear, but that awareness didn't diminish my eagerness to keep learning: I always enjoyed playing on my own. For as long as I took lessons as a child, I gently but persistently resisted the notion that I should play in front of others and, while this attitude was tolerated, I was made to understand that I wasn't really playing the game. My parents never pushed me; five children in a household have a way of defusing the pressure to perform that might otherwise come their way. Mostly I think this was just understood to be part of the system of taking lessons and no one thought to approach music otherwise. Only one or two of Miss Pemberton's students seemed drawn to performing for others, and they were the ones who were most advanced and who were likely to center their lives around music. To the rest of us the recitals were a strange amalgam: half exam, half carnival, with a dreadful thrill of anticipation until the awful night slowly arrived and quickly passed. I sometimes dream about those strange evening encounters; I always forget how my piece begins and Miss Pemberton is nowhere to be found.

7

JOS

As summer turned into fall, the neighborhood streets assumed the changes both big and small so characteristic of Paris at this season. The cafés at the corners of the boulevards pulled in their aprons of outdoor tables, leaving only one or two rows for the stalwarts who took their coffee in the undying hope of a ray of light through the gray-blue clouds. Along the avenues the opposing rows of chestnut trees faded to a rusty brown and reluctantly gave up their leaves, their overarching green tunnels turned into long black nets of branches. The chestnuts littered the pavement in the evening, to be swept into the gutter's remorseless tide at the following break of day; in front of the elementary school the sidewalks showed only leaves and husks since the boys raced to collect the hard brown spheres, perfect for throwing, as soon as the bell rang in the late afternoon. My walks in the *quartier* were brisker as the weather grew chilly, but I always included the atelier on my circuit when I could find time away from my writing. After spending hours in solitude looking at words, I found that I craved the combined pleasures of good company and fine pianos.

Late one morning, I noticed a small truck parked at the curb before the shop, two men preparing to unload pianos from it. Luc was on the phone at the front; we shook hands and he nodded me into the back room, where I found another man wandering among the pianos. Coming from the far side of the back room was the sound of someone tuning: a note would be repeated several times, then another note would be sounded with it, usually a major third, and then the initial note would be tuned slightly higher and then lower before being brought to the true tone. There was something monotonous, dissonant, but also mesmerizing about the sounds, akin to the half-tones and repetition that are familiar to us from Indian instruments like the sitar. And my ear was drawn to the minor variations that were finally resolved to the pure tone, a moment of keen relief before the whole process began again on another note.

Luc came into the back room, having finished his call, and was immediately intercepted by the other customer who began asking him a series of questions about a small Ibach grand, one of the better German makes. They began a long and animated discussion about various advantages of the Ibach's pedals.

Maneuvering my way around the overcrowded room, I found a tall black upright, scuffed and dull with dust, right at the entrance to the atelier. Upon opening the fall board for inspection I was greeted with a grandiose flourish of faded gold script: 'Maxime Frères, Paris & London'. The words were flanked by three gold seals superimposed on either side, with doubtful-looking depictions of Queen Victoria and Prince Albert in profile. The effect suggested a label on some prize-winning bottle of mineral water, showy and a bit pathetic. The cabinet had faded traces of gold stencilling on the black panels, done in Victorian lines and beads. Some turn-of-the-century antecedent of plastic covered the flimsy-looking keys.

Luc passed by on his way to pick up a tool. 'Thank God it says Paris,' he whispered, 'otherwise I'd never be able to sell it.'

'Why is that?'

'The English turned these things out by the shipload a hundred years ago. Mass assembly, cheap materials, low prices: pianos for everybody. Now some of them are still surviving, if that's the term, and they send them to the south.' In French he said '*le sud*' and there was enough contempt to reveal generations of abuse visited upon the peoples of the Mediterranean by the perfidious Anglo-Saxons. 'Greece, Albania, Turkey – they're not too particular about what they take, so long as it's got a keyboard. Many of them end up in tavernas.' This last was offered with a wince that suggested that even for pianos there was such a thing as a fate worse than death. 'We occasionally get them in France, but an English piano of that vintage is generally unsaleable. That "Paris" should help, but it would be a lot better if it said "Londres" instead of "London". The "Maxime Frères" means nothing at all; they'd put the Lord's name on it and call it their own if they thought it would sell pianos.'

Luc had explained this practice to me before, one that is as old as pianos and still goes on today: a mass manufacturer will turn out vast numbers of instruments and then brand them with names which are either defunct or that sound close to the names of the great German, American, and Austrian makes. So it is that there have been numerous downmarket approximations of Steinway ('Stenway' and 'Steinmay') and Bechstein ('Beckstein' and 'Bachstein'), not so close as to trigger a lawsuit for infringement of the brand name but close enough to gull the credulous and the unwary. And 'Maxime Frères' may have had just the right 'continental' feel in turn-of-the-century England to sell pianos to a growing middle class determined to display a hint of sophistication and with little regard for the actual quality of what they were buying.

The movers began bringing the first of four pianos into the atelier. It seemed as if there couldn't possibly be room for even one more, but they moved boxes here and piano parts there, and made a space just the size of an old upright's footprint. This they placed carefully in the oblong clearing, tilting it delicately from the dolly as one might deposit a heavy box of crystal. They disappeared to continue their unloading.

I wandered to the back and in one of the far corners I found a man tuning a Pleyel grand. A closer look showed me that it was Luc's piano in the shape of a harpsichord, the one he had 'settled for', the one that fit. The restoration was by no means complete – the cabinet was sanded to the bare wood, untrimmed felts draped the strings with crimson folds, the brightwork was still dull and tarnished – but the essentials of the mechanics had been completed. New strings gleamed from beneath the angled top and the soundboard shone with the warm glow of resurfaced wood the color of poured honey. The tone, even in the endless repetitions that gave it tune, was clear and bell-like and thoroughly distinctive.

I realized this must be Jos, a Dutch tuner now living in Paris whom Luc had once mentioned to me as being 'one of the best'. He pronounced his name 'Yoss'. With the old man, Desforges, leaving the shop for retirement, Luc no longer had time to tune pianos in the *quartier*. He proposed to send me Jos when my piano next went out of tune. 'He's very good. Just be sure that he tunes your piano in the morning.'

'The morning?' I was willing to trust Luc's judgment, but I didn't follow his reasoning.

I started to ask, but he cut me off with a look of indulgent humor and a pouring motion with his right hand, as if he were holding a bottle. '*Il aime son ballon de rouge.*' ('He likes his glass of red wine.') It was offered with a shrug of the shoulders, but the message was clear: in the morning this man would whisk through the infinitely precise and delicate series of tasks that brings a piano back into tune. Wait until the afternoon and I might have anything from a gently tipsy spirit to a falling-down drunk on my hands.

Luc had told me very few of the particulars concerning Jos, but what little he had sketched was intriguing. Jos had, at some indefinite point in the past, worked in the Bechstein factory in Germany. Following an unspecified period of problems, he had had to leave Germany for France. On the one hand, Luc told me, fate had not been kind; on the other, Jos seemed happy enough and his vagabond existence was perhaps what he needed. Luc told me that he was 'almost a homeless person', sleeping in trains parked overnight in the major stations of Paris. He owed a considerable sum to various hotels and restaurants in the *quartier* after a period of trying to live a more normal life, during which he never managed to pay the bills. But Luc was unequivocal in his praise for his ability as a tuner. Never one given to exaggeration or overstatement, he said that Jos was one of the few who had a thoroughly intuitive sense of pure pitch and so he was always in demand – in the mornings, at least.

I watched him in profile, draped across the front of Luc's little prize Pleyel. I did not approach nearer than a few yards away, a respectful distance from the man who was so carefully concentrating on his work. He had an intensity to his features that was palpable as he listened for the note to come to the true tone. Sitting on the bench with one hand on the keyboard and the other reaching over to the tuning pins, his head was cocked to one side – I couldn't help thinking of the blank intensity with which a robin listens for a worm – as he tightened and loosened the tuning wrench, his gaze on some formless middle distance where the perfect tone lay. When he came to it, his features relaxed almost imperceptibly and the smallest of smiles would play across his mouth for a split second, an island of resolution and release in the sea of dissonance and half-tones. Then it was on to the next note right away. He repositioned the broad felt damping wedges that muted the strings to either side and the whole process began again, filling the space with an insistent repetition of notes and their approximations. In another setting the constant repetition might have seemed boring, even annoying, but in this shop of marvels, all of them having to do with the piano, it seemed a fitting kind of music that drifted over the instruments that surrounded us.

The movers continued to unload their pianos from the truck out front and, inexplicably, to find just enough space to deposit them. Luc and his customer were deeply involved in their discussion about the

Ibach – they had moved from the pedals to a debate over the manner of stringing. Soon a well-dressed older couple came in and politely, discreetly, asked about the 'Pleyel from the 1840s'. Luc excused himself for a moment, pulled some cardboard boxes from the top of a hidden upright and indicated the piano they were asking about, saying that it was 'exceptionally well maintained'. Immediately their curiosity overcame them, and they scrambled over and around the obstacles like bird dogs after fresh game, all vestiges of decorum or age lost in their enthusiasm to see the wonder at hand.

I decided that it was time to drift further back in the shadows, out of the commotion in the middle of the large room, so I headed to the other far corner. I squeezed between three large boxes of blue felt and a disused organ in pieces, the shiny cylinders of its pipes stacked around its console like the exhaust pipes of a dragster. Hidden in the furthest reach of the room was a small mahogany grand, a dark and simple Schimmel. On its music rest was *The Well-Tempered Clavier*, opened to prelude number IX. The fall board was open, the keys shone; everything seemed to whisper 'Play!' but it was impossible to do so with the tuning under way. I wondered if Luc had been playing the Bach.

I turned to leave and discovered that the access to the front had taken on the aspect of a maze with all the moving around of pianos; narrow openings through which I could barely squeeze defined a roundabout way forward. I realized that the activity throughout the atelier had intensified. The movers were bringing in their last piano, muscling it into a tiny opening as if with a shoehorn. The man who had been there when I arrived was stretched out full length on the floor inspecting the underside of the Ibach he and Luc had so animatedly been discussing. The older couple were rhapsodizing to Luc about the cabinet they had somehow exposed from amidst the clutter; the phone rang long and loud before Luc excused himself and answered it.

As I made my way out I passed a piano, half hidden along the wall, which stopped me short. Its top was open, angled towards the back of the room where I was standing, and the wood was a golden blond, richly highlighted in the glow that was suffused through the skylight. Its lines were simple and sinuous, and the music stand was a plain oblong of intersecting diagonals, almost austere in its uncomplicated utility. At first I thought it was oak, but as I drew near I realized that it had nothing of the opaque and flat finish that oak normally assumed; this was all dancing light and golden depths, a sheen close to opalescent. Birdseye maple? I wondered. It was clearly something extraordinary, but I don't know woods well enough to identify any but the most obvious.

I lifted the fall board with the air of hushed expectation that always came over me as if I were opening the door to another world. When I rolled back the long curve of fancy wood I was greeted with the legend 'Gaveau, Paris'. Instinctively, I placed my left hand on the keyboard and formed a chord, realizing as I did so that I couldn't try out the tone of this wonder because of the tuning that was still going on in the atelier. The keys felt cool and slightly irregular beneath my fingers, their surfaces worn by years of playing, and I wondered what I always wondered as I touched the broad expanse of aged ivory: who had played this piano and where, and what music had they made?

While I peered into the dusty insides, Jos got up from his bench and walked towards me, the tuning apparently finished. I now saw him head on: high forehead, deep-set eyes, long chin, and a red flush across his cheeks and nose, as if he had lately been in a strong sun. Although we had never met he greeted me in heavily accented English: 'It's a special one, *ja*? Almost a hundred years old!' Standing now at my side, he peered under the open top where the soundboard swam beneath the strings in a sea of dust, the coats of arms of monarchs and princes dimly visible beneath the grime. 'All those kings and queens, all this dust. They're all gone now' – he turned and gave me a beautiful smile, a flash of enthusiasm coupled with an amused look in his eyes – 'and this beautiful piano is all that remains. Hei, Ho!' This last was a little verbal fillip, sung more than spoken over his shoulder as he walked to the front.

I turned back to the dazzling yellow piano and, seizing the moment now that Jos had finished tuning the Pleyel, I sat at the bench and played. Not wanting to draw attention with all of the others in the atelier, I depressed the soft pedal and tried a Schubert waltz. The worn ivory keys felt strange at first, but soon their subtle ridges and indentations seemed forgiving, even welcoming to my fingers. Although I was playing as softly as possible, the timbre of each note was clear and absolutely even from bass to treble. Most surprisingly, the action was so sensitive that I found I could still modulate each note considerably, from soft to extra soft. I was enraptured, transported by the faint but perfectly limpid tones that came forth from this century-old marvel.

My smattering of Schubert left me frustrated, though, since I kept playing the same familiar pieces by heart whenever I was left to improvise. Wouldn't it be wonderful, I asked myself, to be able to sit down at a piano as fine as this one and to play a Chopin ballade off the cuff? Playing the Stingl at home over the last few months, sheet music and all, had made me realize that if I truly wanted to improve I'd have to take lessons again.

While I was playing the last bars, finishing the waltz with a flourish, Luc was making his way to the back. Seeing me sitting at the Gaveau, he kissed the tips of his fingers and gestured towards the piano as he opened them. 'Lemonwood,' he said, pausing as the surprise crept into my eyes. 'Very rare.'

'And very beautiful, too. I had no idea you could make a piano from lemonwood. Do you have any takers?'

'I have several hesitaters, but no takers for the time being.'

'And what about the rosewood Steinway? I noticed that it's gone.'

'Ah, a *jazzman* came in last week and fell in love with it on the first note he played. It made me very happy that it went to him.' One of his customers asked him a question from the back and he was gone.

So the drama of the magnificent Steinway had ended well. When not so many weeks before he had dolefully observed, 'This piano will go to another,' the story had ended there for me. But for Luc the *jazzman* had been what he needed to make things right, what he wanted in the give-and-take that was his business. I hadn't considered the *suite*, as the French put it, the follow-through to circumstances and events that lends life its air at once poignant and meaningful.

8

HOW IT WORKS

In the first few weeks after the Stingl's arrival I was giddy with excitement each time I came home and laid eyes on this vision in the corner of our living room. I felt the combination of surprise, discovery and delight that comes momentarily with a shiny new car, or a special birthday present, but this seemed both more substantial and more meaningful than just another new possession. I polished its lacquered surfaces thoroughly – Luc told me what special product to use – and I dusted the insides with a soft cloth so that they gleamed.

One day, as I was playing scales with the top all the way open, reveling in the sonorous vibrancy of its voice, my six-year-old son approached the cabinet quietly and peered inside. A look of fascination came into his eyes and his features had the same mesmerized intensity that I remembered from when I first watched the hammers dance so mysteriously as a boy. 'How does it work, Daddy?' he asked when I stopped playing.

I explained the fundamentals and demonstrated the connection between the keys and hammers as he watched my fingers on the keyboard. He seemed satisfied with this basic – and visible – kinetic principle, but I saw that when we talked about it again he would expect more specifics and I was unprepared to explain the complexity of its workings.

For all my love of pianos over the years and my preoccupation with discovering their provenance and unearthing their lore, I realized as I spent more time at the atelier that I had only a rudimentary notion of how this instrument actually produces the extraordinary range of tones and contrasts that are its hallmark. I knew that a key, when depressed, activates a felt-covered hammer which in turn hits the particular string that corresponds to that key. The string vibrates and a sound is produced. That's the basic principle of the mechanism and I have always loved to watch the hammers dance across the strings from below when a grand piano is played with its top open. But beyond that simple association of cause and effect, I had very little idea of what went on inside.

What an astounding result from such a simple movement. It's as if our upper extremities – fingers and hands and arms – were infused with a subtle power that, once concentrated on the keyboard, opens the door to every kind of sound. Seeing the secret innards of pianos spread out before me made me want to know more about the mechanics, not for the utilitarian aspect but for the poetics of it. I wanted to understand how this big machine could be so exquisitely receptive to a basic set of movements that it could give full-blown voice to the balletic hands of a Thelonious Monk or a Vladimir Horowitz. Gradually, as I poked around among the pieces of machinery that occasionally littered the back room, Luc answered my many questions and revealed the basics of how a piano works.

I soon found out that while pianos have been turned out in huge numbers for more than a century (they were one of the first mass-produced consumer items that were also complicated and expensive), their many moving parts and fine woodworking insured that every piano had a distinct character. I sometimes heard Luc volunteer that Pleyels, say, had this particular problem that had to be watched out for, or that Seilers, a good German piano, had a strange design feature that accounted for a certain aspect of their sound. But Luc took it further than the broad category of a particular brand; what really interested him was how an individual piano was different from all others and how he could understand and learn from what he referred to as its *identité personnelle*.

Older pianos were generally more interesting in this regard because they tended to be less uniform. Even the same model by the same maker of the same vintage could differ in ways that were significant to him because so much of the work had been done by hand. Modern production methods have standardized so many procedures that very few modern pianos have what he called *caractère*. Adaptation and invention, I found, are crucial in repairing and restoring pianos since parts aren't always standard and they often wear in dissimilar ways, and it was this unpredictable aspect that captured Luc's imagination. He would say in mock self-deprecation, '*Je ne suis qu'un bricoleur*' ('I'm only a handy-man'), but the born tinkerer's love of a challenge gleamed in his eyes as he said it.

Press key, hear sound: the fundamentals are simple but the particulars very quickly become complicated. The moving part that we see, the part that we touch when we are playing, is the key. Modern pianos have eighty-eight of them arrayed as 'naturals' (the whites) and 'accidentals' (the blacks) across seven-and-a-third octaves of the Western diatonic scale. Push a key and a note sounds, a pure tone with a fixed point of reference expressed in vibrations per second that is the same for all pianos. What we don't see when we push down a key, though, is the ingenious and complicated mechanism that sends a hinged mallet flying upwards to strike the string.

Each key – a refined lever, really – is connected to more than thirty moving parts that are intricately designed and assembled to insure that the motion is uniform. The force with which the player presses the key is directly related to the speed with which the felt-covered hammer strikes the string and this in turn determines the volume of the sound produced. Hit the key hard and a loud, bright tone is produced; hit it gently and the note sounds softly. This property is embodied in the combination of all the hidden parts –

collectively called the action – that translates the downward motion of the key into a tone of variable volume. It was a revolutionary innovation when the piano was invented around 1700 and since then the mechanical system that was first developed has been refined but not fundamentally changed.

When the key sets the hammer in motion it strikes a string stretched with great tension between two points. The vibrations of the string – from 30 cycles per second at the low end of the bass register to 4000 cycles per second at the top of the treble – produce a tone that corresponds to that particular note. This, too, is more complicated than it at first appears. The hammer in fact usually hits more than one string, for while there are eighty-eight keys on the modern piano there are more than two hundred strings. Among the highest notes on the keyboard (the high treble range) each typically has three thin strings tuned to the same pitch and struck together by a single hammer. As you go down the keyboard to the intermediate range (lower treble), thicker strings make for a louder sound and so each note needs only two strings. The lowest notes (the bass register) require only one thick string each since their oscillations produce more volume than a single thin treble string.

Aside from the number of strings, a few underlying mechanical principles must also be taken into account. The length of a string determines its pitch: the shorter the string, the higher the note, so high treble strings are the shortest under the piano's cabinet, the bass strings the longest. The thickness of a string is also directly related to its pitch: thin strings have a higher pitch, so strings are both thicker and longer as you move down the keyboard from right to left. In a grand piano, the strings are all attached to tuning pins running parallel to the keyboard; they are drawn back across the soundboard and attached to the far side of the frame. The beautiful curve we see, therefore, is the manifestation of those graduated points of attachment across the entire range of the piano's keyboard. Perhaps the easiest image to grasp is contained in the phrase coined by the English poet, Leigh Hunt, in the early nineteenth century: 'a harp in a box'. Think of a full-size harp, the kind used in orchestras. Pivot it mentally from the vertical, as it normally stands, to the horizontal and put it in a box shaped to its frame. There you have the shape of the grand piano.

Perhaps most important, the tension maintained on a string directly affects both the volume and the quality of the tone. Greater tension is always desirable and a force of two hundred pounds per string is common on a modern grand piano, a combined torque of over thirty thousand pounds across the entire keyboard. Strings are therefore made of a very high grade of carbon steel with extraordinary tensile strength, and stretched across a cast-iron frame that can withstand the aggregate pull of more than twenty tons. The metal frame is consequently massive, accounting for a third of the weight of a piano. When a tuner adjusts the notes on a piano, he minutely alters the string tension by turning the tuning pin to which one end of the string is attached, thereby raising or lowering the tone slightly.

By itself, a vibrating piano string makes a sound that is weak and lacks resonance, and some means must be found to amplify the string's oscillations considerably. The solution is to transfer the string's energy to a large, thin sheet of wood called the soundboard, which in turn vibrates across its surface and amplifies the tone. It is, in effect, a huge membrane that touches the strings at the bridge, a raised strip of wood glued to its top whose upper edge is held firmly against the strings and transfers their movement to the wooden diaphragm below.

All the subtle art of woodworking now enters into the picture. A feel for wood is crucial, an ability to know how to let the wood sing that brings an instrument alive. This sensitivity to the qualities of wood was as essential to the pioneers of piano building as it was to the great makers of stringed instruments like Stradivari or Guarneri. The wood literally shivers with the sound, passing it along through its fiber. Spruce is the favored wood for good soundboards for its combination of strength and lightness, and craftsmen pay close attention to the straightness of the grain, the regularity of the growth rings, and the flexibility of the entire sheet once it is assembled from carefully glued strips. The soundboard is fixed to the case or 'cabinet' along its perimeter, and the way that the case is assembled and joined to the rest of the mechanism also directly affects the instrument's tone. If the soundboard is built for flexibility and responsiveness as an amplifier, the inner rim of the case must be both strong and stable, a sort of velvet vise firmly gripping the frame, the strings, and the soundboard, and yet allowing a regular resonance to pass throughout its own structure.

The other principal wooden component in a piano is called the pin block. Mounted underneath the front edge of the frame on a grand, it is joined to it by the tuning pins. The pin block functions as an anchor for the tuning pins, a massive laminated block of wood in which they are seated and which must hold them firm and motionless when the pins are slightly rotated to vary the pitch of the strings during tuning. Finally, massive reinforcing struts, the back-post assembly, strengthen the entire piano and focus energy on to the soundboard for a more powerful tone. When a piano is being played, especially at volume, the entire wooden structure vibrates and resonates sympathetically with the tones produced by the strings; not surprisingly, it can feel like a living thing when you lay a hand on it.

The pedals, a later invention, help the pianist control the sound even more precisely. They hang from the bottom of the case and are connected to the action above by simple metal push rods; all are encased in an open wooden housing, called the lyre, which keeps them properly aligned. When depressed, one pedal allows the tone of the vibrating string to be sustained by lifting off the string the felt-covered damper, which usually comes down to quell a note once it has been played. The effect is captivating as all of the tones mix, like a watercolor with hues swirled together, and lovely carrying notes endure long after the fingers are lifted from the keys. Another pedal softens the sound by moving the hammer slightly to the side so that it hits only one of the two or three strings per note. Some pianos have a mute pedal that lowers a strip of felt between the hammers and the strings, muffling the sound to a nearly inaudible level. This feature, called *une sourdine*, is much prized by the French, particularly in Paris where close quarters to one's neighbors is the rule.

Those are the barest fundamentals, and they apply both to uprights and to grands, the principal difference being that the soundboard, frame, and strings on an upright have been pivoted to the vertical plane rather than stretching away from the keyboard on the horizontal. The different mechanical configuration gives the grand distinct advantages: the keys are longer and therefore more responsive; the hammers work with gravity as they fall back, allowing faster repetition; and the soundboard, longer and wider, sends its vibrations up into the room. Since the late nineteenth century there has been a consensus on these basic components of a piano, but how best to combine them continues to be a terrain where opinions vary widely based on quality, practicality, and – not least – the aesthetics of sound.

The weight of the individual hammers, the composition of the felt covering that strikes the string, the counterbalancing of the keys: the possible variations are virtually infinite. So, too, with something as seemingly straightforward as the strings: how best to balance string length, density, tension, and steel quality against the demands of tonal clarity, stress on the frame, labor costs, and a myriad of other practical considerations makes each brand slightly different. This juggling act is perhaps most demanding when it comes to the parts that are made entirely of wood, since the strictly mechanical is left behind and the subtle qualities of this once-living material must be respected and enhanced. Strength, suppleness, longevity, internal resonance, external beauty: all play a part in the extremely specialized carpentry that gives a particular instrument its voice, and the pitfalls and problems are legion.

As I came to understand just how complicated pianos were, I began also to see that much of their appeal to Luc lay in their eccentricity as well as their complexity. On a raised work bench near the back of the space, pieces of the mechanisms of various pianos were usually arrayed neatly for repairs or new parts. Occasionally, however, entire pianos would be disassembled and in plain view. Luc didn't like this arrangement. He said that it distracted from the atelier's aspect as a showroom and it worried potential customers to see *des pianos éventrés* (disemboweled pianos) among the instruments they might buy. Still, there were times when it couldn't be avoided and on such days the atelier showed a different side of its mysteries.

The mechanism suggested the precision and the predictability of an engine, a supremely nineteenth-century invention that relied on the inherent strength and close tolerances of machine parts. The various piano actions lying around the atelier gave the feel of a garage where fine motors were assembled or repaired: shined metal glistened from perfectly aligned rows of faceted parts, specialized wrenches and screwdrivers unlocked hidden workings, machine oils coaxed precise bearings into fluid movement. Seeing all of this close up filled me with a certain amazement akin to what I felt in automobile garages where engines were dismantled – 'How will they ever get it all back together?' – and a wonder that there were people like Luc for whom this was a commonplace.

But the other part of the instrument spoke of fine woodworking and the intuitive feel for the material that lay in the carpenter's art. Alongside the massive cast-iron frames and the endless coils of replacement strings, wood of all sorts graced the atelier: the finely tapered expanse of varnished spruce used for soundboards, the beech and maple laminations used in grand casework, the veneers of exotics like smoky mahogany or satinwood. When Luc had lately been cutting or sanding a wooden component, their shavings would cover part of the floor and a subtle perfume would diffuse in the light-filled room.

A piano builder or restorer, then, has to be part master carpenter and part structural engineer, fitting a mechanism as intricate as the finest timepiece into a wooden cabinet that is strengthened with a massive steel frame. A musical historian I once met commented that the mechanism was as complicated as a clock. 'But the big difference', he pointed out, 'is that you don't pound on a clock.' This combination of delicacy and sturdiness, of finesse and vigor, makes the piano unique, and the skills to build or repair it are not often found in one person.

When we talked, Luc often touched obliquely on the piano's dual nature. He liked that they could be a repository for our dreams and a bauble that can readily be bought and sold, and he often pointed out that the same instrument could be both sophisticated and vulgar, subtle and brash, classical and jazzy. '*C'est costaud!*' ('This thing is tough!') he would say when we strained to lift a solid oak upright across the atelier. '*Ce n'est pas un violon.*'

It was plain that we shared a love of pianos, but it was equally clear that his interest was of an entirely different order from mine. His passion was his profession, while for me it was an avocation, an engaging diversion from my other responsibilities. He was infinitely patient with my questions and I think he saw right away that my curiosity was genuine, not just for the magnificent instruments that abounded, but for his strange merging of art and commerce. What for him was the routine of an ongoing business seemed rare and wonderful to me at the end of the twentieth century: a master craftsman with a personal connection to his clients, his suppliers, and – most intriguing of all – to the very artifacts that he repaired and sold. Without holding up a mirror to his activities, I think the pleasure I took in his atelier reminded him that it was outside the realm of the everyday. This was a form of flattery that he welcomed without our ever talking about it.

I enjoyed the slow unfolding of a friendship where, beyond our conversations about the pianos in the shop, certain things were tacitly understood. Luc and I virtually never asked about each other's personal lives, although details occasionally came out as we talked. This was understood as respect rather than lack of interest, a sometimes surprising notion for an American used to the rapid divulging of facts and the urgent expectation of intimacy in new relationships. The pace was different in the atelier and I learned to give things time.

9

FALL BOARDS

For as long as I can remember I've lifted the long curved piece of wood that protects a piano's keys, the fall board, whenever I came upon a piano, it didn't matter where: hotel lobbies, restaurants, schools, theaters. Something both illicit and tantalizing lurks about the habit in the same way that pulling down a book from a stranger's shelf and opening it can be an act of intimacy. As a child I longed to see the maker's name hidden underneath, the 'Knabe' or the 'Mason & Hamlin', and the name of the city where the piano had been manufactured. How many childhood dreams began with my musing on the strange place names inlaid on pianos? Long before I knew that New York was an important city, or even a very big one, I knew that it was a place where pianos – lots of them – were built. As I came to understand the geography of Western music and culture, I could bring it alive merely by reading the inscription 'Vienna' or 'Paris' on these ungainly instruments that seemed to have arrived, as if by sorcery, from faraway places.

When we lived in France, the exotics were the pianos from New York or Boston. In North America this was a relative thing and discovering 'Richmond, Virginia' on a piano in, say, New Mexico was as big a thrill as a 'London' or a 'Hamburg'. It became a kind of game where the more improbable cities counted for more in the scheme of things. 'New Yorks' were easy to come by in America, but an 'Amsterdam' was truly rare. I devised an entire eccentric history of

74

discovery, exploration and colonization based on my first-hand evidence of where pianos had ended up, a personal notion of the *mission civilisatrice* that had as its sole aim the distribution of hugely impractical instruments throughout the world.

Often I would be shooed away from the pianos I was so interested in opening. But once the keys were revealed, it was an irresistible temptation to strike a few and hear the voice of this particular piano: raspy or trilling or placid, or sometimes entirely colorless. Usually it was only a few notes, or a simple chord, but any sound at all was enough to bring the guard dogs baying. 'No playing!' they would yell from behind the bar, or from the front desk of the hotel. 'The piano is for our musicians only!'

This rang out as a personal affront, a hurtful slap at my notion of the generosities of music. In my mind I *was* a musician because I had taken a few years of lessons and, perhaps more importantly, because I cared so much for pianos. I would close the piano abruptly and mumble an apology, but the reproofs never kept me from trying the next time. It was my own personal form of anarchism and I was nothing if not persistent.

Once – I must have been about ten – my family was leaving a restaurant in Washington, D.C. when I spotted an old upright in the empty bar adjacent to the entrance. While coats were being assembled and my father was paying the bill, I slipped into the darkened room, opened the fall board, and found in faded gold script the words 'Story & Clark; Grand Haven, Michigan'. Where was this place? It sounded like a seaport and I made a mental note to find it on my atlas.

Made bold by the vacant and somber surroundings, I sat down and played a few scales as quietly as possible. I remember that the piano had a beautiful tone, round and full, not at all like other uprights I had played. I continued with furtive enthusiasm, louder now as I thought myself to be alone and hidden. Suddenly the door behind the bar burst open and a man in a white apron sang out, 'How about "Mack the Knife", you know that?'

My hands froze on the keyboard, caught between the shame of being discovered and my embarrassment at being asked to play. I only knew classical pieces; show tunes and popular songs were as alien to me as the surface of Mars. What should I do? I looked at the man in his white apron, his forehead covered with beads of sweat and his smile strangely intimidating and insistent. I smiled back, desperate to maintain the fantasy of my newly conferred status of pianist and performer, yet eerily aware that I might as well have been at Miss Pemberton's on recital night.

'Come on, kid. That was nice, but how about playing something I know?' Then, shouting over his shoulder as he held open the door to the kitchen, 'Hey, fellas, come see; we've got a regular little Liberace out front!'

That broke the spell. Musically it was no compliment, to say nothing of the idea that I would in any way ape the wild showmanship of Liberace. I got up from the piano as two or three men came to the kitchen door, all smiles and jokes. By this time my father was at the swinging doors that separated the bar from the lobby. 'What's up in here, Thad? It's time to go.'

'Just looking at the piano,' I mumbled.

My father looked at the group behind the bar and the cook spoke brightly, explaining the sudden theatricality of the moment: hesitant pianist, expectant audience, weighty silence. 'Aw, we were just hoping for a little concert, that's all.'

Reading the embarrassment on my face, my father answered the man as if he were an impresario with the regrettable task of depriving the audience of a concert in order to protect the artist's delicate temperament. 'Sorry, gentlemen, not today. We've got to take this show on the road.' As he turned to leave, his back to the bar, he winked at me.

Later that night I pulled the atlas from the bookshelf and discovered that Grand Haven was a town on the western shore of Lake Michigan. As I mused about that piano's beginnings in the Great Lakes country that to me seemed so exotic, I thought about being caught at the keyboard. What had I wanted? I had loved finding a piano with no one else around, especially an unknown make – this was my first 'Grand Haven'. But the attention that came with the sudden audience terrified me. I wanted to find a piano unawares and play it in solitude and in peace, alone with my own imaginings and challenges. Even when I practiced at home, there was almost always someone else in the house. I didn't want other people around, I realized. No recital, no grinning adults and special requests; just me and the unexceptional playing that swelled into intricate fantasies of triumph and transcendence.

Only once was this child's dream realized. My mother and I were picking up my sister at her school and I was told to wait in what they called the music room, an oak-paneled room that overlooked the garden. Carved oak shelves covered the walls bearing piles of sheet music that lay flat on special sliding trays. A dozen music stands stood open at one end of the room, as if a small chamber orchestra had recently been rehearsing. Flanking them was a large grand piano, its case also of carved oak which, I realized, subtly echoed the curves of the room's panelling. The top was open and sheet music stood on the music desk.

To my amazement I had been left alone in a room that was like a dream. I walked over to the open piano with a mix of urgency and inevitability that creates a kind of fearless calm. Above the keyboard I read the polished brass letters: 'C. Bechstein – Berlin'. I sat down on the bench and started playing, instantly lost in the perfection of the moment; I was elsewhere.

I played whatever it was that I was studying at that point, some simple melody from Mozart or perhaps one of the uncomplicated Schubert dances. The piano was heavenly compared with the old upright I had been playing: a Bechstein grand in perfect tune with a touch that was like waves of silk. Everything sounded different, better, clearer, and I no longer felt like a twelve-year-old at his music lesson. This felt authoritative, like real music, and I felt like a musician. After playing for a while I looked to the far side of the room and saw a woman standing near a door that I had not noticed before. I stopped playing and started to get up, embarrassed and flustered to have been found out. How long had she been there, I wondered.

She crossed the room, smiling and reassuring me in a low, throaty voice, 'I'm terribly sorry to have interrupted you. That was lovely. Will you be here for a while?'

She was an older woman with very thick glasses, so thick that her eyes were distorted behind them. She was carrying some sheet music – had she been planning to practice? – and she continued to smile at me as we stood in front of the piano. I told her that I was waiting while my mother and my sister met with one of the teachers. 'Sara never told me that she had a brother who was a pianist. Well, if you're like me you prefer to be left alone when you play. Let me close both of the doors so you won't be disturbed.'

It was as if she had read my mind, had looked right inside, and seen specific instructions under the heading 'What This Boy Wants' and was following them. As she turned to leave she looked back and said, 'It's a wonderful piano, isn't it?'

'Yes, ma'am, it is. It's wonderful.'

I sat on the piano bench in silence, amazed that a total stranger had instantly understood something about me that even my family didn't fully comprehend. On the way out to the car I asked my sister as nonchalantly as possible who the woman with thick glasses was.

'Oh, you mean Miss Killian. We call her Old Coke Bottles' – for a split second she mugged blindness – 'She teaches music and chorale. She's actually really nice.'

'Yeah, she is.'

★

As I got older I came to use attitudes about pianos as a measure of a person's worth. With that relentless seriousness that youth so often mixes with unconcern, I made sudden and obstinate judgments: if Miss Killian was a kind of angel, then the woman I met in my last year of high school was a genteel sadist. She had plenty of ideas about pianos and music, ideas I abhorred, and early on we fought a battle of wills.

Her name was Mrs Palmer and she was the wife of the headmaster at the boarding school I attended for my final year of high school when my parents were again living overseas. All of us boys were obliged to be nice to her in public, but she was privately loathed. She was inventively mean. One of her favorite tricks was to corner new boys at the headmaster's welcoming reception and pour them a cup of tea. She would then encourage them to squeeze a wedge of lemon into their steaming cups. 'You'll need lemon for the winter ahead!' her voice would boom out. A few minutes later she would reappear with a cream pitcher and again make the rounds, foisting 'a splash of cream' on all those present. The cream – naturally – curdled and this was her chief delight, to mock us for our pliability.

As everyone stood around with an undrinkable concoction in his hands, she would make a little speech about how you sometimes had to have the 'gumption to say no', that life was like that and we'd have to learn to think for ourselves sooner rather than later, and that that was what made the school great, the insistence on being independent and free-thinkers. It was a peculiar inversion of what was in fact the prevailing attitude at the school, and I don't think there was anyone who wasn't aware of her hypocrisy.

As she spoke my eye fell on a beautiful old Chickering grand in the main room. Chickering was one of the great American builders in the late nineteenth century, although the name is now used on modest instruments made elsewhere. This was one of the originals: it sported late-Victorian detailing in the black cabinet work, fluted legs and an elaborate music desk with fancy tracery. While the other new boys huddled together or were accosted by our eccentric hostess, I examined this piano with a jealous eye. I knew that I would have to play a few notes, and thought the stifled roar of teenagers crammed into a formal room would be good cover. As I surreptitiously formed a chord and gently depressed the keys, I was startled by her shout from behind me: 'Carhart, do you play?'

'Uh, yes. I mean, no. Not very well, that is.'

'Well, which is it? Do you or do you not play the piano?'

This was too categorical a formulation to shrink from; it was a point of honor. 'Yes, I do,' I heard myself say in a clear voice.

'Splendid, then you can play hymns for us on Tuesdays.'

I started to say that I wasn't good enough for that kind of sight-reading, but she cut me off. 'Come now, no false modesty around here. If God gave you a gift, He did it for a reason. We'll put it to good use. That's the spirit of the school!'

For the next several Tuesdays I played hymns for the school's church choir, presided over by Mrs Palmer. The music itself was straightforward and fun to play: effortless chord progressions marching forward with the same relentless beat, over and over, the choir's voices making two- and three-part harmonies over the uncomplicated melodies. The atmosphere, however, was insufferable. Mrs Palmer gave us constant lectures on the meaning of the hymns – she might as well have been in a pulpit – and her railing didn't stop when the music started. She stood to my right, facing the twenty boys arrayed before her and frantically yelling out directions over the verses: 'Now, let me HEAR you! "A MIGHTY fortress is our GOD!"'

Then she would berate me for not playing loudly enough, thumping the side of the Chickering as I pounded the keys, her face a study in Christian indignation. 'Carhart, are you UNDERWATER? Let me HEAR you! That's what a BIG piano like this is FOR!'

After four weeks I was desperate to escape. I had cut the index finger on my left hand at soccer practice: nothing serious, but it bled profusely, as superficial cuts sometimes do. I put a bandage on it and went to choir practice that evening. After I had played a couple of hymns, she began to rant at one of the boys for not going low enough in the bass line. I put both my hands under the piano's key bed and loosened the bandage; then I squeezed my finger vigorously until I felt a liquid warmth. I stuck the bandage on loosely and waited.

'All right, I want them to hear the second verse in BOSTON! Carhart, give us some POWER!'

After five or six chords pounded out at full volume, the bandaid flew off and a fountain of blood gushed out. Mrs Palmer was concentrating on crushing the spirits of the boys facing her. Something in their faces finally alerted her, though, because she yelled at one of them – 'DOLAN, what's the MATTER?' – and then followed his line of sight to the keyboard. I played on, although in fact my finger was starting to hurt and from the corner of my eye I could see that the ivories in the bass registers were more red than white.

'CARHART, for heaven's sake, stop bleeding on my PIANO!'

I looked at my hand in feigned shock as it dripped like a leaky faucet. As I got up I managed to spatter a nearby footstool covered in white and black petit point. That sealed my deliverance.

'GET OUT! Go to the infirmary and have that taken CARE of!'

The doctor told me that it didn't need stitches, just another bandage, but I was officially off choir duty for good. Secretly I resolved to avoid other people's demands and expectations, and I even stopped taking lessons after I went away to college the following year. I continued to open fall boards whenever I encountered a piano, though, and I always was drawn to the Miss Killians of this world, although they seemed rare.

Years later, when I rediscovered the importance of the piano in my life, I imagined someone like her, an intuitive teacher who could draw out the music from within rather than drilling it into me. Instead of relying on a chance encounter, though, I saw that I would have to seek out such a person and make clear my needs and expectations if I were to enjoy playing as an adult.

10

THE WORLD BECOMES LOUDER

No one knows exactly when the piano was invented. The generally accepted date is around 1700, although evidence exists that some models were built as early as 1694. There is little doubt, however, about its inventor, an instrument maker at the Medici court in Florence named Bartolomeo Cristofori, who developed a way of making a struck string resound loudly. Before Cristofori, keyboard instruments were unsatisfactory for different reasons: clavichords, whose strings are struck, were small and delicate, and their greatly reduced volume made them suitable only for small gatherings. Harpsichords, while larger and therefore considerably louder, had one overriding limitation: since the string is plucked, the force with which the key is depressed is unrelated to the volume of the sound produced. Dynamic control of each note was not possible.

What was needed − and what Cristofori invented − was an instrument as large and robust as the big harpsichords that would also allow the dynamic range that before had only been available on the flimsy clavichords. The first piano was described by a contemporary musician in 1711 as a '*gravicembalo col piano e forte*', a 'harpsichord with soft and loud'. This was the essential breakthrough, but it took decades for the seed to find fertile ground, and it did so not in Italy but in eighteenth-century Germany.

German instrument makers incorporated Cristofori's break-through into a series of increasingly powerful keyboard instruments that were true pianos. Johann Sebastian Bach was impressed by the first piano he tried, but he pointed out limitations that still needed to be worked on: a heavy action and a treble that was not loud enough. Two of his sons, Carl Philipp Emanuel and Johann Christian, championed the instrument in the next generation; by the time that Johann Christian Bach gave the first solo piano performance in England in 1768, the triumph of this new keyboard instrument over the harpsichord was assured. Social attitudes took a while to evolve, however, and even Voltaire dismissed the piano as late as 1774: '*Le pianoforte est un instrument de chaudronnier en comparaison du clavecin*' ('The piano is a boilermaker's instrument compared with the harpsichord'). For a while composers marked their scores with the notation '*pour le clavecin ou le pianoforte*', but gradually they wrote exclusively for the piano's new and seductive voice. The age of the baroque was giving way to the classical era and the piano was the perfect medium for music's new expressiveness.

Now the role of the keyboard as a solo instrument came to the fore musically. It was no longer just another part of the ensemble and its unique volume freed it from the confines of the drawing room to which the harpsichord had always been consigned. Haydn and Mozart both wrote masterful sonatas for the new instrument, its keyboard was greatly expanded, and its dynamic range – the single feature that most distinguished it from the harpsichord – was exploited fully. A whole new technique stressing fluidity was developed for the piano and Mozart wrote: 'It should flow like oil.' Solo concerts became the norm rather than the exception, and a class of instrumentalists with technique and power arrived on the scene. In a letter he wrote in late 1777, Mozart enthused about the tone of the new pianos: 'In whatever way I touch the keys, the tone is always even. It never jars, it is never stronger or weaker or entirely absent . . .'

What had been a tinkerer's offshoot among harpsichord makers became an industry in its own right. London and Vienna were its focal points. The Seven Years War in Germany drove many instrument makers to seek refuge abroad in the 1760s, and a second wave of émigré specialists – this time French, fleeing the Revolution – arrived in England in 1790 to pursue their business. The two capitals gave rise to distinct schools of piano building, the principal difference having to do with how the action – the intricate mechanism that activates the hammers to strike the strings – was conceived and assembled. Viennese pianos were generally softer, with a refined singing tone that allowed the melody to come to the fore; the pianos themselves had delicate cabinetry. English pianos, on the other hand, had a more robust tone, with a stronger action and greater tension in the strings; they had solid cases and sturdy frames. The great Viennese composers of the classical era – Haydn, Mozart, Beethoven – played Viennese pianos, but the transition to the stronger instruments of the English school can be seen in Beethoven's last piano sonatas.

Beethoven was known for the increasing dynamic contrasts in his works for piano, from whisper to thunder, and he sometimes destroyed the fragile Viennese pianos when playing his music. He had a strong influence on the direction of piano manufacture and, as early as 1796, he expressed his frustration with the overly delicate styles of playing that were a hold-over from harpsichords: 'There is no doubt that so far as the manner of playing is concerned, the pianoforte is still the least studied and developed of all instruments; often one thinks that one is merely listening to a harp . . . Provided one can feel the music, one can also make the pianoforte sing.'

Many have speculated that Beethoven attacked the keyboard with such fury in order to feel the vibrations of his music through the piano's cabinet as he gradually lost his hearing. In 1818 Broadwood, the pre-eminent English manufacturer of the day, offered him a grand piano that incorporated all of the latest features: stronger case and frame, trichord stringing, more responsive action. This piano, too, Beethoven damaged with the fervor of his playing (a contemporary reported that 'the broken strings were jumbled up like a thorn bush in a storm'), but he remained attached to it until his death in 1827. Descending into deafness, he imagined music unlike anything his contemporaries were writing; the *Hammerklavier* sonata from this period still strikes us as a revelation of the piano's extreme limits of power and expressiveness. The longest of Beethoven's thirty-two piano sonatas, the *Hammerklavier* is generally acknowledged to be his most difficult and his most visionary composition for the keyboard, a technical and poetic tour de force whose fugue finale still startles listeners to this day. The composer predicted as much when he wrote to his publisher, 'Now you have a sonata that will still keep the pianists busy when it is played fifty years from now!' In a sense, Beethoven was composing for an instrument that didn't yet exist. Within a generation it would and the piano would reach its apotheosis.

Two of the most imaginative piano manufacturers who spent time in London at the end of the eighteenth century were French, Sébastien Erard and Ignace Pleyel. When the fires of the revolution subsided they returned to Paris and established what would become the most important piano houses of the early nineteenth century. They were both firmly committed to the stronger, more robust action that was gradually supplanting the Viennese style and Erard, with a sensitivity to a musician's needs, refined the design of the new breed of pianos. His inventions include the modern pedal mechanism for more expressive control; the use of metal bracing bars over the soundboard to allow a considerable increase in string tension, thereby enhancing the tone's power and volume; and, most famously, the double escapement action that keeps the hammer close to the strings. This ingenious design, used by every manufacturer in substantially similar form to this day, allowed for the first time the extremely rapid repetition of a single note. The new Romantic music required not only a wider compass of notes and a greater amplification of the sound, but also mechanical solutions for the speed, power and contrast of the new soloists.

America made its contribution, too, in the first half of the nineteenth century, first with a one-piece cast-iron frame patented by Alpheus Babcock in 1825 and improved upon and successfully manufactured by Jonas Chickering in 1843. More than any other breakthrough, this design allowed Romantic music to be played with abandon without fear of damaging or destroying the instrument. The machine age had finally brought its technology to bear on some of the piano's fundamental structural problems and the result was a tough, resilient mechanism fitted to a massive structure. Henry Steinway, a recent immigrant from Germany, consolidated these improvements and added his own: diagonal cross-stringing of bass notes, an innovation in 1857, allowed much longer and more resonant strings to be used.

The successful development of the piano in the United States demonstrated that the wealth, the manufacturing capacity, and the ingenuity of America had to be reckoned the equals of Europe. The piano was a distillation of inventiveness, craftsmanship, cultural seriousness, and marketing prowess, and within two generations of its appearance in the New World Americans were producing instruments that were unsurpassed.

The new music that emerged in Beethoven's shadow was nothing if not dramatic and Liszt was its avatar. As a performer he was the first of a new breed of itinerant *virtuosi* who created excitement, even uproar, wherever they went. His playing was not just energetic; it was obsessed, enthralling, and – for pianos, at least – destructive. At the beginning of his long career when pianos were not yet iron behemoths with a wooden shell, Liszt commonly had one or two pianos in reserve at each of his concerts. They would be carried on in turn as their predecessors fell beneath his hands, offerings to the god of louder, faster, more emotional music. At the end of the concert the stage was littered with dead pianos, as if after some latter-day approximation of gladiatorial combat. The halls, too, were littered, not with pianos but with hysterical women swooning before the first hero of the concert stage.

As pianos became stronger Liszt sampled them all and his endorsement, like that of great athletes for sports gear today, was jealously sought. Erard long claimed that their piano was the choice of Liszt, but Liszt also played and owned most of the great makes: England's Broadwood, America's Steinway and Chickering, Germany's Bechstein, Austria's Bösendorfer.

Chopin was Liszt's opposite when it came to his style of playing. He preferred Pleyels, finding them conducive to a softer, more subtle way of addressing the keyboard than was currently popular; he hated public recitals and performed very little. Volume and raw power did not interest him. Instead, he developed an entire music that required a revolutionary technique in playing to reveal its harmonic and rhythmic subtleties. '*Souplesse!*' he urged his students in Paris. 'Suppleness above all.' His compositions almost define the term 'pianistic'; indeed, none of his melodies is really convincing when transposed for the voice or other instruments.

More than any other composer's, Chopin's music directly addresses the central paradox of the piano: how to make a percussion instrument sing. This is the basic riddle that any serious pianist faces, to find a way of using the piano's machine precision to bring forth a continuous stream of notes that cast the enchanted net we call music. It is in some important sense counterintuitive, and specific techniques have to be learned and assimilated to create the illusion of flow. Overlapping successive notes, clever finger work, use of the pedals, and tonal shading: all are important in developing the singing line that brings Chopin's compositions alive. His music was born on the keyboard and it has remained popular throughout the world since he wrote it, more so by far than that of the showman, Liszt.

Liszt was the vanguard for a whole piano phenomenon that swept the rapidly industrializing West. While Chopin and Mendelssohn and Schumann composed masterworks for the solo piano and a small army of performers took their works around the world, the piano also lent itself to the hands of those who were far from virtuosi. It became the single most important engine of entertainment that the Western world knew.

Think of a world with no electricity: no radios, telephones, stereo systems, televisions, films, cars, or computers. All of the diversions that we now take for granted were still to come, and yet the rapid industrialization of Europe and America meant more money and, with it, more leisure time for a fast-growing mercantile class. There was more time to see one's friends and neighbors, and more money with which to entertain them; music-making at home was increasingly popular and the piano was the ideal social lubricant.

Manufacturers realized this early on and as the piano-making business grew in the early nineteenth century, the output was destined for the changing household far more than for the conservatory or the concert stage. A vast quantity of popular music was written for the piano and most of it was played for entertainment in the home. The piano came to be regarded as one of the indispensable 'accomplishments' that made women of the new middle class charming, attractive, and – not least – marriageable. For many this was a mixed blessing. Some idea of the piano's prevalence in polite society can be gleaned from Oscar Wilde's comment at the end of the century: 'I assure you that the typewriting machine, when played with expression, is not more annoying than the piano when played by a sister or near relation.'

Unique among instruments, the piano was also a piece of furniture and this was crucial to how it was marketed. At the beginning of the nineteenth century there were two principal designs with different shapes: the square and the grand. The square piano (an oblong, rather) resembled a large, thick table with a keyboard inset in one of the long sides. When closed it was often disguised as a sideboard or a desk. Musically, however, its relatively small soundboard and delicate tone made it ill-suited to the louder and more chromatic interpretations that were current, and by mid-century it began a rapid decline in popularity.

The grand piano's singular and unmistakable shape, developed first by Cristofori, was patterned after the harpsichord. The Germans call it '*ein Flügel*' ('a wing') while the French refer to it as '*un piano à queue*' ('a piano with a tail'). Unlike the square piano, it resembled no other piece of furniture. Anyone who could afford a grand, though, wouldn't want to hide it. Aside from its advantages musically – larger soundboard, stronger frame, longer keys – much of its appeal lay in the fact that it was massive, elaborate, and demonstrably expensive, an island of gentility in the parlors of the new bourgeoisie.

The other shape of piano, the square, was gradually displaced by a new design, the upright, in the middle of the nineteenth century. The rectangular shape of the new upright made it easier to fit against a wall than the curved grand, an important consideration for the small interiors of so many nineteenth-century houses and apartments. And it was considerably cheaper than its aristocratic cousin.

The history of the piano's development in the nineteenth century is, in some measure, the history of the Industrial Revolution. Changes and refinements in the instrument's capabilities closely followed the technical breakthroughs of the Machine Age that made them possible: cast iron for the frame, fine metalwork for precision parts, stronger adhesives for laminations, and so forth. What in 1800 was a piece of lightly reinforced cabinetry that most resembled the harpsichord from which it derived, finished the century in its fully evolved form, a massive assemblage of machine parts and technical finesse.

In line with the technical advances, popular tastes concerning the tones a piano produces evolved rapidly. Western industrialization was just dawning in the 1820s and with it a world of powerful sounds that no one at the time could even suspect. When one of Mozart's piano sonatas is played today on a perfectly restored Viennese period instrument, although we hear the same tones as they did in the late eighteenth century, we cannot hear them in the same way. What for a contemporary ear was remarkably loud after the soft tones of clavichords and virginals, sounds to us as delicate, almost ephemeral. Such a pronounced difference has as much to do with the way we hear things as it does with the evolution of piano building methods.

Luc regularly contrasted the 'sweet' tones produced by his early nineteenth-century pianos with the acoustic landscape of modern life. 'The public will no longer settle for the original mellow sounds, no matter how accurate and pure. The tone always has to be loud and bright, whether it's jazz, classical, or pop. We can't go back, even if we wanted to.'

He likened it to the way we look at Notre Dame in contrast to the way someone from the late Middle Ages would have seen that same structure. We live with it at the heart of Paris, we know everything there is to know about its construction, the art of its sculpture, the methods used for its stained glass. But its scale is, in itself, unimpressive in our day of skyscrapers and Eiffel Towers. We can't possibly see it standing alone.

'Now,' he continued, 'imagine someone coming to Paris for the first time in, say, 1350. As he came down into the Bassin Parisien he would see a good-sized town straddling the modest river, with simple houses and public buildings not exceeding three stories. And there on one of the islands in the stream would be an immense and unique structure, alive with statuary and gleaming white in the sun, one of the handful of truly large structures – all of them cathedrals or chateaux – in northern France. When he entered the colossal doors and walked under its vaults, it would feel different from anything he had experienced before, perhaps sublime, quite possibly like the house of

God. I think that's something like what it must have felt to hear Beethoven on his Viennese Graf.'

The whole world has changed around us in ways we can only guess at. In an age when any stereo system can re-create the full range of tones audible to the human ear, is it any wonder that piano tuners are expected to make the instruments bright and clear, and, above all, loud? In this sense, the modern ear can be seen as a response to the assault – both in volume and in sheer quantity – of noise in our time, and it's a process that began nearly two hundred years ago.

A piano boom began in the 1850s, fuelled by increased production, rising affluence, and easy terms. A piano was one of the few luxury goods available to a majority of consumers and it was among the first to be available through financing schemes allowing payment over time. Suddenly there was a piano for everyone, and the rise in both output and sales was dramatic. In 1850 worldwide production was around fifty thousand instruments a year; by 1910 that figure topped half a million, of which three hundred and fifty thousand represented the production in the United States alone.

This was the piano's high-water mark, a time when a piano could be found not only in every respectable home, but also in every school, bar, club, church hall, steamship, café, and roadhouse in the West. In the deft translation of manual dexterity into loud tones it perfectly distilled the technological genius of the age; its successful marketing was a precursor of all the consumer goods that were to follow. It's no coincidence that when the Eiffel Tower was built in 1889, the first artifact to be hauled to the small rooms at the top was a piano, a small Pleyel upright, reflecting the futuristic structure's blend of engineering and art.

The piano wave crested at the beginning of the twentieth century and the flood gradually subsided. There were about three hundred makers of pianos in the United States in 1910; by 1950 that number was closer to thirty. The decline in European production was equally dramatic. New forms of entertainment and transportation meant the home was no longer the center of social life, and radio, television, movies, and recorded music – all more passive forms – displaced many keyboards. Musically, the piano was brilliantly exploited by a generation of black players and composers who invented uniquely Afro-American forms that were born on the keyboard – blues, boogie-woogie, and jazz – and were central to the birth of rock and roll. Songwriters still use the piano when they compose, classical artists continue to interpret the repertoire, and countless youngsters have their introduction to music seated in front of this strange piece of furniture. But the days of its unquestioned supremacy, its omnipresence throughout the entire society, are over.

Certain conventions adhere to the piano, not all of them explicitly practical, some of them hard to fathom. For instance, black is the color invariably associated with the piano. One thinks of Henry Ford's dictum concerning the Model T: 'You can have any color so long as it's black.' In fact, pianos were not originally black. They were neither painted nor lacquered; their cases were made of fine wood and the grain was left revealed. As with harpsichords before them, stains and veneers, marquetry and inlays were extensively used, but the most common color, until well into the nineteenth century, was of highly polished wood in tones of brown and chestnut. Rich whorls of mahogany or cherry were treasured for their beauty, just as they were in any other fine piece of furniture. The fact that many of their makers began as master woodworkers counted for much in this practice.

Gradually, over the course of the nineteenth century, pianos were painted and lacquered rather than being left in their natural state. This was partly due to the fact that with greater and greater numbers of pianos being produced, the quality of the wood in their cabinetry was not what it had been in the days before mass production. Paint and lacquer covered a multitude of sins at the low end of the market. The finest pianos, however, became more and more idiosyncratic. Finishes and colors were offered to match the suites of expensive furniture that filled the salons of the bourgeoisie, whether Louis XV, Regency, or Victorian. The culmination of this trend was the art case piano, a grand piano whose carved case was decorated with elaborate paintings and filigrees.

The great manufacturers – Steinway, Erard, Bechstein – commissioned piano cabinets from famous cabinet makers. Some extraordinary objects resulted. One of these, a Steinway model D decorated in high Victorian style in the 1880s, recently sold at auction for $1.2 million, 'the highest price ever paid for a piano', as the newspapers trumpeted. Another Steinway D from the 1930s, encased in natural mahogany and sitting on three gilded legs in the shape of eagles, is the official White House piano. Every musical instrument collection features them in one form or another, as do museums and palaces throughout the world. They are, in effect, the ultimate bauble: Napoleon III gave a fancy Bösendorfer to his Empress, Eugénie; Czar Nicholas offered Alexandra a Bechstein that was decorated like his gilded coach.

More recently, Bösendorfer has produced a limited edition of modern art case pianos designed by the well-known architect, Hans Hollein. With angular brass legs and red undersides to the black fall board and lid, it looks like something the Russian Constructivists might have imagined. Its principal curiosity is a conceptual detail made possible by current technology: instead of a prop stick, Hollein designed for the massive lid special bracing and an electric motor run by a car battery so that it could rise and sit fully open with no apparent support. I once happened upon one at a New York dealer's showroom and asked the elegant, blonde-streaked saleswoman if I could take a look at the insides.

She reached underneath the case and flipped a switch. There was a whining sound and the top started to lift, but after an inch or so it fell back down. It did this several times in rapid succession, like a giant castanet. Finally there was a clicking sound and its convulsions stopped. 'Dead battery,' she declared with a deadpan look. 'Why don't you come back tomorrow and we'll fire this baby up.'

The irony today is that the more elaborate the case and the more gimmicky the decoration, the greater the derision from serious musicians. There is a practical consideration: ormolu fittings and elaborate inlays, metal music desks and carved cherubs weigh on the case and can detract from its ability to resonate. But principle is a stronger argument. Real musicians want a piano that is entirely an instrument, in the full sense of that term, a medium that is stripped down to the mechanism and with a craftsmanship that will produce the sounds they intend. Nothing should distract from that purpose, either functionally or visually, and so the standard is invariable: unadorned, elegant in its simplicity. The painted and carved and inlaid cabinets that the great makers turned out are fine for the furniture collector and there is a thriving market in them as investments, but for the dedicated pianist they'll always seem like a classical sculpture clad in a ruffled silk dress.

The preference for simplicity developed at the beginning of the twentieth century. As the spirit of modernism dawned, a convention emerged that concert pianos should be stark, unadorned, and shiny black, a perfect mirror for the gleaming insides. Black, the non-color, the always-elegant foil to light and movement, carried the day and so it has remained the standard. An even more rigid convention – there are virtually no exceptions – is that of the key colors, black and white. There has always been this pronounced contrast between the two kinds of keys, but in the eighteenth century it was very often reversed: the naturals were black and the accidentals white. The present arrangement has prevailed since the beginning of the nineteenth century. What's needed is visual contrast, but there is no particular reason that keyboards couldn't be configured in, say, blue and yellow or red and black. But even on fancy custom pianos with elaborate casework, black and white is the rule.

How many elephants died for the ivory that covered keyboards until quite recently? The plainest answer is 'Too many'. Only in the past twenty years has the indiscriminate slaughter of elephants for their tusks troubled piano lovers. It's one of those cultural conceits, like bird-of-paradise feathers for women's hats in the late nineteenth century, that now seem unimaginable but at the time were seen as perfectly normal, indeed necessary. Now laws have been passed and synthetic substitutes have been developed to take the place of elephant tusks. They differ from ivory in two ways: look and feel. Many pianists, particularly concert artists, prefer ivory because it is said to absorb sweat from the fingers and to have a 'softer' feel than polymer-based replacements. Beyond such a practical consideration, the look of real ivory is a more immediate attraction. The natural material has very slight irregularities in the grain and a tendency to yellow gently over the years, the edges of the key tops rounding with use. Plastic looks white and stays white, and it shows very little wear. Ivory keyboards are unquestionably beautiful and full of *caractère*, but it's hard not to see all the millions of pianos that have been built over the last two centuries as an elephant graveyard.

Like so much of Western culture, the piano has since been projected far and wide on the planet: at a time when colonialism went unquestioned pianos were sent up the Amazon, across the Sahara, and into the frontier settlements of the American West. Its history is comparatively recent and since it tends to be long-lived, many of those pioneer pianos survive in one form or another. Perhaps the ultimate proof of its missionary status is that by far the greatest number of contemporary pianos come from Asia. Yamaha, Kawai, Young Chang, Samick, Dongbei: all are familiar brand names and increasingly respected. Japan, Korea, and China lead the world in production.

Electronics and metal alloys, computer chips and state-of-the-art plastics: all have been applied to the piano's design, but they don't improve the original appreciably. It is what it is, a perfect articulation of an idea that occupies a kind of cultural cul-de-sac. It's the ultimate expression of one strand of our mechanically clever culture (think of the typewriter or the computer keyboard) joined to our specific notion of music based on the diatonic scale. Its great genius is to translate the merely mechanical into the realm of music.

11

LESSONS

When at last the Stingl had become acclimated to our apartment it became part of the household landscape. It was not quite a member of the family but more, somehow, than a pet. I wanted it to be both accessible and respected, so we set up some ground rules that mirrored Luc's suggestions: no food or drink near the piano, no pounding on the keyboard, no radio or loud talking in the same room when someone was playing. Otherwise the new arrival was open to all and my daughter in particular liked picking out melodies on the keys when no one else was around. I played it every day for those first weeks and even my haphazard doodlings could transform the moment into a dream of escape and inventiveness: the keyboard became music's secret pathway to another world.

Now that I had a piano, the first I had ever owned, I felt both giddy and intimidated by the responsibility it implied. This was a substantial step, like buying a house or a new car, and I wanted to use it to transform my life, to rediscover music. I harbored no illusions about being able to take up where I had left off; it had been fully twenty years since I had last practiced with any regularity and it seemed unimaginable that I had ever played Bach two-part inventions or Mendelssohn songs. But now the Stingl was in tune, its keyboard beckoning me each time I passed it. At first I began with simple scales and progressions of chords, the dutiful student dimly remembering the outlines of a long-ago practice routine. I recalled a few well-loved pieces whole – Schubert waltzes came readily to mind – and some passages from others, but soon my frustration grew as I was only able to reproduce the snatches of memory that had stayed with me. I could see clearer than before that I'd make no progress without a teacher.

Teachers for young people abound, since youth is the time when our brains most readily absorb the language of music. But would I find someone prepared to take on an adult of medium ability, who could give me an honest evaluation of my level? I wanted to make the most of whatever had remained to me from my childhood studies and gradually work on filling in the large areas in which I was ignorant or lacking confidence, such as sight-reading and harmony. I was even ready to hear that I would have to start over as a rank beginner, but not before a competent musician had properly analyzed my status.

Most important, though, I wanted to change the basic approach that I had known as a boy, to escape the form of genteel tyranny I had encountered with Miss Pemberton and be forthright with my teacher. There would be no expectation of a career or even recitals, no promise of undiscovered talent waiting to be fulfilled. The bargain would be clearer this time, I decided, and more personal: I'd choose pieces that would deepen the pleasure I found in music and that enlarged my sense of the world. If I reveled in that freedom, though, I also felt a different kind of responsibility, to take seriously the framework of lessons so that I could learn to express myself at the keyboard. I was no longer trapped in a child's world; if I chose discipline, it had to be worth it.

I asked around about the possibility of piano lessons for adults, but most of my friends and acquaintances were familiar only with the rigidly hierarchical system of the French *conservatoires*, where age limits and an early start were the rule. One day I mentioned my need to a French friend, Claire. 'Why, I've got a wonderful teacher,' she said, 'and I did just what you want to do: I went back to the piano after leaving it behind when I finished my studies at the university.'

Claire's words surprised me: although we had known each other for some time, I had no idea that she was a pianist. It turned out she was currently working on a Brahms intermezzo, which told me she was light years ahead of my level, but she insisted that her teacher, Anna, took students at all levels and was particularly good at figuring out where there was work to be done. She taught in one of the municipal conservatories close to Paris, but she also taught private students at her house. I took her number and called her a few days later. In her heavily-accented French – Anna was a Lebanese émigrée who had lived in Paris for a decade or so – she agreed to meet me at her house the following week for what she called '*un rendezvous de premier contact*'.

Anna lived in the *proche banlieue*, the near suburbs, just across the Paris city line. Like most of the communities on the city's outskirts, it had once been a small town with a real center: town hall, town square, town church. As Paris had grown, however, these had been overrun by development so that it was now a mishmash of modern apartment buildings and older facades housing small grocery stores, modest restaurants, and laundromats. Anna lived on the ground floor of an older three-story building. A direct metro line stopped nearby and so it took me less than half an hour to arrive at her doorstep. I could hear a piano from behind the door and when I rang the bell the playing abruptly stopped. A short, slender woman with long, auburn hair pulled back into a bun opened the door. She was wearing black pants, a black turtleneck, and a bright-yellow vest that was elaborately embroidered with silver thread. 'You must be Claire's friend. I am Anna. Please come in.'

Cordially, but with a certain reserve, she showed me into the *séjour* (a small living room) of a modest apartment. A few pieces of furniture skirted the wall – a small couch, some chairs, a bookcase, and a desk – but the room's main feature was a large black Bechstein grand set at a slight angle to one of the interior walls. Stacks of sheet music lay in piles on shelves and chairs. Anna invited me to sit down on the bench, and she pulled up a chair alongside and asked me about my musical background.

I began tentatively, describing my beginnings in Fontainebleau and talking about the different teachers I had had throughout childhood and adolescence. She listened attentively to what I had to say and then she asked a number of precise questions: Had I studied harmony? Had my teachers favored one method or another? How often had I practiced? What music did I prefer? How long had it been since I had played regularly? What were my objectives in returning to the piano?

'Fine,' she said after I had briefly sketched out my experience. 'Let's turn to the keyboard and see where you are today.'

She invited me to play a C-major scale, slowly and with an emphasis on a very consistent rhythm. The scale was easy, I thought as I began to play, but the regular phrasing that she asked for was not so obvious and my hesitation came out in the notes. She watched carefully as my fingers moved across the keyboard. We then spent most of the remainder of the hour on intervals. After I played a minor fifth, say, she would ask me to sing it, then to sing the corresponding major fifth in the inverse order. It was challenging but fun, and I found myself concentrating intensely on the logic of the keys and the tones and half-tones that separated them. After a half-hour or so of this, she said simply, 'You must be able to hear precisely in order to play precisely.'

I was not aware of how much effort had gone into my listening carefully to the tones and the distances between them until we finished the hour. By then, Anna would have me play a single note, say an F-sharp, and then she would say 'minor fourth, descending' and she would expect me to sing the second note that corresponded to the interval she had named. I made many mistakes, but I surprised myself to discover that this kind of mental calisthenics had awakened a sense that had gone unexercised for many years. I was also strangely captivated with the rediscovery of the French terms that I had learned so long ago. Not since my first hesitant steps with Madame Gaillard in Fontainebleau had scales been *gammes*, piano keys *touches*, flats *bémols*: all the rest of the specialized vocabulary that music calls its own fell readily into place. It surprised me to find how quickly it jumped back into my mind.

At the end of the hour, Anna turned to me and gave me her assessment. 'You have a very good ear and you are lucky for that. With your big hands you could easily play Brahms – the notes at least – but your touch is very imperfect. If you like we could work together and try first to identify your blind spots, and then concentrate on filling them in before we worry about your level of interpretation.' I felt encouraged by her words but also somewhat embarrassed to hear the specifics of what I already sensed: there were major gaps in my understanding of the fundamentals of music. But her manner was reassuring and her willingness to take me on as a student sparked a keen ambition to work hard.

We agreed that I would come to her apartment once a week for a lesson and she told me to bring a blank music notebook the next time. From then on I spent an hour each week with Anna, shoring up the unsteady foundations of my musical education. Initially I took a lot of time to reacquaint myself with the keyboard, principally by playing intervals, scales, and harmonic progressions. Anna had me draw the *Cercle de Quintes*, a graphic representation of the interrelationship of the various major and minor keys. She called it my 'Rosetta Stone' and often she asked me to describe the exercises I played in terms of their place on the circle.

She told me from the outset that she would like me always to be working on two different pieces for the variety and for the challenge. For starters she chose Bartók's *Mikrokosmos*, a collection of progressively difficult pieces that highlight various pianistic challenges, and *The Notebooks of Anna Magdalena Bach*, an assemblage of compositions by Johann Sebastian Bach and some of his friends, to be played by his youthful second wife, Anna Magdalena. Together we worked through their sections, beginning with the Bartók. Some of the pieces seemed deceptively easy, but Anna insisted that I under-stand them harmonically before going on to more complicated things. Understanding the structure of even simple compositions was new to me and when I would express my frustration she wrote in my note-book, '*Etre patient avec soi-même!*' ('Be patient with yourself!') She made me understand that being able to play all the notes without understanding what was going on was a hollow accomplishment; technique as an end in itself was the antithesis of her approach.

Much of her time was spent developing my ear, which she said was particularly sensitive. She would have me sing the melody voicings as I played harmony and vice versa, and even in simple pieces she continually exhorted me to hear subtle harmonies and dissonances. We practiced a form of musical gymnastics, which consisted in having me say out loud the name of the next chord as I played harmonic progressions, faster and faster. It was nerve-racking at first, but it was strangely thrilling as I came to know the sequences not just with my hands, as before, but as an idea that the mind could grasp while the piano gave it a voice.

From my very first lessons with Anna I experienced a satisfaction and a kind of pleasure that I had not expected. Even the simplest figuration in those first pieces – a change of key, an unexpected chord – could fill me with joy as I grasped with my ear and my mind what was intended, however straightforward. This was a new kind of experience for me: not just fingers on the keyboard but a deeper level of comprehension and, with it, of beauty.

Very often I made mistakes or I misapprehended a piece's structure terribly but Anna would methodically go over the problem with me and have me take it slowly. '*Travailler par petits bouts*,' ('Work in small pieces') she would write on the score and we would go on. '*Pas d'accents*!' was a constant refrain and I had to concentrate fiercely to avoid drawing attention to notes that were not meant to be emphasized.

I worked on some early pieces by Schumann, one of Anna's favorite composers, as well as some Schubert dances, pieces that I was able to master completely; eventually, Anna proposed that I try some of the Beethoven bagatelles and a fantasy of Mozart that intrigued me with its strange dissonances. When I worked on them I had for the first time a real sense of trying to understand music that was challenging, profound, and beautiful. Mozart and Beethoven wrote much that was far more difficult, much that I'll never play, but these pieces nonetheless seemed challenging and serious, and the rewards they gave me were commensurate with my efforts. I was no longer a beginner.

Playing Anna's Bechstein was an added delight. Good as the Stingl was, my piano simply didn't have the same kind of resonance as this masterpiece of German artistry that dated, I learned, from 1906. It had come through the convulsions of Europe's two world wars intact, and now it graced Anna's modest apartment with a power and a dignity that inspired me even when I played the simplest exercises on its ivory keyboard. At times it seemed like Anna's alter ego; when she occasionally played through a Chopin or Haydn piece for my benefit, the piano and Anna were indivisible, each the extension of the other as the music poured forth.

One of the revelations of taking up the piano again as an adult was to find that, other than in musical matters, my teacher was my peer. Gone were the empty, childish excuses for not having practiced; gone, too, the sheepish reliance on others to make me work. The fundamental rule was simple enough to grasp without ever being articulated: if you practice, you get better. It was as simple – and as demanding – as that. It was an unexpectedly pleasant form of self-discipline: this travail wasn't for my parents or for the teacher or for the year-end recital. This was for me. Anna and I talked about this only obliquely, but she gave me to understand early in the process that there had to be a fairly serious commitment from me if our time together was to be worthwhile.

I hadn't formulated clear goals for myself and at first I thought this was a mistake. I didn't have in mind one day to play a Beethoven sonata, say, or to work my way up to the *Goldberg Variations*. The challenge of individual pieces from which I learned something new was somehow enough; the whole question of accomplishment was beside the point, as it hadn't been when I was young.

One day, as I was gathering my music from the Bechstein's music desk, Anna told me that she had a small gift that she thought would be helpful in my approach to music. She took out a little paperback book called *Zen et l'art chevalerèsque du tir à l'arc (Zen and the Chivalrous Art of Archery)* and offered it to me. 'As you're beginning to see, it's one's attitude that counts.'

I read the book excitedly that evening, recognizing in oblique form some of Anna's precepts. Its philosophy put contemplation at the heart of mastering a demanding activity – in this case archery – that seemed rooted in the merely physical; it placed the emphasis on concentration and on an appreciation of the process of learning. Each new skill, however modest, had its own revelations and satisfactions, and mental discipline counted as much as the aesthetic pleasure in the undertaking at hand. The student must respect the master, it said, and accept a rigidly hierarchical relationship. In particular, one had to practice a form of alert detachment in order to give expression to one's art. 'Stop thinking about relaxation!' cried the master to the student. 'It's only because you're not really detached that you feel tension. And yet everything is so simple!'

This attitude embodied Anna's approach to music; both challenging and realistic, she taught me a way of using internal concentration to know a part of what we call beauty. 'You have to look at the works of a Brahms or a Schubert and recognize them for the masterpieces they are. And then be grateful if one small part of those masterworks lends itself to your skill at interpretation. It's a way of looking at life, isn't it? There is no such thing as perfection.'

12

CAFÉ ATELIER

As my friendship with Luc grew, I felt more and more at ease at the atelier and found, with pleasure, that although I was often hailed affectionately by Luc as *l'américain du quartier*, there were times when I became an honorary Frenchman. Late on Friday afternoons, when Luc had finished up for the day or had concluded a particularly satisfactory transaction, the atelier would take on the atmosphere of a good café. Customers, friends, acquaintances: all would linger for an extra half-hour. Luc held forth in the back, sometimes provoking arguments with half-serious assertions and wild claims, as half a dozen conversations motored along under the high skylight.

He conducted a minor ritual at the end of every Friday. Like a lesser clergyman seeing to his aspersions, he sprinkled water around the wooden floor of the atelier from a large zinc bucket. He said it was to keep the dust down and it no doubt helped to do that, but he also said it was his unscientific way of humidifying the atelier over the weekend. The worn wooden floor, shredded in places by the constant friction of pianos being dragged across it, would turn a dark brown as the water seeped in, absorbing the moisture like a thirsty sponge. When one of his customers pointed out that spreading water on a wooden floor would eventually ruin it, he laughed at the thought: 'This floor will last a lot longer than I will, no matter what I put on it!'

In the few minutes it took him to slosh the water around the atelier, one or another of us in the back would open a bottle of wine and scrounge a few glasses from among the messy piles all around. When he finished his sprinkling and the sweet, dank smell of wet wood rose in the air, we poured a glass together and toasted the end of the week. This was the signal for a collective breathing out, and the stories and gossip and jokes could begin. Sometimes as many as ten or twelve people gathered amidst the rows of pianos, and an enthusiastic din would explode as people paired off and engaged in one of the Frenchman's favorite pastimes: talk.

One of Luc's customers, a thin, balding man with an austere air, was a student of what he called '*l'aspect social*' of the piano and he seemed knowledgeable about the growth of its popularity in the nineteenth century. By the 1880s, he claimed, it was often used by devout Catholic families to accompany the singing of hymns before meals. At the turn of the century, however, the balance had shifted from religious to secular uses, a transition made possible, according to him, by the success of the *Francs-Maçons* in breaking the hold of the Church on French society. And pianos were part of the change, free to be the untrammeled engines of enjoyment and pleasure with no need for a liturgical justification. Hymns before dinner gave way to light melodies that were popular in the new music halls.

At this point several people jumped in. The historian had mentioned a key word that, while puzzling to an American, was charged with gunpowder for a Frenchman: '*Francs-Maçons*'.

Opinions range across the entire political spectrum as to whether the Freemasons are a force for good or evil, but no one would deny their importance and their continuing influence in the institutions of French public life. It was one of the few times I heard Luc express an opinion that sounded political, although when I later thought about what he had said I realized that his strongest sentiment seemed to be almost anarchic. 'Religions at least give hope; that's something, even if it's based on dreams. But those who promise heaven here on earth, whether it's Communists or Masons, they're the worst of the worst.'

'In France the Masons don't promise heaven on earth! All they promise is the supremacy of the Republic!' The historian was irate.

But Luc's response was thick with sarcasm: 'Ah, yes, the holy Republic. With them pulling the strings, of course. It's the monarchy all over again, dressed up in democratic clothes.'

The discussion went on like this for a while. It wasn't really an argument, although the opinions expressed were strongly felt. A series of words and phrases are, for the French, filled with deep feeling: *La République, Francs-Maçons, la monarchie, la tradition laïque*, the secular tradition. It was unthinkable for those present not to have a point of view on these matters, although there seemed to be by common consent an unwillingness to force one's opinions on those who disagreed. Rather, it felt like the important thing was to get one's turn to disagree without directly attacking anyone else. The pot never boiled over, but it bubbled along noisily for some time.

As was so often the case, I was absolved from participation by being a foreigner. Americans in particular are often regarded by the French with something between fascination and bemusement, naïfs who can't possibly understand the complexities of domestic politics. This could be annoying, amusing, or – most often for me – useful. I could ask questions that would be thought too direct or provocative if posed by the Frenchmen present.

Gradually the intensity of the discussion subsided as more wine was poured out and another man, an older customer of Luc's with a shock of white hair, brought the subject back to pianos. He had a whimsical metaphor for the insides of grand pianos, a theory that only a Frenchman could espouse. For him they were like the packaging of champagne bottles, from the label to the foil wrapping around the cork. The reasoning he brought to this conceit was intense, formal, and rigidly intellectual. 'Look, they're both highly stylized systems of signs, organized around an unspoken convention that is nevertheless strictly adhered to. And the variations, while limited by the rules, give play to creativity and a certain circumscribed sense of beauty.'

Now there was silence as this categorical pronouncement was taken in with amused astonishment by all of us present. He led five or six of us from one grand piano to another, opening the tops with Luc's permission to illustrate his thesis. He pointed out how the subtleties of finish on a piano's cast-iron frame recalled the differences in the foil used by champagne houses to wrap the necks and corks of their bottles. For the piano, gold or bronze paint is invariably used as a final coat on the metal frame, but within that standard there are myriad variations. 'Think of the foil on a bottle of Moët Brut or Roederer Cristal or Taittinger. If I showed you the foil, I'll bet you could identify the brand simply from that feature.'

The others nodded in agreement. I remembered that some bottles of champagne had foil textured like snakeskin, others had smooth and shiny wrappings, but I could never have said which was which. As the group shuffled to the next piano that would illustrate another aspect of this theory, I stayed behind, lingering near the table where the wine bottle stood open. Luc said in a low voice, 'Well, the seminar has started and the professor is on stage.'

'He's done this before?'

Luc took a long drink from his *ballon de rouge* and sighed quietly. 'He teaches linguistics at the Sorbonne. Just don't say the word semiotics or we'll never get out of here.'

While the members of the seminar peeked into another piano at the back, we joined a conversation that was under way between a mustached man in a blue work smock and a blonde-haired young woman who lived in the apartment next door to the atelier. I had thought from his work clothes that he was one of the movers who regularly appeared at the atelier, but it became clear from what he was saying that he was a car mechanic. Luc told me later that he worked in the Renault garage down the street, and that he loved pianos and stopped in occasionally to see what was new.

He was drawing an analogy of his own, but rather than an academic theory with universal application, this was an impression that was offered hesitantly, drawn from his own experience. He described how for him opening the top to a grand piano is much like opening the hood of a car: the innards are where both the machinery and the art that make the thing go are laid bare.

Yes, I thought to myself, with this essential difference: a piano's top is opened not just when there is a problem and it can't be used; rather, an open top more often shows that a piano is ready to be played. Luc caught the same image and interrupted with a laugh: 'I'd hate to have to drive a Renault with the hood up!'

'Ah, my art is in the repairing, not the driving,' the garageman replied, 'although there are times I'd rather drive one of your pianos than some of the heaps my customers bring me to work on.'

'And I could sooner play Mozart on the dashboard of one of those heaps than on some of the disasters that pretend to be pianos!'

Laughter rose up and we poured out what remained in the bottle of wine. Looking around at the disparate group, it occurred to me how rare it was in France to mix freely with so many people from different backgrounds. You see it sometimes in the cafés, a rough approximation of camaraderie at the counter, but the groups who regularly meet at their favorite bar can most often be found in the booths and tables at the back, homogenous and closed to all but the initiates. The atelier fostered something else altogether, a coming together of people whose common points were Luc's approval and a love of pianos.

We started to clear up and I remarked that there were many fewer pianos than the last time I had stopped by.

'Oh, yes, I got rid of a lot recently. This isn't a music conservatory; after all, it's supposed to be a profit-making business!'

It felt as if Luc was trying to convince himself of this more than saying it for my benefit. When pianos began to pile up and the atelier became impossibly cluttered, Luc would abandon the quest for symmetry in the transaction and focus instead on selling a lot of pianos in a hurry. In another business this would be termed 'clearing the floor' or 'moving the stock', but I never heard Luc refer to it in the conventional terms of the retail trade. He 'got rid of a lot recently' or 'cleaned up the atelier' and the result would be that ten or fifteen pianos might be sold inside a week. I doubt that he actually lost money on these sales, but neither did he hold out for full price or even a worthy buyer. When this mood prevailed he was like a bulldozer that carried all before it.

And yet even in this house-cleaning mode he held on to a few favorites until the right moment came. They were the *rescapés* – the survivors – from the wrecker's ball and he saved them until a suitable customer appeared. Nothing made Luc happier than the balanced deal, the sale that left him with a decent profit and satisfied him that the piano had been placed with the right person. When I asked him about the lemonwood Gaveau that had been so dazzling, his eyes lit up. 'I sold it to a Japanese collector last week who wants to have a piano that is representative of each type in the world. He also bought a Pleyel upright and now he's looking for old Erards.'

This was virtually the ideal customer. Doubtless he had paid good money for the Gaveau and he was having it restored before sending it to Japan. He would likely buy more pianos from the atelier and the idea of a collection seemed wonderfully attractive to Luc, as if it insured that the instruments would be well cared for. And it appealed to him that these masterworks of European artistry were being sent off to the Orient, a kind of personal *mission civilisatrice* to a culture whose rigor and finesse he respected. 'Look,' he told me, 'we collect their chests and lacquer ware and swords. You can go down to the Faubourg St Honoré right now and find exquisite Japanese antiques from hundreds of years ago. Why shouldn't we send them some of our finest instruments? There's plenty for everybody.'

As we were leaving, I lingered in the narrow front room while we slowly filed out, talking and drinking the last of the wine. Along the wall of shelves stuffed to overflowing with the bolts of felt and various parts of piano mechanisms, I noticed a closed paper bag with a single word written on it in bold black marker: 'sitars'. I asked Luc what it contained. 'Why just what it says. Strings for sitars.'

We all stopped and stared at the paper bag, as if it would contradict Luc's words. 'So you supply East Indian musicians with their materials too!' The mechanic had a rich irony in his voice.

'Not by design. It happens that sitar strings are also appropriate for harpsichords and spinets, at least for part of the register, so we sell them to both. East meets West, if you like.'

Luc went on to explain that the strings were not as thick as piano strings and they were very much harder to come by. As a consequence, they were quite expensive. I asked where they were made and his answer was a kind of lilting singsong that I didn't understand: '*Ce sont des sitars des cisterciens de Cîteaux.*'

Now we all exchanged puzzled looks; none of the others present had followed either. Luc smiled and explained the improbable facts. There is still a community of Cistercian monks at the ancient abbey of Cîteaux. As one of their means to a livelihood they make sitars – and sitar strings – which they sell to musicians and collectors. Luc had come across their strings through a musician friend; he found them to be of excellent quality and he sold them as part of the comprehensive inventory he tried to keep on hand for keyboard instruments. He liked the fact that they were also serviceable as spinet strings. And what he called the *poésie* of the Cistercian connection was very special in his scheme of things. It had nothing to do with religion, he said, but with tradition, with making things painstakingly by hand because it was the right way to do it. That, he declared, was increasingly rare.

113

13

UN MATCH AMICAL

Now that I was taking lessons with Anna and practicing at home, I found that I was intensely aware of every scrap of piano music that drifted my way, as if my hearing had been sharpened to detect this one special kind of noise. I listened to things with a ravenous ear, things I wouldn't have noticed before, eager to imagine how others approached particular problems I was struggling with. I'd hear a piece on the radio and wonder how the pianist had worked out the fingering, or what pedaling had given a certain mysterious quality to the music.

One evening in the spring I was walking home across the Ile Saint-Louis, the smaller and more residential of the two islands in the Seine, when I heard loud piano music surging from an open window. As I drew closer I recognized Beethoven's *Diabelli Variations* being played forcefully and with a strange urgency. I held my breath in surprise and delight: to come across this piece is rare enough in the concert hall, much less by happenstance in the street, and the history of its inception is one of the great Beethoven stories.

In 1821 a Viennese music publisher, Anton Diabelli, sent a waltz that he had written to fifty prominent composers asking each of them to contribute a variation; among their number were Schubert, Hummel, Czerny, and the ten-year-old Liszt. Initially disdainful of the project, Beethoven decided to use the unassuming little tune to showcase his protean capacity for invention. In thirty-three masterful variations on the theme, he parodies the styles of lesser composers, alludes to works of Bach and Mozart, anticipates Chopin, and finally reaches heights of such sublime beauty that all other compositions for the piano pale in comparison. In short, he summarizes his entire art in an hour-long piece that is by common consent one of the towering works of the Western imagination, as great and fundamental a manifesto for the classical era as Bach's *Goldberg Variations* are for the baroque. Only the greatest pianists can give a convincing interpretation of this masterpiece and here was someone in full command of the music, pouring it forth in waves of subtle beauty.

By stepping across the street I could see through the open window the profile of a young woman at a grand piano. She was more than halfway through the thirty-three variations, and the arm of someone I couldn't see would periodically reach up to the music desk and turn the score. Her playing was technically superb and the depth of the tone color she projected in the various passages was breathtaking.

In my excitement I wanted to stop passers-by and make them take notice: 'Hey, listen to this! This is a phenomenal Beethoven!' But silently I continued to hang on each note as people hurried by, cars stopped and started; one of the immense *bateaux mouches*, the tour boats that Parisians derisively call *porte-avions* (aircraft carriers), glided noisily under the adjacent bridge, the Pont Marie, its klieg lights transforming the trees and buildings into cardboard movie sets. As the blazing light faded, the unseen page turner rose and walked to the window. She was an older woman wearing a bright-red sweater, and she pushed the hinged window closed, latched it firmly and pulled the drapes against the intrusions of the city. 'Oh, no!' I cried to myself. The music continued but it was now reduced to a distant tinkling with no poetry or verve to those of us outside. I had heard five, perhaps six, of these superb variations and that would have to do. Such revelations were rare and I appreciated them as special delights that couldn't be planned, another rich layer that Paris sometimes offers to the passer-by. I was therefore agreeably surprised when I discovered by chance some musical offerings in the building where I work.

My office is a small room on the courtyard side – *côté cour* – of a big seventeenth-century building near the Sorbonne. Unlike the residential *quartier* where we live, the streets nearby are thronged with life: cheap restaurants for students, clothes shops, and cafés lie next to some of the oldest buildings in Paris, dating from the late Middle Ages when Latin was the lingua franca of what we have come to call the Latin Quarter. The Tour Clovis, a Gothic bell tower, marks the site of a monastery that sheltered Abelard. Across the way the carved stone facade of Saint Etienne du Mont contains the remains of Pascal and Racine.

The building where I work dates from the 1600s and is made of the same massive, pale-yellow stone blocks that were used to build all of the oldest structures in the *quartier*. A modern-sized door is cut into one of the two enormous wooden portals that block the entrance arch and beyond this barrier the arch is extended to form a kind of sallyport that passes through the building to the inner courtyard. This courtyard is covered with massive old paving stones, their tops rounded with centuries of wear; they look like slate-colored pound cakes laid down in an uneven pattern.

While the street outside is bustling, loud, frantic with activity, the courtyard is a much more peaceful place. Its resonances are less frequent, softer, more intimate: a child playing ball at the far end, a window being closed, a cat scrambling up the trunk of a chestnut tree. One of the chief pleasures of writing in my small studio is that, with the quiet that prevails, I can overhear my neighbors practicing their musical instruments.

I had changed offices after buying the Stingl, setting up in an inexpensive space away from our apartment so that I could work on a book. When I first moved in it was early fall and rainy, and I heard very little. Windows were kept shut against the chill and damp, and I

116

caught only the occasional, tantalizing piece of music when one of the *voisins* would open his windows briefly in order to pull closed the shutters in the evening. With one floor below me and several above, it was next to impossible to pinpoint which window was giving forth music in the few moments before the sound was cut off.

As so often happens in Paris, spring arrived late and then, all at once, it was upon us. Before their leaves opened, the sober paulownia trees that dot the small parks and squares of the Left Bank suddenly exploded in showy violet flowers, like giant wisteria parasols, and the restaurants and brasseries along the narrow streets pushed every available table on to the sidewalk for the noonday meal. Flower vendors reappeared at some of the big intersections and groups of tourists began again to poke their way down the *ruelles*, the alleys and tiny streets that surround the Sorbonne.

With the first sunny days people threw open their windows for as long as there was light. The cold, gray Paris weather had weighed on us all and as soon as there was the suggestion of warmth in the air we invited it in. The unspoken rule still applied – no overly loud music – but during the day that was more flexibly interpreted than at night or in the early morning. Now a vibrancy welled up from the courtyard as music drifted from the welcoming windows, and I quickly made a catalog of who played what and when.

A jazz guitarist played in the mornings, his strumming filtering from the small window set at ninety degrees from mine and over-looking the same zinc roof of the single-story *pavilion* below. A very good flautist practiced scales in the late afternoon from an apartment at the far end of the courtyard. From the three-story building flanking the right side of the courtyard the low thrumming of a harp drifted down from one of the upper floors in the morning. The harpist would invariably start with a tuning across the entire diapason and then move on to scales. After twenty or thirty minutes of warm-up, though, he or she would play elaborate compositions, continuing for an hour or more. This was not the simple plucking of the troubador's harp or the forthright accompaniment for folk melodies. It was harp playing of the first order, a real virtuoso's repertoire, from baroque to modern. Once I recognized the harp solo from Berlioz's *Symphonie Fantastique*; most often the pieces were unknown to me but no less impressive. There is something about the resonance of a harp's plucked string that is deeply mysterious and thrilling: even to hear the mounting approximation of tones that came with the instrument's tuning was a delight.

I became accustomed to working with the sound of my neighbors' music wafting in from outside. Only when something was truly extraordinary – the Berlioz solo, for instance – would I turn my attention fully to what I had been overhearing, and this interruption was a small price to pay for the pleasure of little epiphanies that were all the sweeter for being spontaneous. On the occasional rainy days, windows were less frequently opened and I found that I missed what I had only dimly apprehended: a kind of secret sharing of what I imagined was the inspiration behind each piece of music. This oblique world of sounds had become very real to me. I felt as if I knew each of these unseen musicians; we had a bond that only I was aware of, and yet I felt as if they had withdrawn something to which I was entitled when they closed their windows against the wet.

On one of those first early spring days, I heard a piano coming from somewhere in the courtyard. Rather, I first heard a singer – a throaty contralto singing a *bel canto* aria – and realized that she was being accompanied expertly by a pianist. I listened carefully as passages were repeated two or three times by the pianist and then the singer would try them with a new musical accent or a changed rhythm. It seemed like a class, but I couldn't be sure. An assurance about the playing left no doubt that the piano really was taking on the part of the entire orchestra and yet the balance with the voice never seemed distorted.

There were good singers, there were bad singers, and many in between. Occasionally I would hear a melody that I knew sung beautifully. Once I overheard an extraordinary rendition of '*Libiamo . . .*', the drinking song from Verdi's *La Traviata*, and it had everything that one could want: a beautiful, pure tenor, dramatic phrasing, and an energy that was confident, forthright, and high-spirited. When they finished I wanted to applaud, to yell 'Bravo!' from my window for a performance that was unexpectedly ravishing.

Once in a while a singer was truly awful. This was a peculiar form of torture: not only could I not ignore the melody, but I was impelled to follow every note closely and to measure mentally just how far off the true pitch the singer had strayed. The worst was a soprano who struggled through an aria from Mozart's *Don Giovanni* with catastrophic results. From the very first note she was horribly, hopelessly, irretrievably off key, and with each high note the problems were exaggerated. 'Good God,' I would yell to myself, 'you're flatter than a mashed cat!' At one of the dramatic climaxes the music suddenly stopped and the pianist hit the right note – one full step higher than what she had been singing – five or six times and then sang along with it himself: 'La, la, la, la!' So it was a man, and although his voice's tone was not beautiful, the pitch was correct, and he was insisting that the soprano stop and take stock.

In that instant there was forged between me and him a bond. I felt gratitude and relief that he should haul the uncertain singing of the soprano back to a resemblance of what the composer had written. The soprano now tried the right note herself – 'La, la, la, la, la!' – and, magically, she sang it on key. Suddenly all was right with the world and I wondered at the patience of anyone who could gently correct the execrable.

For some time I had had it in mind to introduce myself, and when I heard the singing stop and noticed a woman clutching what looked to be sheet music leave through one of the doors on to the courtyard, I hurried down to the entryway to his stairwell. He resumed playing.

I hesitated for a long moment outside the apartment's door but finally knocked. The door was almost immediately opened by a young woman. 'I've come to see the pianist,' I offered hesitantly.

I could see him through the doorway behind her, seated at a large upright, a fine-featured man in his thirties with tortoise-shell glasses and a shock of unkempt hair. He immediately stopped playing and looked at me from the piano bench with a mixture of resignation and dismay. The woman's face lost its smile. 'I'll close the window,' he responded abruptly.

'Oh, please don't do that. Then I wouldn't be able to hear your wonderful playing.'

There was a moment's hesitation followed by relief as they determined that I was in earnest. He rose from the keyboard and introduced himself – Jean-Paul – and his wife, Odile. He was a professional accompanist. 'You're welcome to knock any time with compliments,' he said. 'It's the opposite reaction that usually shows up at my door.'

He invited me in for a glass of wine, assuring me that he had finished his practicing for the day and now needed to relax. We sat in the small *séjour*, where the piano held the place of honor against an interior wall. It was a Petrof, he told me, a very good Czech piano that he was particularly fond of. It had a very full tone for an upright, it didn't take up too much room in their modest apartment, and it had the added advantage of what the French call *une sourdine*, a mute pedal. This allowed him to practice at night without disturbing his neighbors.

I remarked on how many musicians there were in our courtyard, judging by what one heard with the windows open. He assured me that it was only happenstance that accounted for the large number of gifted musicians. He knew them all and he gave me a brief *catalogue raisonné* of my musical neighbors.

The jazz guitarist was, in fact, American and he played in clubs around Paris. It was his back window, however, that opened on to our courtyard; his entrance was from another courtyard altogether, so he was not known to those on our side save for the sound of his music floating out the back way. The harpist above Jean-Paul's apartment was actually two harpists, a wife and husband, both of whom were principal harpists with different orchestras in Paris. They practiced frequently and for long periods, so one was apt to hear a lot of harp in the morning. The flautist was an adolescent boy who was very gifted and very lazy – 'a classic combination,' Jean-Paul said – but when he played there was what he called 'magic in the air'. Besides the musicians whom we heard, he went on, there were several who lived in the buildings around the courtyard but who did not practice at home. 'You've got a very well-known mezzo living just down the hall from you, but she never sings a note outside the concert hall or the conservatory.'

Jean-Paul pulled out a bottle of wine and two glasses, and proposed that we drink to music. As we drank, I told him a bit of how I had bought my piano from Luc and I asked him how he had come to be a professional accompanist.

'I played the piano before I chose it,' he said quietly. 'In a sense, I was baptized before I wanted to be.'

He went to the conservatory and did exceptionally well: prizes, concerts, 'a career of great promise' opened up before him. But then, after years of preparation, it failed to blossom as all expected it to. Without elaborating, he said simply, 'I can't sell myself, so I'm not a soloist.'

There followed 'some difficult times' before one of his professors proposed to him that he consider becoming an accompanist. His sight-reading had always been superb and his ear was sensitive in that strange, almost uncanny way that we call perfect pitch. I asked him what exactly it was like to have perfect pitch, and he drew the distinction between what he termed *une oreille absolue*, absolute or perfect pitch, and *une oreille parfaite*, what in English we call relative pitch. Perfect pitch he described as the capacity to produce and name a note, any note, from a void, while relative pitch is where a specific sound triggers an association, and you can then recognize and name the musical intervals that exist relative to that sound. What was it like in practice, I wanted to know; how did it change his daily life, if at all? 'Ah' – he smiled wanly – 'it is my delight and my prison. I can't *not* hear!' Ironically, his *oreille absolue* was, in fact, falsely absolute insofar as it was keyed, from long years of playing, to the current diapason of 440 cycles per second, the prevailing standard frequency of vibration for A above middle C to which almost all pianos are tuned. When recordings or concert artists tuned their instruments to a higher reference pitch, as they sometimes did to produce a higher, brighter sound, he was lost. 'It's deeply disturbing, like an assault on one's innermost beliefs. And yet it's just a physical principle whose basis has been changed.'

The best antidote to the specificity of his ear's sensitivity, Jean-Paul said, was song. While a piano has specific tones with very clear intervals between all of the notes, song provides an infinite variety of tones with no abrupt transitions from one pitch to another. He spoke about the frustration of being limited to the specific tone quality of each of a piano's eighty-eight notes, so different from the human voice or a stringed instrument, where infinite modulation is the rule. 'I found that I need both. The piano is clear, precise, perfect in the narrow sense of the term. But song lets me dream.'

He had sung a lot as a boy, in choirs and on his own, and it was only later in life that he understood that song was in some measure the antithesis of what the piano presented him with. 'I realized later that being an accompanist gave me an entry into the world of song and it diminished the piano's tyranny. Of course, we all try to make the piano sing, but it's a losing battle. You're playing a percussion instrument, no matter how you look at it. The voice, on the other hand, is infinitely supple. I really believe that the brain is concentrated in different areas for piano and for song.'

Here Jean-Paul was describing the basic challenge that any serious pianist faces, to get beyond the piano's overly precise notes, to conjure the poetry of melody. Unlike most other instruments, a given tone on a piano cannot be directly altered for pitch. A violinist, a trumpet player, and a flautist can all push the pitch of their instruments by a half-tone, a quarter-tone, an eighth-tone – the possibilities are limitless. A pianist is tied to the purity of the tone produced when he depresses the key: he can't force it even slightly up or down, it is what it is. Specific techniques have to be learned and assimilated to create the illusion of flow so that the mind can construct a continuum from the separated parts. The most important of these is called *legato*, literally 'tied together', the art of depressing one note before releasing the one that precedes it so that the tones overlap and sound connected. 'Here the melody is a river, not a lot of raindrops!' Miss Pemberton would proclaim as I struggled to master *legato* phrasing.

'In the best case', Jean-Paul continued, 'you work with a singer who not only has a good voice, but who is also musically intelligent, and our instincts and ideas match and complement each other in interesting ways. We provoke each other and it brings out something new.' He likened it to a *match amical*, a friendly contest, in which the pleasure comes from the new territory that is explored together. 'Most often, though, you're in a strange situation where you know far more musically than the singer you're working with and yet you have to be careful how you assert yourself. You must earn the confidence, the respect, and the trust of notoriously wilful and self-centered performers.' The human qualities an accompanist needs most, he told me, are tact, humility, and kindness, but also a firmness about musical principles.

Jean-Paul claimed that accompanists were systematically misunderstood by singers and public alike. Singers too often develop the notion that their natural talent is everything and so they neglect their musical education. He contrasted this with the renowned singers of the past. Farinelli the great castrato, for example, had a profound understanding of harmony, counterpoint, melody, and sight-reading, and he used all of them to perfect his interpretations. 'It's almost inconceivable today that a singer would have that deep an orientation to his music, whereas a serious instrumentalist is expected to be a master of all those disciplines.'

As he was talking a bird trilled in the courtyard and we heard its song through the open window: sharp, clear, and high. Jean-Paul stopped in mid-sentence and pointed to the outside, a look of wonder crossing his features as we listened attentively to the insistent repetition. '*Ça tout seul, ça vaut un instrument.*' ('That in itself is as good as any instrument.')

He poured out more wine and continued. As far as the public is concerned accompanists are all but invisible when, in fact, musically and intellectually they're responsible for at least half the performance. 'All I can tell you for sure is that when it works, neither of you is conscious of the various elements. It's like a wonderful conversation where anticipation and communication merge. It's almost as if you are breathing together and the music is your breath.'

It heartened him to remember that Sviatislov Richter had spent many of his early years in Odessa as an accompanist in clubs and for light entertainment; Richter had always made a point of saying how it had taught him a way of hearing music that was entirely different from what the conservatory offered. Some things came out only when you were forced to join the discontinuous notes of a piano to the ceaseless stream of the voice.

After our meeting I listened to Jean-Paul's rehearsals with new interest, appreciating more fully the dialogue going on between the two musicians and the tact Jean-Paul used to convey his musical ideas. I was sorry when August came and he stopped for the summer holidays; it was as if our long-distance musical conversation had come to an end.

14

TUNING

As Luc had warned me, my piano gradually went out of tune over the course of the several months after it was delivered. I therefore arranged for Jos, the Dutch tuner who occasionally worked with Luc, to come by and tune the piano properly. This would be the first time that Jos would come to our apartment and while I relished his reputation as one of the best, I was wary of the consequences of his drinking. He agreed to stop by at eleven in the morning and in this I was following Luc's advice to catch him before noon, before the *ballons de rouge*.

At half past eleven Jos had not showed up and I began to be concerned. Just then my wife returned to the apartment for lunch and I explained the situation. She sympathized and then she added with a dawning awareness: 'Wait a minute. When I came into the courtyard a few minutes ago there was a guy in front of the neighbor's door looking confused. I stopped to talk to the concierge for a few minutes and he just stood there. When we asked him if he needed help, he said no and then he walked out to the sidewalk.'

'Tall and thin, with straggly hair and a red nose?'

'Yes, a very red nose' – inwardly I winced – 'and he was carrying a satchel that looked like a doctor's bag. I thought he was a delivery guy at the wrong address.'

'That's our man. Which way did he go?'

'I have no idea. He just wandered out to the street.'

This did not augur well. Despite my detailed written instructions,

Jos had taken himself only as far as the neighbor's apartment. Another five meters and he would have been at our front steps. Now there was nothing I could do; I would just have to wait to see what developed. I didn't have to wait long. A minute or two later the phone rang and Jos greeted me in a loud, affable voice. He spoke slowly in his Dutch-accented French. 'I have been at your door, but you were not there.'

'No, Jos, you were at the neighbor's door. We're the next one down on the right, just before the back of the courtyard.'

'Ah, it says "second-to-last door on right"' – he was obviously reading from the paper I had given him – 'but that's where I was.'

There was no point in arguing the detail, so I proposed that he come by and I would wait for him in the courtyard. 'All right, then, I'll come right away. I'm just using the phone in a nearby café.' He hung up and as I held the receiver with its droning dial tone I cursed my stupidity.

'What's wrong now?' My wife had overheard my side of the conversation.

'Our tuner is settled into a café somewhere nearby and I let him get away. He's supposedly coming right over.'

Another twenty minutes passed, during which I kept an eye on the courtyard from our windows one floor above. Finally the *portail* creaked open, and a slender figure made his way through the entrance and into the small courtyard. I ran down the stairs to intercept him before he took another false turn.

Jos was smiling broadly. His face was as flushed as when I had met him in the atelier and he seemed more interested in the potted plants in the courtyard than in coming in to tune the piano. 'Ah, you have wisteria! Such a difficult plant to grow in pots, at least in Holland. Does it bloom for you?'

'Those plants are the neighbor's, actually, and yes, he does get them to bloom in the spring. Shall we go inside?' Finally he was in our front door and headed up the single flight of stairs; he was positively effusive as he came into the living room and laid eyes on the Stingl. 'What a beautiful little grand!'

He was curious about its builder, surprised that in his twenty years of what he called 'piano work' he had never before come across this maker. Jos was intrigued by one or two of the mechanical elements that he could see under the open top – he pointed out the distinctive curvature of a few dampers in the middle registers that he said was characteristic of Bechsteins. I was both pleased that its apparent aspects satisfied him and vaguely disappointed that he had not brought me the story of a distinguished pedigree known only to a few, a Stingl renown that had not traveled beyond Central Europe. I left him alone to work, relieved that he seemed to be sober.

The long series of repeated notes began, climbing and descending the scales by half-tones as each note was brought into tune. Occasionally I would hear a laugh or an exclamation from the main room where Jos was working, most often when he was sounding a full chord. Then the individual notes would resume again with the subtle but insistent distortions that straddled the note before the true tone was captured, as pure yet as fleeting as a swallow in flight. After an hour the individual notes ceased and Jos sounded a series of loud chords across the whole keyboard. The tuning was finished and I returned to the main room to hear his assessment. 'What a tone! You've got a real prize!'

His enthusiasm was unqualified. The sonorous tone was to him very unusual for a baby grand and the feel of the piano had also captivated him. This, coupled with the fact that he had never heard of Stingl pianos, left him excited at the new discovery. His delight was infectious and when I played a few scales on the piano that was now perfectly tuned, the effect was even more impressive.

As he put his tools away and prepared to leave, Jos cautioned me not to use the pedals vigorously until the '*barre stabilisatrice*', the stabilizer bar was installed. He pointed out the holes which revealed the absence of a slender iron rod that should be fixed diagonally from the piano case to the lyre to brace the pedal housing. Without that bar in place, he warned me, the pedal mechanism could damage the action. I recalled that Luc had told me that the bar was missing when I first bought the Stingl and I made a note to ask him about it. I paid Jos for his services and said goodbye. He smiled engagingly and then descended the stairs and was gone. I watched him from the window as he shuffled through the courtyard, stopping once to pull down a lilac branch and bury his nose in the cluster of blossoms that hung heavily from its tip.

Tuning is a prodigiously difficult job. Consider the basics. A piano has more than two hundred strings, each of which must be individually tuned to a particular pitch. Each pitch must in turn relate to the pitch of the other strings so that a regular series of tonal intervals is produced across the entire range of notes, from the lowest bass to the highest treble. In one sense it is pure physics – mechanical, to use Luc's term – since the regularity of a vibrating string is predictable if all the other elements are constant. (In the real world, though, that's a very big if.) Everyone uses the same starting point: A above middle C is almost always tuned to 440 cycles per second, the number of times that a string oscillates to give its particular tone.

What keeps it from being a purely mathematical proposition, however, is the intricate mechanism that receives and processes the sounds produced, the human ear. It happens that we do not hear perfect intervals as perfect music; the human ear, in fact, hears high tones as if they were lower than their actual frequency. Put another way, a piano that is tuned to a mathematically perfect and regular series of intervals – every third and fifth and octave with exactly the same difference in frequency across the entire keyboard – sounds hopelessly wrong to the human ear used to Western music.

This presented fundamental problems as Western music evolved, but the means to reconcile it were not obvious. This was yet another of Johann Sebastian Bach's insights, that keyboard instruments had to be tempered, or slightly distorted, across their entire range so that the ear would hear harmony rather than dissonance. His comprehensive set of preludes and fugues, *The Well-Tempered Clavier*, is both an illustration and a manifesto for the adjustments that must be undertaken in order for music to be made with the same instrument in a wide variety of styles and dynamic ranges. Thus a piano must be tuned so that the intervals, rather than being uniform across the keyboard, are gradually expanded as you move into the upper registers.

What this really means is that tuning is always an approximation, an attempt to reconcile two notions: that of the mathematically pure with that of the musically appealing, the one empirical, the other intuitive. What the tuner is above all aiming to achieve is balance, a mean between the dissonance of theory and the pleasing tone of what the ear is used to hearing.

So much for the technical demands, complicated and irregular as they are. A further complication arises when one considers that no two pianos with different stringing scales – and different manufacturers typically attach their strings to the frame slightly differently – have their strings tuned in precisely the same way. And a variety of other considerations peculiar to the individual piano have also to be taken into account. Stiff strings, for instance, will slightly raise the pitch and this must be factored in when tuning.

Perhaps most important, there is also always a human dimension. Is the piano a sturdy upright that is banged on by children and played occasionally by their parents? Or is it a concert grand being prepared for a major public recital? Is the customer someone who has his piano tuned regularly, or is this a case where infrequent and overdue tunings are the rule? These and countless other considerations enter the equation and determine how a good tuner will achieve the equilibrium that is a good tuning. Part of the equation is anticipating how long the piano is likely to stay in tune from the kind of playing it is used for.

Luc's comment on different approaches was characteristically inclusive and non-categorical: '*Accorder un piano, c'est comme de la cuisine: chacun a sa recette.*' ('Tuning a piano is like cooking: everybody has their own recipe.')

It is, in fact, possible to tune by machine; this is an increasingly popular approach in the United States. But the results are often less than satisfactory. The point of departure – A above middle C – is clear enough and the machine with a digital read-out can as easily pinpoint 440 cycles per second as the traditional tuning fork. But a machine cannot take into account the minute changes that occur to the complicated mechanism of a piano between tunings. Strings stretch, hammers soften, wood swells – these and a thousand other factors will have an effect on a piano's tone.

The phrase 'bringing a piano into tune' best captures what is at the heart of tuning, namely, that it is above all a process, one whose aim is to bring all the elements of this instrument to a delicate point of equilibrium and to encourage this balance to remain within a range acceptable to the human ear for as long as possible. When a piano has been rebuilt, for example, or even when it has been moved from one environment to another, it requires a series of successive tunings to reach a true tone because the wood has absorbed different levels of humidity, the tuning pins have slipped, the keys have altered slightly. Only once it has been acclimated fully to its new environment will it hold a tuning for any appreciable period, and in any event the process of change and degradation of the moving parts begins again immediately. In this sense there is something capricious, almost alive, about the newly tuned piano.

Not playing a piano at all is worse than playing it hard and regularly, Luc contended. Aside from the sentimental consideration that pianos were built to be played, there is a practical consequence of leaving the keyboard idle. Unlike modern machines, many of the piano's thousands of moving parts are made not of metal but of wood. The wood matures and 'seasons' by itself over time, but it also has a subtle interaction with all of the other parts. When a piano is played, all of the parts are subjected to the vibrations that emanate from the soundboard. Over time the effect of these vibrations on the ensemble of parts is more or less uniform: tuning pins seat themselves in a certain way in the pin block, hammers respond to keys with regularity, the soundboard flexes and vibrates within the spectrum of movement for which it was built.

Left unplayed, none of the parts moves and the only factor acting on the whole is the long, slow process of deterioration with changes in temperature and humidity, and the relentless pressure of the strings to unwind themselves. The important difference is that these changes then act irregularly on the pieces; there is no balance, no uniform reaction. In this sense, too, the piano is very much like a living organism that needs the stimulus of playing in order for all the parts to breathe together through sympathetic vibrations.

One consequence of this is that a brand-new piano needs a breaking-in period during which the instrument is acclimated not only to its new environment, but also to the style and frequency of playing. A piano that is played frequently and well will most often reach a perfect balance and an optimal tone within the first few years of its acquisition. Properly maintained, it can continue to respond properly for many decades, even generations. The overall rule, though, is slow deterioration after an initial period of seasoning.

This is why most major concert halls rent rather than buy the pianos used by visiting artists. A concert pianist wants to use an instrument that is at the apogee of its transient existence, suitably broken in and seasoned, and yet not less than mechanically perfect. This period lasts for only a few years at best and a rental piano can then be exchanged for another instrument in optimal condition.

So a tuner is part scientist, part artist, and part psychologist. It is best if he knows the basic physics of harmonics and wave dynamics, if he knows his clients and can ascertain their needs, if he has the sure touch of a fine mechanic when he takes up his tuning wrenches. These are all desirable characteristics, but the one indispensable element is what is called a good ear. This is the ability to discern minute variations in tone and pitch across the full dynamic range of the piano's keyboard, from bass notes grumbling at 30 cycles per second to the very top of the seventh octave where treble notes shimmer at over 4000 cycles per second.

How does one come by a good ear? It is clear that some people are born with better powers of perception than others and hearing is no exception. But the ear can be developed. This needs to happen at an early age or it doesn't happen at all; twenty or twenty-five is the outside limit for awakening and nurturing this capacity. Before that age the ear can better grasp and confidently learn the infinite subtleties of changing pitch. Like pure mathematics or quantum physics or – not surprisingly – music, this particular form of specialized discernment is the territory of the young. It requires enormous powers of con-centration, almost like an athletic event. Curiously, though, this capacity is not generally lost as the hearing begins to deteriorate and lose its ability to discern the limits of the normal human register. Once the distinctions are learned, it is almost as if they were hard-wired; an older tuner will still hear the subtleties he needs to do the job properly.

While a good ear is the *sine qua non* of tuning, training that ear is less problematic than training the hand, that is, the means by which the infinite gradations of pitch are achieved. Learning to feel the tuning pin, to anticipate its slippage and to compensate accordingly, to turn the wrench as little as possible and still reach the desired pitch is surprisingly complicated. The hand, the arm, in a sense the whole body have to feel what the tuning pin is doing and to anticipate its natural tendency to retract under tension in order to move it to a correct and stable position. To further complicate matters, some say that while the ear and the right hand are important, the truly critical facility is in the left hand, the hand that strikes the keys while the right hand turns the wrenches. The left hand has to be perfectly controlled and consistent in the way it strikes each of the notes so that the appropriate resonance can be attained in a uniform manner across the entire keyboard.

Bringing all of the notes into tune is just the first part of a comprehensive tuning. The subtle art of voicing is what actually gives the piano its distinctive tone, its character: its voice. What makes for a pleasing voice is far more subjective than whether the pitch is correct across the instrument's entire scale. Voice varies according to the setting; a piano voiced for a household would sound wrong on the stage of a concert hall. More of the technician's skill and weight of experience is therefore brought to bear in getting the balance right. 'We all have our own bag of tricks for voicing,' a tuner once told me. 'It's like being naked; I don't want others around while I'm voicing, especially colleagues.'

Some of the arcane techniques for changing a piano's voice include pricking hammer felts with needles to soften them and reduce a bright tone, or remedying an overly mellow tone by applying chemical hardeners to them. The shape of a hammer can be minutely changed by sanding, its position adjusted by heating and then bending the parts. A piano can be perfectly in tune, but if it is not properly voiced it can have a strange, even unnatural sound to the human ear.

I asked Luc what made a good tuner, thinking that he would enumerate a list of tricky skills and improbable approaches that would distinguish a special tuner from one who was so-so. In retrospect his answer should not have surprised me since it cut through the theory and much of the practice to the essential point in his world of tuning: 'A good tuner is one the client doesn't call back right away.'

It happens that tuners in Paris have a reputation for eccentricity.

More than once I heard of the capriciousness or follies of tuners, usually followed with a quick insistence that these things no longer went on, that French tuners were now like everyone else in the business, *très correct*. I told Luc that I had come across the story of the tuner who was called to tune the Pleyel upright that Gustav Eiffel had brought to his tiny apartment at the top of the Eiffel Tower soon after it was finished in 1889. The tuner was asked to pay an admission price to go up to the top. He refused and left on the spot, indignant that his professional services were not properly appreciated. *Le Figaro* covered the story approvingly.

Luc chuckled and said that the principal eccentricity of tuners these days was their inclination to play around with their clients in bed. All the jokes about plumbers and postmen could as easily be applied to tuners: they come to your home during the day, they need to be there for a considerable amount of time, the work is complicated or, at least, unfamiliar to the layman. And the client is often at home alone. When I sketched out this formula, Luc – practical as ever – observed: 'Sure, some tuners are there for four hours when it really takes fifteen minutes. And they're not exactly just polishing the piano. But those guys' – he turned his palms outwards and shrugged his shoulders in the universal French signal that the world is a strange place – 'they don't make any money.'

This reminded me of something else Luc told me about tuning: the best tuner is the one who turns the tuning pins the least. In other words, a good tuner does quick work. With a good ear and a sure hand, he or she should be able to bring the ordinary piano back into tune in an hour or an hour and a half. The longer one takes (unless there are structural problems one must allow for), the worse it is for both piano and tuner. 'They tire out the pin block, they tire themselves out, and the ear is no longer fresh.'

Until recently tuning was learned exclusively by apprenticeship to a master. Increasingly there are specialized schools and programs designed to prepare one for the profession, but everyone agrees that there is no substitute for hands-on experience with someone who knows the field. Once exclusively a male preserve, tuning is gradually attracting qualified women to its ranks. It's a world with its own traditions and lore, some of which are hidden within pianos themselves.

When the Stingl was first tuned, I was intrigued to discover a hidden message inside. Luc had removed the fall board to make an adjustment, revealing the long wooden key extensions that ran back from the ivory-covered tips. On one of these in a fine and formal hand was inscribed in pencil a name and the serial number of my piano: 'A. Weychaky, 32324'. Luc said that it was fairly common to find names and dates, and sometimes even short messages on the insides of pianos, occasionally the name of the tuner/technician together with the date on which he had last tuned or voiced the piano. These signatures were a kind of bookkeeping reference for the fellowship of technicians. Less common were the names and dates that were found on other hidden parts of the piano.

What was this strange tendency to sign the innards of a piano, I wondered, particularly where it would never be seen unless the piano was disassembled? These scribblings were not meant for players of the instrument or even for dealers. Luc's analogy was apt. 'For me, it's like the stonemasons who carved the cathedrals.'

Many of the statues and gargoyles on the great Gothic cathedrals are so far up on the facade that they could only be seen by another stonemason: the artisan doing the next row of statues, say, or someone come to clean or repair the work hundreds of years later. For Luc the interesting thing is that the detail is as rich and complete on the stonework high up as it is on the more visible statues at ground level. 'The Church says that they were doing it for God, who sees everything. Faith was certainly part of it, but I agree with those who say that they did it for each other, too.' Signatures on pianos convey some of that same sense of defying time's dominion. A mature technician who has rebuilt a fine piano can, with some reasonable certainty, assume that the piano will outlive him.

The famous grand piano presented to Beethoven by its maker, John Broadwood, in 1817, was signed by five of London's leading pianists as a special dedication from the English community of musicians. More personal and more whimsical, too, are the inscriptions found on the soundboard of Edward Elgar's Broadwood. Along with the names of some of the pieces he composed on this small piano, including *The Dream of Gerontius*, appear the words 'Mr Rabbit'. While it is in Elgar's hand, there is no known composition of his bearing this title. There is speculation that the words refer to his daughter's pet, but no one knows for sure.

Nor is it only the woodwork that is sometimes autographed. Luc once showed me a pin plate that had been signed by the man who had cast it. Bending close, I read in a fine nineteenth-century hand of violet paint worked as ink, 'Leguessier'. Each tuning pin hole was labeled in the same delicate curves, 'A', '#', 'b', etc., the violet tracery against the gold paint like a perfectly rendered crackle on an antique glaze. 'I often see that on the oldest pianos. It's from the time when artisans used to do piece work and they generally signed every piece. That was especially true at Pleyel, even for the metalwork.'

A friend's piano tuner in California told of working on a piano that was full of the family's history: births, deaths, weddings, and all the attendant dates, written in a variety of hands on the piano's insides. It was like the family Bible, a place where life's turns and rhythms were set down as a record in a place that was private if not altogether secret. And performers sometimes sign the pianos they play. Paderewski's Steinway, a concert grand that he hauled from one end of America to the other on his triumphal tour of the New World, sits in the Smithsonian in Washington. On its gold-painted frame, in delicate strokes of black ink, it bears this inscription: 'This piano has been played by me during the season 1892–1893 in seventy-five concerts. I. J. Paderewski.'

On a visit to the Steinway showroom in New York, I saw Henry Steinway, the last member of the family to be connected with the company, take out a felt-tip pen and sign the painted metal frame of a piano for an enthusiastic customer. It was like watching a baseball player sign a ball, or an author his book, and seemed in keeping with our age of celebrity.

When I then visited the Steinway factory in New York, I asked if employees sometimes signed the new pianos in unseen places. 'Of course, we have no way of being certain,' the factory guide told me, 'and officially it's not encouraged. But there is a long and informal tradition that seems to be current once again to make a mark in a place that the customer will never see.' My host seemed to hesitate between official censure at the thought of unauthorized initiatives and respect for a practice that was part of the highly personal world of the master craftsman. He then told me a story that tipped the scale in favor of the latter.

A voicing apprentice came to work at the Steinway factory one day to find his master, a man of great reserve, in tears. The master was standing before the disassembled action assembly of an old Steinway grand that had been sent back to the factory to be reconditioned. 'What's wrong?' asked the apprentice. 'How can I help?' The master then explained that when he had removed the action assembly from the piano, he had found the name of another Steinway technician hidden on the inside, the signature of his late father.

Now, the factory guide told me, master craftsmen were allowed to apply an ink stamp with their initials in a hidden part of the piano. He showed me one. It was rather like the calligraphy stamp that one finds in the corner of Japanese prints: square, graphically stylized, and understated. I preferred the idea of taking out a pen and signing the wood itself, an extravagant practice to be sure for those of us accustomed only to paper. But then how many of us are competent to shape and tune and voice metal and wood into the intricate miracle that we call the piano? For noble work, a noble gesture. What a precious discovery, like finding a pearl in an oyster, to read the hand of someone who cared for and repaired the instrument that he then sent back into the world, a messenger with no certain destination and bearing only one meaning of which we can be sure: 'I was.'

15

LE MOT JUSTE

One Friday I stopped by the atelier late in the day to see if Luc would be able to advise me about my missing *barre stabilisatrice*. Luc's closing time of 6.30 was posted on a small handwritten sign in the window, but I knew that was an approximation of when he would actually pull down the old metal shutters and lock up. The little bell rang as I closed the front door, but rather than coming out, Luc yelled from deep within the shop, 'Come in! We're in the back!'

I opened the door that led to the atelier and found Luc with three people standing around a baby grand piano covered with an old canvas drop cloth. On the cloth were arrayed the makings of the classic French *goûter* for the late afternoon: a large *saucisson*, half of which was cut into slices; two pieces of cheese peeking out from under the wrapping paper used by *charcuteries*; two baguettes, one of which was half gone; and two bottles of wine. There was even a small candle flickering in an old brass holder with a finger loop.

'And here's our local American!' Luc said warmly, handing me a glass.

He introduced me to the others: a black-haired woman in her thirties with a wide smile called Mathilde whom he referred to as 'a client and a friend'; a short man by the name of François with a round face and a halo of curly blond hair whom he called a '*mélomane*', the French word for music lover; and an elegantly dressed older woman, Danielle, whom he introduced simply as a '*voisine*'. I poured myself a glass of wine and listened to the conversation as they took up where I had interrupted.

Mathilde was talking about the piano she had had throughout her childhood and as a young woman. Somehow – this was unclear, I had missed part of the story – she had 'lost' this beloved piano and she hoped against hope for its return one day. 'I dream of finding it again. The image that keeps coming back is that one day I'll just open a door and it will be there.'

Her features were inexpressibly sad; she had about her the inconsolable sense of frustration shared by everyone who has lost a treasured object. A long silence followed and then Luc spoke in a voice I had not heard before, low and soothing: 'You have to forget that piano; it's gone. We'll find you another.'

She gave him a look that was initially defiant, but then it softened. 'It went to England. Maybe someone will send it over here and you'll buy it second-hand.'

'Do you realize what the odds are against that? And besides, they only send us their junk; they keep the good stuff.'

François, the *mélomane*, then told a story about how another piano had been lost. Six men showed up at one of the leading concert halls in Paris wearing uniform shirts embroidered with the name of a reputable moving company. They were there, they told the management, to take the concert grand piano for repairs, as arranged. No one questioned the undertaking – it was the beginning of the lunch hour and the director of the hall was absent – and they removed the Steinway model D from the wings of the stage. The entire operation took no more than fifteen minutes. They drove off in a large truck and were never heard from again. The piano was conservatively worth half a million francs.

We all snickered in amazement at the audacity and the deftness of the ploy, but Luc interrupted. 'There's just one problem with that story: there's a version of it current in every city of the world, it seems, and the details are too similar for coincidence. It's always a Steinway model D, there are invariably five or six uniformed men, and they always get away in a rental truck. But where are you going to sell a nine-foot piano worth that kind of money? It's hard to hide, it's hard to transport, and there's a very limited market. And pianos have their serial numbers hidden in many places other than the metal frame, so the first time you need it tuned or serviced you risk discovery.'

Luc acknowledged that it made a good story, but he contended that the real duplicity occurred with more modest instruments and under more conventional circumstances: a newly bereaved widow letting her husband's piano be taken for an evaluation; a church or a school unaware that it has received back a similar, but inferior, piano after a reconditioning; a large hotel or a convention center that discovers only at the end of the year that its inventory of pianos is short by one or two. 'Look, a piano is bigger and heavier than a wardrobe cupboard and just as hard to hide. It's not the first choice of the petty thief. Most of the stealing is an inside job by someone who has a way of selling it quickly.'

'Like you!' Danielle sang out, a challenging smile on her face as she refilled her wineglass.

'Ah, I'm too old and slow for those tricks. And I don't need the aggravation.'

'You mean to say you've never had a stolen piano in this atelier?'

'Never knowingly, absolutely not. But who knows where some of the used pianos I buy started out their journeys? I make it my business to buy in good faith and to sell the same way. But I can't launch an investigation into the origins of every piano that comes to me from an auction or a warehouse sale. You do what you can and that's it.'

This seemed reasonable to me, and I helped myself to bread and *saucisson*. We were standing not far from the immense – and immensely ugly – wood-burning stove that dominated one side of the atelier. Its massive superstructure towered above it in an impossible contortion of pipes, tubes, and Y-shaped fittings so that the heated air circulated as much as possible as it rose. The whole thing was painted a metallic gray, but years of dust and nicks and rust gave it the look of some disused piece of fantastic machinery, or of the long-lost wreckage of a plane recently found in a remote forest.

Its efficiency as a heater was dubious, but this mattered little since it was the only source of heat in the atelier and winter mornings could be bitterly cold. Pianos and their parts were never allowed near the stove, so it sat in its own clearing, isolated in a rough circle that never became anything other than mildly warm. Luc told me many times that cold would not harm his pianos, but direct heat would be their death, so he didn't mind coming to the stove to warm his hands before returning to the cold perimeter to work.

I used to kid Luc about the monstrous stove, telling him that it put me in mind of one of the pieces of bad modern sculpture that were so common in the parks and squares of France. Once I even showed him a version of his stove in a picture of Brancusi's Paris studio.

Luc was unimpressed. 'Sculpture, my foot; these things were as common as the kitchen table at the turn of the century. It shows nothing more than that artists get cold, too.' He paused and gave me a sudden conspiratorial look. 'But it's interesting to think that Brancusi probably burned some of his wooden sculptures in it to keep warm.'

He smiled as he contemplated this paradox, art going up the chimney in the service of the practical needs of the moment, but I was unaware of the parallel in his observation until I returned a few days later to find him stoking the stove with sticks of wood. It was early December and, overnight, winter had replaced fall: a biting wind howled through the leafless trees and cafés pulled in the last tables against the gusts of rain that hammered the streets. 'It must be below freezing out there. Do you mind if I warm up for a minute?'

'Not at all. Besides, 1925 was a very good year for English pin blocks!'

He couldn't suppress a laugh as I looked in surprise at the piece of wood in his hand. The regularly spaced holes at one end showed that it was undoubtedly a part of the massive piece of wood to which a piano's tuning pins are fixed. 'Don't look at me as if I were a cannibal. I'm just keeping myself from freezing to death. And I'm saving the world from dead pianos in the bargain.'

For this man who gave pianos a kind of life, there was also such a thing as a death: final, irretrievable, and sure. It happened that, more often than he liked, he acquired pianos that simply couldn't be repaired. Almost always they came in a batch with some good pianos and he was obliged to take the lot. Once he ascertained that nothing could be done to make them playable again, they were disassembled, stripped for usable parts, and reduced to kindling that was stacked neatly by the stove.

Everyone present was apparently aware of Luc's practice of burning pianos that could not be repaired. Luc called them *les combustibles*. He walked over to the strange-looking stove with the improbable series of pipe fittings ascending to the skylight. Putting his hand on its cold metal top, he turned to the group and said with an air of mock solemnity, '*C'est ce que je voudrais pour mon corps; il faut laisser de la place.*' ('This is what I'd like for my body; you have to leave room for others.')

'Ah, when you go we'll pile up all your pianos and put you on top of the heap and burn the whole thing. We'll dance around the fire and howl at the moon. *Siegfried* meets *Rite of Spring*.' Danielle, the neighbor woman, had a feisty air about her, as if the joke nevertheless contained an image that appealed to her.

Luc laughed with the rest of us. 'That sounds like a waste of good pianos to me. Better to use the ones that are beyond hope; there will always be plenty of those.'

'No, a hero has to have a sacrifice that means something, that hurts. And you'll need those pianos in the afterlife, no?'

'Sometimes my idea of heaven is where there is no such thing as a piano.' Luc took a long drink of wine and looked around at the circle of faces. 'But that's only on days like today.'

He then told us about how he had spent his afternoon. A woman had called him the week before about the possibility of selling an old Erard. He had gone to see it after lunch and found an aged widow in a small apartment near the old *Opéra*. The piano, an upright from the 1880s, had pride of place in the modest salon. The woman had had it since she was a girl; before that it had belonged to her aunt. 'I can no longer play it,' she told him. 'Look at my hands.' They were palsied and deformed with arthritis. 'If it's worth something, I'd rather use it to continue to live an independent life than to have it for a headstone.'

At first sight the piano looked to be in good condition. The cabinet, like the rest of the heavy furniture in her tiny living room, had been regularly polished and waxed. But when he opened the top to examine the mechanics, he found a catalog of horrors. 'The hinges of the front panel separated from the wood as soon as I pivoted it and a thin powder of wood dust fell on my hands. But the worst was the odor. It was if I had unplugged a toilet; I was almost sick on the spot. But the old lady was oblivious to it.' Inside he found that vermin had infested the piano long ago. The felts had been almost entirely eaten by moths, the wood was riddled by termites, and mice had happily lived inside for many years; one of their rotting bodies no doubt accounted for the stench. When he played the piano, it was not only out of key, but certain notes gave no sound at all because the strings had broken. 'It was a complete and utter wreck, but the outer shell looked presentable. I'm sure that piano hadn't been moved one centimeter in the last fifty years.'

'So what did you tell her?' Mathilde voiced the question that was on all our minds.

Luc winced, as if the memory were physically painful and he took a long drink of wine. 'I was tempted to offer her a thousand francs for the fall board; the Erard name plate from that era is worth something. But literally nothing else on the piano was salvageable for me and I didn't have the heart to tell her the truth. So I told her it wasn't the type of piano I handled.'

The atelier suddenly became quiet as we all shifted uneasily, eager to show our concern and our sympathy for Luc, for the old woman, for the absence of a clear or graceful resolution. 'Well, that was true in a way,' I offered.

'In a way,' Luc repeated softly, staring into his wineglass for a long moment.

'So what will become of the ruined Erard?' Danielle wanted to know.

'Oh, I called Le Coq and explained things. He'll salvage the ivory and the fall board, and maybe the pedals. She'll see two, maybe three thousand francs. But the moment they try to lift that piano it will be a pile of kindling.' Luc looked at us sourly and added, 'And I don't care to be around for that.' The woman had a daughter who lived on the outskirts of Paris with whom she would likely be obliged to move in before too long.

More poignant still was when someone had decided to sell a piano, but wasn't in fact ready to part with it. They often showed the same apprehension as those who had to place well-loved pets, needing to hear that the person they chose would care for and honor their trusted companion in the same way they had. Luc was, of course, a business-man, but his attitude about his transactions counted for a lot to people in that uncertain territory between relief and regret.

This could lead to extremely delicate conversations where every word had to be weighed and where Luc's manner was at least as important as the price that had been agreed upon. '*Dans ces cas, il faut trouver le mot juste; il faut respecter la poésie du piano au sein de la famille.*' ('In those cases, you have to find exactly the right word; you must respect the poetry of the piano in the heart of the family.') Oftentimes the difficulty arose because the piano bore the imprint of someone now dead who had played it regularly.

Luc described his visit years before to the home of a widow to appraise the piano she wanted to sell, a beautiful Pleyel grand. In order to test the action and the sound, he began to play Schumann's *Träumerei*, only to have his hostess burst into tears. 'I'm sorry,' she sobbed. 'My husband used to play that for me.'

Music and memory: can there be a stronger amalgam weighing on the heart? No wonder it's hard to leave behind a piano that one has loved, or that one associates with friends and family, when circumstances force the abandonment of this supremely unportable possession. Several dealers in Paris and New York told me the same bittersweet tale: a client would insist on finding a used piano of a particular make, model and finish, and the cost was not a major concern. Refugees, émigrés, victims of the fortunes of war: they'd had a whole world wrenched from them, very often together with the loved ones who peopled it. As their material circumstances improved one of their first instincts was to find a duplicate of the piano that had been at the center of their home, but things seldom worked out as they had hoped.

A New York dealer recounted how he had found and restored a Grotrian-Steinweg grand from the twenties, a rare enough German brand in America. With unbounded delight his client set this exact model of piano from her girlhood in Europe in her living room. As she played it and lived with it, though, she discovered that the resemblance was only cosmetic, that the features she missed were not to be had for money no matter how faithful the restoration.

'A piano is just too personal,' the dealer told me. 'What people actually remember – a certain raspy tone, a lightness in the treble, a pedal that sticks slightly – are the kind of things that only one piano in the universe will combine. And they're often just the kind of things that get fixed with a professional restoration.'

We invest it with our dreams, we touch it offhandedly as we walk by, we crown it with favorite photos and treasured objects until it becomes a kind of domestic shrine. But when it is gone from our lives, it can't really be replaced, not for what it encompasses as part of a life's progress. Time moves on and the piano, like us, wears down or, less frequently, is destroyed in fate's spiral. We can start over and a good instrument will still open the way to the realm of music. But the associative power of this thing, this great hulk of wood and metal, resides in the individual specimen.

After Luc told us about some of the intractable situations he encountered, his face resumed its expression of slight mischief. 'There are times I won't even pay the minimum salvage price only to pull apart the piano and burn the rest. If I think the customer can face it, I tell them the truth. Then I suggest that they have a barbecue in the backyard and burn the piano themselves. Invite the neighbors and all the family members who played the piano. Buy a couple of kilos of sausage and make a party of it. Better that they make it a ritual for themselves than that they take a few miserable francs to have someone else do the dirty work.'

Luc's features were more relaxed now as he described a situation that clearly was not as painful to him as the no-win proposition that the old lady represented, the wreckage of dreams with no suitable end. It seemed fitting to him that a family should make of their old piano's demise a kind of party, like an Irish wake, to celebrate a completed life and to share some of the memories evoked. And, not surprisingly, his idea of having a shared meal over the pyre had about it that uniquely French capacity to use food as the basis for almost any rite of passage. 'Of course,' he added, 'I tell them not to cook the sausage until the varnished parts have been burned. It spoils the taste.'

Gradually the talk died down and we started to clear off the leavings of our snack from the top of the piano. As Luc was closing up the shop, I asked him about the stabilizer bar for my piano's pedals. He promised to see if he could find a spare, assuring me that the lyre would brace the pedals adequately as long as I didn't use them too vigorously.

We all stumbled out on to the sidewalk, wishing each other '*Bon weekend*' and promising to continue our discussion when next we crossed paths in the atelier. I turned to go and noticed Luc and Mathilde together, heading in the opposite direction.

16

SCHOLA CANTORUM

Not long after I began my lessons with Anna, my daughter started to show interest in this big musical instrument that was now installed in one corner of our living room. Her curiosity took the form of playing a few notes when no one else was in the room, but we would hear her from other parts of the apartment and try not to interrupt. I asked her if she would be interested in taking lessons and she answered, with a tentative air, that it might be nice. I knew not to press her shyness beyond its limits, so we agreed only to look into it.

I thought at first that Anna might take her on as a beginner – Anna counted children as well as many adults among her private students – but it was impossible given the time involved reaching her apartment on the outskirts of Paris. So we had to find a good teacher closer to home. My wife and I agreed that we didn't want to try the municipal music conservatories in Paris that offered lessons to children. These schools are notorious for their highly competitive approach. We wanted to find a teacher who could help our daughter to discover the fun in music.

This wouldn't be easy. The teaching of music in France is taken very seriously; while admirable enough in itself, very often it veers towards an overly formal and academic approach. From the earliest age, great emphasis is given to theory, and *solfège* – the practice of sight-reading and singing at the same time – is almost always required. This allows for a very well-rounded musical education, but most often

150

its benefits are reserved for those children who are already highly motivated and talented: it does little to develop that motivation and talent. Many children take music lessons for a while, pressing on doggedly in joyless sessions of theory and practice, only to drift away as soon as they can. We wanted our daughter to have a solid basis in music, but we also wanted her to experience a sense of adventure and discovery. She should practice for a love of music and not to impress her teacher or her parents. The right beginning was crucial.

One day, while this search was going on, I walked home from a friend's apartment in the Latin Quarter by a roundabout way, purposely taking the narrow street that leads past my favorite church in Paris, Val de Grâce. It lies on the rue Saint Jacques, a small but noisy thoroughfare that has led south since the time when Paris was the Roman city of Lutetia. Its current name derives from its use as a route in the Middle Ages for pilgrims heading to Santiago di Compostela in Spain; or, in the usage the French prefer, *Saint Jacques de Compostelle*. Val de Grâce is a large late Renaissance church that is unusual for Paris; its exuberant carvings and animated facade are more typical of Rome, and the most beautiful dome in the city graces its undulating mass of light yellow stone.

I love walking down the cramped and busy sidewalks of Saint Jacques, suddenly to come upon an unexpected widening of the street and the glory of this Renaissance pile set back behind gold-tipped iron pickets. This, too, is more like Rome than the Paris of Haussmann's broad boulevards and triumphal esplanades. It's extravagant, voluptuous and very grand, and yet its setting is strangely intimate.

I took in this sight once more, with the sense of visiting an old friend whom I saw infrequently, and as I walked back into the narrow passage on the far side of the tiny square, I saw before me a large doorway set in a high wall with two Latin words cast in bronze on its lintel: '*Schola Cantorum*'. A small brass plaque affixed to one side of the heavy wooden doors bore the engraving: '*Ecole Supérieure de Musique, de Danse, et d'Art Dramatique*'. As I considered what this could be, there was a lull in the noise of cars rushing by and I heard the sound of a violin coming from beyond the wall. I crossed the street to get a better view, and from the far sidewalk I could see an old building set back beyond the walls, four or five stories tall. Its facade had some of the grace of architectural detailing that is typical of old Parisian *hôtels particuliers*, private mansions, from the seventeenth and eighteenth centuries. The windows were delicate, the slate roof was steeply pitched. It was far from a gussied-up mansion, however; there was a fire escape attached to one side, and I could see through one of the upper windows that faced the street a semicircle of music stands facing a semicircle of empty chairs.

'Very solid, very imaginative,' one friend told me when I asked him about the school, 'not like the rat race of the conservatories.' But *poussiereux* (dusty) was another assessment, although when I pressed for details this opinion was directed more towards the *tristes lieux* (sad premises) that the school occupied than the approach to music. An American friend told me that Cole Porter had studied there after World War One. Finally I asked Luc if he knew about the school on the rue Saint Jacques. 'Why of course I do; it's one of the very best music schools in Paris. Debussy, Messiaen, and lots of others taught there. It has a reputation for caring about music, first and foremost. It's private, though' – here he shrugged his shoulders – 'so they don't have a lot of money.'

This pronouncement suggests how France differs from America in this respect. In the United States, private institutions – schools, conservatories, hospitals, universities – are very often the richest and most prestigious of their kind, while this is rarely the case in France. The government-run conservatories are showered with resources while their private counterparts must make do by raising money in a country where there are few private foundations and little tradition of giving for activities that are regarded as the province of the state.

I called the Schola Cantorum and asked to visit the school to explore the possibility of arranging lessons for my two children. The next week I took a break after lunch and walked over. This time the large wooden doors were open, revealing a small gravel-covered courtyard. The building at the other side had a simple doorway leading to a vestibule and a central hall tiled with the stencil designs that were so popular in France in the late nineteenth century. From behind a series of doors one could hear the faint sounds of instruments being played.

I made my way through the entrance hall to the back of the building and there the look of the place changed considerably. In place of the tiles at the front, the floor was paved with white marble squares, worn and cracked, and graying with age. At the end of the hall a staircase rose in an elongated spiral, an elegant banister of beautifully proportioned ironwork curving along its inside edge. The walls were covered with wooden panels painted shades of white and gray, and there were a number of elaborate architectural embellishments worked into the plaster above the panels. Among these was a large scallop shell, perhaps a reference to the same device used for centuries by the pilgrims of *Saint Jacques de Compostelle* to identify themselves. The proportions of the space were grand without being pompous, and yet it was by no means perfectly maintained: several of the wooden treads on the staircase needed replacing, the walls wanted a new coat of paint, the plaster detailing was chipped.

To one side of the staircase a pair of glass-paneled doors led to a garden and I walked out into the hidden world of a large inner courtyard. By Paris standards it was large, perhaps a quarter of an acre, an almost unimaginable luxury in this *quartier* where the apartment houses were so densely built. And yet Paris sometimes reserves this kind of surprise: on the side of its buildings away from the street – *côté cour* – there are still old courtyards that have not been given over entirely to new buildings or to parking lots. The astounding thing about the Schola garden was that, like the elegant staircase, it was not perfectly manicured. Rather, it gave the appearance of a garden that had once been fancy, but that nature had now partly reclaimed. This is a rarity in Paris where the infrequent gardens that remain in private hands are most often subjected to the French fervor for formalism and order in making things grow just so. I walked around the quiet garden and then sat down on one of the benches to read a brochure about the Schola's history that I had found in the hall.

The buildings – or at least the site – had a long history, not in itself surprising since this is one of the oldest parts of Paris. It began as the *Hôtel des Bénédictins Anglais*, a convent for English Benedictines that became the refuge for Stuart loyalists in the late seventeenth century. The story was full of the Byzantine turns that for so long invested the relations between the French and the English when religion became the matter for war. The little brochure related that in 1701 the body of James II was interred there and his grave became an attraction for pilgrims, and then added with the cryptic air of the mystic, '*Dieu a daigné opérer des cures merveilleuses auprès du tombeau de Jacques II*' ('God deigned to perform miraculous cures around the tomb of James II'). None of the cures was described.

Benjamin Franklin had apparently spent some time within the convent's walls, writing out the preamble to the Constitution of the United States. During the Revolution the convent was turned into a prison and subsequently used as a cotton mill, then a preparatory school for the *Ecole Polytechnique*, until in 1896 it began its vocation as a private school for music, dance, and theater. Satie, Debussy, Albéniz, and Messiaen had all been associated with the Schola, and its philosophy was consciously informal and forward-looking. I particularly liked the rationale it advanced for renouncing the tradition of competitive *concours*: '*On ne fait pas de musique contre quelqu'un*' ('One does not make music against someone else').

I sat in the garden, looking back at the Schola through the trees.

The main wing was made of the light yellow stone that is so common for French architecture of the eighteenth century, with full-length windows on each floor set into the stone. A slate mansard roof, delicate wrought-iron balustrades at the windows, and simple detailing on the upper stories completed the vision of a domain belonging to the Enlightenment. What had this same pavilion looked like as a prison during the Revolution? It wasn't hard to imagine that this quiet inner courtyard had witnessed scenes of unmentionable dismay and despair in that convulsion of fervor that was concentrated in Paris.

I considered this place, as secret in its way as Luc's atelier; it seemed to embrace the past without being lost in it. It was old but not in the least stuffy, and I reflected that the same friend who had labeled it dusty had referred to the 'sad premises'. I found them anything but sad. Dilapidated, yes, but exhibiting the kind of shabby gentility that was expected with an old mansion. From the look of it, what money existed had been used for the teaching of music. Vitality filled the air as students of all ages hurried by on the staircase, carrying their instruments and chattering about music. If Ben Franklin had looked up from the garden or down through the same wavy panes of glass, he wouldn't have been altogether disappointed to see what had become of this enclave set back from the noise and hurry of a world that turned faster than the one he had known.

Our son wanted to play the recorder ('Something I can hold!' he insisted) and our daughter had chosen the piano. Early in our first conversation the piano teacher asked if there was a piano in our home and whether my wife or I played. When I told her yes, that I had taken up the piano again, she was enthusiastic. 'It's much easier when there is already music in the family.'

When September arrived, we took the children to the Schola and met their respective teachers. A matronly woman greeted our daughter with smiles and at once addressed her with the somewhat old-fashioned French endearments, 'ma puce' ('my flea') and 'ma biche' ('my doe'). Her lessons were given on the ground floor of one of the small pavilions that flanked the front of the Schola on either side of the gravel-covered courtyard. She taught on an Erard upright and through the windows I could see the two of them sitting side by side, my daughter on the bench, her teacher on a chair, as they began their half-hour together. I had a strange intimation of myself sitting next to Madame Gaillard so many years ago, not quite déjà vu, but a parent's recognition of the preciousness of these beginning steps along music's broad path. When asked afterwards how things had gone, our daughter replied with the non-committal 'Fine', but in the following days we noticed that she eagerly opened her music notebook when she had some free time to practice.

Occasionally, when I waited for the children I would read a book in the entrance hall or, if the weather was nice, in the garden. Sometimes, though, I would find an empty practice room on one of the upper floors and play the piano available there. Many of them were Pleyel grands and it occurred to me that it was very French, if not simply eccentric, to fill one's practice rooms with old pianos that were no longer made. Each possessed a distinct feel and sound, what one could even call a personality, and no two had exactly the same cabinets. It was fun sitting in the old empty rooms with their tall ceilings, fireplaces, and an atmosphere of history and intrigue, trying my modest repertoire on different keyboards.

Our Wednesday visits to the Schola Cantorum became part of the weekly routine. I looked forward to being there in much the same way that I looked forward to stopping by the atelier, although for slightly different reasons. Luc's presence dominated the atelier and I always enjoyed talking to him, and to his friends and customers. The Schola's appeal was less personal, but it shared with Luc's shop a respect for music in all its forms. Both were nice places simply to be, to step outside the ordinary pattern of things, to breathe in and absorb a different rhythm.

In the middle of the fall trimester, I found myself one day in the Schola's office when the director, Monsieur Denis, walked in and introduced himself. He was a middle-aged man with a slight stoop to his shoulders and the look of chronic worry that often marks those responsible for small private schools. His features became animated, however, as soon as he started talking. He wore the uniform of academics and administrators throughout France: a blue-gray suit, a gray V-neck sweater, a white shirt, and a dark-blue tie. He talked about both my children by name and said that he had received good reports of their progress. I told him I was surprised that he maintained this level of familiarity with beginning students but he insisted that every student was important at the Schola and he hoped that beginners would eventually become what he called '*vétérans*'. There needed to be more flexibility in the French approach to teaching, for music as well as for other disciplines. 'The system needs to be changed from top to bottom. I like to think that here at the Schola we're pioneers.'

He had himself attended the Schola, studying piano and organ. I asked about the well-known composers who had been associated with the school and he said that many famous ones had indeed taught there but that it was not good enough to rest on one's laurels. His biggest challenge, he confided, was making the necessary improvements to the buildings and the equipment so that the Schola remained in the first rank of music schools. Like administrators everywhere, he avowed that the buildings he had inherited were both a blessing and a curse, but they helped to make the school distinctive and able to foster a feeling of community.

So, too, were the pianos found throughout the school; the great variety of instruments was a necessity that he tried to turn into a virtue. Some schools had all Steinways or all Yamahas but that wasn't possible at the Schola. 'Consider that pianists don't, as a rule, play their own instruments the way violinists or flautists do, so adaptation is part of becoming and being a pianist.' Feeling the different action of a Pleyel or the tone of a Schimmel, even if in some respects they were not the finest instruments available, taught a pianist much about how to listen and how to play. This was at least as important as developing technique for its own sake because it had to do with the very notion of interpreting music at the keyboard.

What about the Steinway concert grand in the main hall? I asked. It looked to be brand-new and its cabinet was certainly distinctive. He nodded. 'It's very beautiful, isn't it?' It was a one-of-a-kind walnut cabinet that had been made to order for a client in New York. I asked how it had ended up at the Schola and he put up his hands in mock defensiveness. He had acquired it himself, he said, and he had been very lucky. The details were unimportant, he assured me, but a single word would suggest the turn of fate that had brought this world-class instrument to the school. He leaned across the desk and whispered: 'Divorce.'

A few weeks later I met Monsieur Chavatte, the tuner/technician who kept the Schola's pianos in tune and in good repair. A compact man in his forties, with trim black hair and an inquisitive look, he had the confident air of a specialist who is called in to consult on troublesome cases. Beside him on the bench his tool bag lay open, a large leather sack with a patina that came from years of use; each of the tools was perfectly shined and held in its place by loops of leather. The contrast with Jos, with his disheveled appearance and sloppy tool kit, could not have been greater, and I doubted that Monsieur Chavatte favored a *ballon de rouge* in the afternoon.

The two pianos that stood in front of us, he said, were among the finest of their kind. The Yamaha was a superb example of a type of piano that would excel in a setting with many different kinds of players. The Steinway concert grand was, for him, unsurpassed for the virtuoso. I told him that it surprised me that Steinways were so consistently the choice of artists for both live recitals and the recording studio. Monsieur Chavatte shrugged his shoulders, neither agreeing nor disagreeing, and said simply, 'Their sound is beautiful, but it's only one kind of sound.'

Steinway is the exceptional case of a maker that has come to be regarded as the standard of reference by professional pianists and by the public as well. From the very beginning these pianos featured innovative designs, new approaches in construction methods, and an unsurpassed standard of workmanship. To these advantages the Steinway family also brought clever marketing techniques and an assiduous attention to the preferences of the great virtuosi of the day. By the end of the 1800s they were pre-eminent in the field and so they have remained for a century. No one seriously questions that they are superb instruments. Luc regularly told me that Steinways that passed through the atelier, both in design and in workmanship, were like a separate category of piano altogether: they were that much better than all the other brands.

The vaunted 'Steinway sound' unquestionably has appealing features: a powerful bass, a clear treble, and – perhaps most important – immense power in sustaining tones. Even mass manufacturers seek to reproduce this particular tonal landscape. But is its tone so vastly superior?

In a sense the question is parallel to that of the value of hearing music played on restored vintage instruments. If there are advantages in hearing Haydn, say, on Viennese instruments of his day, surely there are also advantages in hearing different kinds of modern pianos. Bechstein, Yamaha, Bösendorfer, and several others make superb pianos with tone qualities that vary considerably from the Steinway sound. Different kinds of pianos project different aesthetics of sound; we hear things differently when there is a different kind of instrument sending forth the notes.

Of the pianos scattered throughout the practice rooms, Monsieur Chavatte pointed out, many were older Pleyels and Erards from a time when French pianos were still among the finest. 'Now they are orphans, but they still have wonderful qualities even if they are growing old. Their voices are certainly distinctive.'

He explained that the French piano business was virtually moribund. In the middle of the nineteenth century it had been at the very summit of innovation and quality, but there was a long downhill slide once the Germans and then the Americans came to the fore. Names such as Pape, Erard, Pleyel, and Gaveau had been the equal of Steinway or Bösendorfer, and they had managed to limp along well into the twentieth century, producing fine pianos but enjoying no great commercial success. Finally, Erard, Pleyel, and Gaveau all merged in an effort to preserve their tradition, but it was too late for the new company to remain independent. In 1971 it was acquired by Schimmel, a reputable German piano maker, and the days of fine French pianos drew to a close.

'Unfortunately, those wonderful tonal qualities will not last for ever. They're machines as well as fine woodwork. And the machine eventually wears down to where I can no longer really repair it.'

This was a good time, I thought, to be at the Schola. The Steinway and the Yamaha that graced the stage were, in any reasonable scenario, where the school would be headed in renewing its instruments. They were fine pianos, among the best, but they were also predictable and a bit homogenous after one became too familiar with their considerable qualities. The Pleyels and Gaveaus would continue for a while yet to give forth their particular sounds, their special touch, and the students who were lucky enough to know them in the quotidian task of lessons and practicing would know something that was going out of the world.

17

SMOKING GUN

At the end of the summer Anna called to ask if I knew someone who could tune her Bechstein and I immediately thought of Jos. It seemed a lucky coincidence that he had once worked in the Bechstein factory in Berlin, and I told her what quick and good work he had done on my piano. He was a bit eccentric, I told her, and he had no fixed home where she could call him. I gave her the number at the atelier and told her that she could perhaps reach him through Luc.

When I returned for my lesson the following week, Anna opened the door to me in a state of agitation. Before I had put down my things she hurled herself into an account of what she had been through. Jos had just left, more than two and a half hours after he had arrived. He had shown up at Anna's door almost an hour late. He was drunk, or at least well advanced towards that state, his face flushed crimson, his words indistinct, his steps unsteady when she let him in. 'He kept smiling and smiling, a big wide smile. I could smell that he had been drinking, but I thought that perhaps this was his ordinary state, what you called his eccentricity. Some people are able to concentrate that way, you know. And so as soon as possible I left him to tune the piano.'

Still visibly upset, Anna talked about the ensuing two hours as one might describe one's sufferings at the hands of a subtle and merciless torturer. She had busied herself in the kitchen, trying in vain not to listen to the tuning under way just down the hall. Each tuner has his own way of working, she told me, but this was something altogether different. 'He pounded on each note, louder than I've ever heard, louder than the loudest *fortissimo*.'

Her face was pained, her voice almost cracking as she recounted what must have felt like an attack on a dear friend. 'After half an hour he still hadn't moved from the middle registers and I knew something was seriously wrong. So I prepared my lunch and ate it, the radio turned up as loud as possible to drown out the horrible sounds from the front.'

Two hours later Anna finally ventured out and told Jos that she had a student coming and that he would have to finish up. He was apparently full of enthusiasm for everyone and everything, and most of all for Anna's Bechstein, which he persisted in calling 'a black beauty'. He spent no more than ten minutes on the bass registers and he managed to break a bass string – the lowest G-string on the keyboard, Anna specified, a long and expensive one to replace. Finally it was over; she paid him his three hundred francs almost gratefully just to be rid of him, and then she sat down and wept.

She was close to tears now and I didn't know how to console her. I felt it was my fault to have proposed Jos in the first place. I awkwardly tried to focus on the practical side to the debacle. 'How bad is the tuning?'

She shot me a look that mixed reproach, disbelief, and disdain. 'It's unplayable; it's as simple as that. Go ahead and try.'

How bad could it be? I asked myself as I sat down on the bench. *Surely it must be close to a proper tuning*, I thought, *with maybe a few false notes that could be individually adjusted to make things right.* I played a simple scale across four octaves, rising and then descending. I did the same with chords, arpeggios, triplets, all sorts of different combinations, and the effect was the same.

It was not a matter of a few false notes, or even many false notes. The entire keyboard was skewed to a false timbre, and yet there was a

162

strange and indecipherable structure to it, as if the distortions had been minutely calculated and executed. Even in major keys it sounded as if it would be suitable only for a Dr Caligari, a warped simulacrum of how a keyboard should sound. This was a piano as it might have been tuned by a fanatic, or by someone with no knowledge of Western music. Or by a drunk.

Anna smiled sardonically. 'Try the low G.'

I struck the key and a hollow tone issued forth. Only one of the two strings for that note was sounding: the other had been broken. 'This is a mess,' I admitted. 'Let me talk to Luc and see what he suggests.'

Since no melody sounded true on the keyboard, we decided that my lesson would be devoted to finger exercises and pedal work. I sat down and extended my feet to the pedals, ready to begin the first set of triplets Anna had set before me on the music stand. As I played the first notes and depressed the damper pedal, I was startled to hear a dull thunk from below the piano and a long hollow sound as if something were being wound slowly and noisily on to a spool. Anna and I stared at each other with wide eyes. When we looked below the Bechstein's case, we saw a wine bottle slowly rolling away from the lyre in which the pedals were housed. It continued its lazy roll across the irregular wooden floor, bonked lightly against the wall, and came to rest.

Anna gave me a pained look, the kind I had seen some of her Lebanese friends use when something struck them as both inescapable and absurd. She turned to me and said sweetly in her accented English, 'I believe you say "smoking gun" in your country, no?'

I went directly from Anna's to the atelier, eager to ask Luc what he suggested I do in this situation. Anna's piano was both the source of her livelihood and the most precious thing she owned. It had to be tuned properly as soon as possible. I was also concerned that Luc understand that I didn't consider him accountable for the mess Jos had created. He had warned me amply and I had assumed that my good experience would be repeated for Anna as a matter of course.

Luc greeted me as if he knew why I had come. 'He's not here. He was falling-down drunk. I threw him out.'

'That's probably just as well. I need some advice.'

Luc listened to it all and when I got to the wine bottle hidden behind the pedals, he couldn't suppress a smile. 'Well, I give him high marks for audacity, but he fails in execution.'

'That's putting it mildly. Can I pay you to tune her piano again?'

'You mean she actually paid him?'

I explained how Anna had been frustrated and not a little fearful at so bizarre a situation. Three hundred francs, while a lot of money to her, had seemed little enough in order to get rid of Jos. But she couldn't continue her lessons, nor practice her own playing, on the instrument Jos had so strangely distorted.

Luc felt strongly that Jos should return, sober, and tune the Bechstein properly. He insisted that there was no one better when he was serious about his work, and he thought he should face the consequences of what he called his *bêtises*. As he talked about Jos, Luc's voice rose and he slapped the top of an upright with an impatience I had never seen before. But the anger in his voice quickly subsided and he shook his head slowly, muttering '*Ça, alors*' with a protective, almost paternalistic wave of his arm. It clearly saddened him that Jos could not seem to be consistent and use his considerable talents to make his way in the world. 'You know, at heart he's a good guy.' In French he said '*un brave type*', a simple phrase that was one of Luc's infrequent compliments. He proposed that I accompany Jos to Anna's on some pretext or other to make sure that he was sober and that he undertook the tuning correctly. He told me to come by the following morning and meet Jos in the atelier. 'That is, if he hasn't gone off to Clermont-Ferrand on the night train.'

'Why on earth would he do that?'

Luc reminded me that Jos regularly slept in train carriages left on sidings in the major stations of Paris. It happened sometimes that his carriage would be coupled to a departing train in the middle of the night and he would wake up somewhere in the provinces. Nantes, Toulouse, Macon – it might be anywhere and, once expelled from the train, he had to cadge a ride back to Paris. This he always managed to do, but what Luc referred to as his '*aventures*' were legion. 'So come by in the morning and we'll see if he shows up, and in what condition. He's not touching another one of my pianos, though, until he makes good on this one.'

The next morning at ten I found Jos at the atelier with Luc. He was embarrassed to see me and yet, when I told him that I thought he needed to tune Anna's piano again properly, he expressed surprise: 'It was fine when I left her yesterday.'

'No, Jos, it was not fine. It was terribly out of tune and it still is. It needs to be tuned right away.' We went around like this for a few minutes, with him denying that there was anything the matter and me insisting that it was unplayable. He seemed abashed and cowed by our talk, and I decided that he needed to have a pretext for being unprofessional, a graceful way out that would explain what we all so obviously knew: he had been phenomenally drunk. 'Jos, I have a feeling that you were celebrating a little too heavily the night before.'

He looked at me, shocked, almost offended, and I was afraid I had miscalculated. *You can open a door*, I thought, *but you can't make anyone walk through it.* Eventually a slow awareness worked its way on to his face and the look of injury turned into a sheepish admission. 'Well, maybe I was partying a little too much that night.' In French he said '*Je faisais la fête*', an expression that covers everything from a sedate drink with friends to a yelling, screaming debauchery.

'Suppose you and I go to Anna's today and see if you can make the Bechstein sing as it should. I need to pick up some sheet music that I left behind.'

165

'*Ja*, we could do that if you think it's really necessary.'

A quick call to Anna took care of the details. She agreed to play along with the story that Jos had been feeling the effects of a good time. 'Remember,' I whispered, 'this isn't the time for pointing fingers. Let's give the guy a graceful way out and hope he takes it.'

'All I care about is that my piano be in tune again.'

I returned to the back of the atelier and told Jos that we should go right away. His look showed both surprise and relief, as if it were hard for him to acknowledge that he had made a mess of things and yet was grateful for the chance to make amends. He put on a ragged jeans jacket and we walked to the door. As we were leaving, however, I noticed that his hands were empty. 'Jos, won't you need your tools?'

He looked at me as would a ten-year-old who has been caught at some mischief, put his hand over his mouth in a pantomime of horror, and returned to the atelier to get his slender bag of tools. As I waited I wondered just what condition he was in and if this expedition would, in fact, solve the problem that he had created.

When we arrived at the metro station Jos put his satchel under his arm and walked past the ticket counter. I realized that he was preparing to jump the barrier rather than pay and I hurriedly bought four tickets – two for him, two for me. 'Jos, here's a ticket for each direction. Let's keep things simple, okay?'

He looked at me with amazement, as if the prospect of actually using a ticket to board the metro were a strange and mysterious concept. 'There's no need, really. I go everywhere like this.'

Yes, I thought to myself, *to Clermont-Ferrand or Bordeaux on the night train*, but all I wanted to do was to get him to Anna's without incident. I grabbed his arm before he could jump the barrier and moved in close, placing the little green metro tickets in his hand. 'Jos, just humor me on this one, please.'

Reluctantly he acquiesced, untensing his wiry body for the leap that would not now be necessary. He took the tickets as if they were vaguely unwholesome, gradually inclining himself to the prospect of riding the metro like a respectable person.

On the metro, Jos started to chat nervously. There really had been nothing wrong with the Bechstein when he left it; Anna must have done something to it since he had tuned it. He was sure, in any case, that even when he had celebrated, it didn't affect his capacity to tune perfectly well. He had done it before, and on and on.

He reminded me of a youngster who has done something wrong and is being taken by his parent to apologize to the offended party. He was by turns defensive, sorry, contemptuous, frightened, and defiant. His face was flushed as red as a radish now, and it occurred to me that his anxiety and his embarrassment probably were giving rise to a powerful impulse to have a drink. It was all I could do to hold his attention; I was afraid that he would lose his composure and bolt, spoiling my efforts to control the damage done so far. By the time the metro stopped at Anna's neighborhood, I was exhausted. We walked the short distance to her apartment; I might as well have been dragging Jos on an invisible leash.

Anna greeted us as if nothing were amiss and I decided I had better voice the issue before us, however obliquely. 'Anna, Jos has come to make a few adjustments to your piano after Monday's tuning. And I want to pick up that sheet music I left behind.'

Anna suppressed with difficulty a skeptical look and walked to the Bechstein. 'Let me show you where I think the problems are.' She sat at the keyboard and played a scale from the bass to the treble, covering most of the keyboard. She then descended in octaves, stopping and sounding the notes loudly when one was clearly out of tune. As she did so, she turned her head and gave us a stiff nod that invited us to acknowledge just how badly the piano was off key. By the time she finished, the problem couldn't have been plainer and we all listened to the notes fade in the quiet room.

Jos had said nothing since we arrived; his eyes were focused on the worn carpet at our feet and he never once lifted his gaze. It was a moment when anything could have happened. And then I decided to *trancher*, as the French say, to cut through the atmosphere and get on with things. 'Well, Jos, we'd better leave you to do your work. We'll be in the back if you need anything.'

Jos seemed suddenly relieved, and he laid his skinny satchel on a table and started to remove his tools. In her tiny kitchen Anna and I closed the door and exchanged smiles. The irregular thrumming of the piano's middle registers sounded through the thin walls and we both knew that a delicate pass had been negotiated.

'Can he fix the broken string?' she asked.

'That's more complicated than I had thought.' I had been surprised to learn from Luc that replacing a broken string was not a simple matter of buying a generic substitute as it would be, say, for a guitar. Since each piano maker strings its instruments differently, each has different strings across the full range of the keyboard. A Bösendorfer's low A, for example, is not the same as a Steinway's or a Yamaha's; they have different lengths and different thicknesses, depending on the maker and the individual model. It happened that there was in the South of France one supplier of strings for older pianos; he would certainly have the necessary string for the Bechstein, but it would take up to two weeks to secure and would cost about a hundred francs.

Nor was installing it a simple matter of winding it on to the tuning pin and tightening until it sounded the proper pitch; that was only the beginning. Because of the enormous stress placed on piano strings, they stretch gradually when they are new and must be retuned until they reach an approximate equilibrium. It would require two or three tunings in the first few months in order for the note to sound true. Luc volunteered that an interim repair could be made by tying a knot in the part of the string that did not 'sound', or resonate, when struck by the hammer, but the aesthetics were dreadful (the knot would be plainly visible when the cover was open) and he dismissed the possibility out of hand for a fine piano: 'It would not be right for a Bechstein.' Luc had also pointed out that, while regrettable, a broken string was not an uncommon occurrence when a piano was being tuned. In this case it might well have been weak to begin with and the incremental increase in pull had been enough to make it snap. Or it could have been that Jos had applied far too much pressure in his altered state and had, in effect, popped the string himself. We would never know for sure.

All of this I explained to Anna, who sighed heavily as she served me orange juice, ginger biscuits, and strong tea, and listened to my account. 'I can live with the broken string. I just need my piano to be playable again.'

About half an hour into the tuning, Jos had moved out of the middle registers and was working his way up the treble. There was no telling yet if the overall effect would be an improvement, but he was certainly working methodically and fairly quickly. Anna said pleasantly, 'You know, if it's still wrong I'll kill him with my bare hands.'

'You'll be killing a corpse, then, because I'll beat you to it.'

As we sat in the kitchen she described how, ever since childhood, the world of her piano and her music had always been a place to which she could escape merely by playing the notes. 'Family, politics, adolescent worries, illness – anything at all could be left behind when I entered that special place.' She assured me that the piano still had that strange power for her to transform and to transcend the ordinary world that fills our days. 'Now I perhaps have to be a bit more conscious of the change, to will it to happen, to want to go elsewhere. But I can still do that readily and, once I decide to leave, I'm gone. It's like a train – it leaves the station and you're already somewhere else.'

About three-quarters of an hour into the tuning, I became aware that there was less noise coming from the front room and the occasional notes were all in the lowest registers. Jos must be finishing up. I gave Anna an encouraging look, opened the kitchen door and followed her to the salon. Jos was removing the felt damping strips from the strings and replacing his wrenches in the small satchel. 'All finished?'

'*Ja*. There were a few slipped strings, but all is right now.'

Anna sat down at the keyboard and played some scales, then a passage from a Chopin ballade. The Bechstein again sounded like the beautiful instrument that it was; Dr Caligari had gone back to his cabinet. She nodded her head in approval as she rose from the bench. 'I am glad to have my piano back.'

18

THE DEAL

Luc had found a spare *barre stabilisatrice* for me in the atelier, slightly bent, and he had suggested that I have it straightened at the local *ferrailleur* and then fasten it to the piano's frame. A small hinged piece at one end had to be welded so that it was immobile. 'The locksmith around the corner from you is also a *ferrailleur*,' he said, exhibiting once again his limitless knowledge of the *quartier*. 'You can tell him I sent you.'

The *ferrailleur* is an institution in every *quartier* in Paris, a metal-working shop that has something of the village blacksmith about it, a dark and disorganized place where modern equipment has for the most part replaced the forge's ever-stoked furnace. If you have to get something welded, if you want iron bars put on your ground-floor windows, if you need to fashion a metal ventilation hood around your stove, the *ferrailleur* is the person you see for custom metalwork. Most often combined with a *serrurerie*, a shop specializing in locks and keys, a *ferrailleur* is an indispensable part of life in every neighborhood.

The *ferrailleur* in our *quartier* was a Romanian in his forties, with a very enthusiastic and welcoming manner when I entered his cluttered shop on a side street. He listened patiently as I described to him what I needed: the twisted metal bar that I was carrying had to be straightened and the hinged end welded so that I could place it at a forty-five-degree angle between the pedals and the body of the piano. He seemed puzzled by its importance, but when I assured him that its function was vital to the piano's pedals, he agreed to do the work. 'Unfortunately it will have to wait, though.'

'Why is that?'

'I'm missing a part for this kind of welding.'

'When do you suppose you might have the part?'

His reply in French was '*Dans les jours qui viennent*', which is much more vague than its literal English translation: 'In the days ahead.' The Stingl had been without its bracing for months, perhaps years, however, so I figured that a few extra days would do no harm. I left the piece with him and agreed to check back in a week.

Despite the fact that the job was relatively straightforward, I found it impossible to get the gregarious Romanian *ferrailleur* to give me a date when the bar would be repaired. I would arrive at the shop to be greeted by a hand-lettered sign stuck inside the locked glass door: '*Absence Pour Cause de Dépannage Urgent*' ('Gone for Emergency Repairs'). Since he was also a locksmith, this was plausible enough, although it was hard to believe it was always an emergency. On the rare occasions when I found him at his shop, he always greeted me loudly and warmly, immediately taking the initiative to add that the piece was not yet ready because the special part for welding was still missing. I resisted asking for the bar to be returned to me since I knew that finding another *ferrailleur* would entail going to another *quartier* and Luc had told me that this man did good work.

I explained all of this to Luc and he listened with a bemused air. After hearing the last account of how I had missed the *ferrailleur*, he grimaced comically. 'We have to put an end to this!'

He stalked across the atelier to a shelf that was cluttered with every variety of piano part, piles of documents, and several bolts of fabric. Into this mass he thrust his arm up to the elbow, moved it around as if he were catching a caged animal by feel alone, and then yanked his arm out abruptly, brandishing a strange piece of machinery. 'Take this to our Romanian friend,' he declared, 'and tell him I want it fixed right away.'

'Fine. Do I ask him what it is, or do I just beat him over the head with it?'

'For God's sake don't beat him over the head with it; this thing is one of a kind.' He paused and turned the object over slowly. 'Besides, I'm going to tell you just exactly what it is.'

Patiently, Luc told me that the bizarre piece of metalwork was '*un appareil "looping"*', a piece of fine machinery that allowed him to turn loops in piano wire before they were fixed to the tuning pins. He put the strange device in a large plastic bag and thrust it into my hand. 'Tell him that I need it right away,' he repeated. 'That should make a difference.'

When I stopped by the *ferrailleur* the next day, he greeted me enthusiastically, as if he had been hoping I would show up. I waited patiently as he finished his by now familiar disquisition on the infamous welding mechanism, and then I set the plastic bag on the counter before him and removed Luc's broken looping machine.

'I've brought you this on behalf of Luc at Desforges. He was wondering if you could repair the hook.' I indicated to him where the piece was broken, and he picked it up and examined it closely.

'It will need to be welded,' he said more to himself than to me, as he turned the tool in his hands. He looked up and said, 'When does *Monsieur* need this?'

'Right away. Apparently it's very important for his work.' I embroidered a bit with this last detail, but I saw that it was unnecessary as soon as I said it.

The *ferrailleur*'s manner was concerned, as if Luc's needs took priority over everything else. 'Please tell him that it will be ready tomorrow,' he said. Almost as an afterthought, he added, 'Your *barre* will be ready then, too.'

When I came back the next day, he took both pieces from behind the counter and showed me just how he had done the work. Both the looping machine and my stabilizing bar were expertly repaired. I went directly to the atelier where I found Luc in the back. I handed him the plastic bag with his repaired tool. He took it out and looked it over carefully, nodding his approval. 'Lirana does good work.'

'Yes, when he gets around to it. If you don't mind my asking, why did he suddenly get so motivated when it came to a little job for you?'

'Let's just say that we have done business before and he has reasons to want to help me.'

I didn't resent Luc's preferential treatment and realized that it belonged to the complicated network of local relationships that it was extremely difficult for a foreigner to penetrate. Just as it had been hard for me to get into Luc's atelier, so it was not easy to get shopkeepers in the *quartier* to put my business first. But it also felt encouraging to know that Luc was prepared to be my sponsor in this intricate world of mutual trust and obligation. I saw just how much he had come to trust me on the day that he allowed me to witness one of his business transactions, something that had never happened before.

On that day two movers were in the shop unloading a series of pianos from their truck parked out front. As I wandered about looking at the new arrivals, Luc held the door open for them as they pushed the final upright, balanced on a small dolly, up the narrow ramp and into the back, easing it into place behind the door. The younger of the men had an expectant air and I saw that he wanted to talk to Luc. His companion made the classic French gesture, although it was only eleven in the morning: '*Tu as le temps de boire un coup*? ('Do you have time for a drink?')

The younger man, a husky guy in his late twenties or early thirties, nodded and waved him on. 'I'll join you at the café on the corner in a minute.' Then he turned to Luc and said in a low voice, 'I've got an extraordinary Erard from 1820 for you, a perfect Louis XVIII.'

He leaned across the back of the Pleyel he had just delivered and brought his face close to Luc's. With a conspiratorial tone he explained that he had seen it only that morning and it was something very special: squared wooden cabinet, lots of marquetry and even some gold leaf, ivory naturals and ebony accidentals, and, a detail he mentioned more than once, three beautifully tapered legs of solid mahogany. At the end of his description he lowered his voice to a whisper and said with a matter-of-fact air, 'Twenty-five thousand francs, cash. I can have it here for you tomorrow.'

Luc didn't blink, nor did he indicate any undue interest. Instead, he asked a series of questions. What was the shape of the legs? What sort of detailing did the woodwork show? Where was the gold leaf? How many keys in the keyboard? Did all three legs touch the ground or was the cabinet warped?

I got the feeling that he was interested in these points, but that it was also his way of buying time, of feeling out the contours of a possible deal, of assessing whether there really was something *extraordinaire* on the other side. At the end of the litany of questions and answers, the young man said, 'Luc, I'll show you that I can deal: twenty-three thousand.'

Luc paused and considered, then he asked if that included delivery to the atelier. The man assured him that it did and still Luc pondered, scratching his beard. 'How about a photograph of this one? A quick Polaroid to get a better idea?'

The young man's reaction was swift. 'No, I can't do that. This client won't allow a photograph, I'm sure. I don't want to scare him away.'

Luc looked uneasy and held his silence. I sensed that this was a delicate moment and I quietly walked to the other side of the atelier as they looked at each other. A few moments later I heard a low voice with what sounded like a pleading intensity. 'Okay, my last price: twenty-one thousand. No photograph; cash today, it's here tomorrow.'

Soon Luc disappeared into the tiny alcove that was hidden in one corner of the atelier. The young *commerçant* bent over the double keyboard of a modern harpsichord that Luc was refinishing and played a beautiful little baroque piece – it might have been Couperin – from his standing position. It was the last thing I expected, to see this man with the build of a rugby player and the manner of a horse trader celebrate the closing of a deal by playing a convincing flourish of seventeenth-century counterpoint on the instrument that looked like a toy next to his bulk.

Luc returned with a fat envelope in one hand. Together they hunched over the back of one of the pianos as Luc counted out bills. When he finished, the young man recounted them, pocketed the wad, and announced in a voice that was clearly meant to include me, as if a formal notice were being given: 'That's it; tomorrow at nine fifteen we're here.'

There was a long handshake and then he was gone to join his companion at the corner café for *un coup*. I wondered if the drink would be the standard *ballon de rouge*, or a *coup de Calva*, a shot of the strong apple brandy from Normandy – Calvados – that was favored locally on cold mornings such as this one.

As he closed the front door, Luc turned to me and shook his head. 'I'm taking a big risk.'

'What's the risk, that it's not the model you're imagining?'

'That too, but above all that that may be the last I see of him and of the cash.'

Despite his expressed reservations, he didn't seem regretful or even nervous. Instead, his air was analytical, almost bemused by what had transpired in the previous twenty minutes. A simple delivery of an unremarkable upright had taken a potentially interesting turn; now it remained for him to wait and see what fate served up the next day. I saw that this was how he did business, that the gamble was in some sense what he needed to maintain his enthusiasm. The uprights would always roll in the door, but the unusual piano, the unexpected deal, is what quickened his imagination. Luc turned to go to the front of the atelier and as he did so he said over his shoulder, '*On verra ce qu'on verra.*' ('We shall see what we shall see.')

19

BEETHOVEN'S PIANO

Two days later I returned to the atelier, curious to know what had materialized after Luc's spontaneous transaction. When I entered he led me immediately to the back, as if he were in the middle of doing something. 'Your timing is perfect. You can help me move a piano.'

In the far corner I saw an old grand piano with wood the color of tanned leather. Its case was squared and narrow, and it stood on three delicately tapered legs with rounded flutings carved into the wood. I couldn't resist asking Luc straight out, although he seemed pre-occupied with other matters, 'Is that the famous 1820 Erard that had you wondering the other day?'

'That's it. It's not Louis XVIII, it's Charles X. But it's old and beautiful all the same.'

I was tantalized by this lovely object, so different from the other pianos that were in the atelier, and I wanted to know the story of what had happened on the day after the deal was struck, but Luc seemed unenthused. Like many Frenchmen, he dated things down to the decade by reference to the monarch who had then ruled France, but the specific age of the Erard now appeared to matter little to him. 'I've got something better than that next door.' I saw now that he was very excited as he gathered the dollies and packing blankets we would need, and I understood that the Erard, while still captivating, had been eclipsed by something even more unusual.

I followed him out on to the sidewalk and waited as he unlocked the next door down from the shop front. He entered and motioned me to follow him into a small dark room filled with upright pianos. The metal blinds were drawn over the one window and there was apparently no electric light, so I waited a moment for my eyes to adjust to the sliver of daylight that came in through the half-open door. Gradually I made out the shape of a long, skinny grand piano lying on the floor on its flat side. Luc made his way to the other end and together we lifted it on to the low dolly he had brought. While it was bulky and somewhat unwieldy, there was nothing about its weight that resembled that of a modern grand piano; it was surprisingly light for its size and the two of us lifted it easily. Next Luc had me position a small wooden ramp at the front door so that we could roll the dolly down on to the sidewalk. With that in place, he pushed while I pulled and slowly our load emerged into the pale light of a cloudy Parisian morning.

I saw a long, sinuous curve of burled wood the color of tortoise-shell whose surface had that slightly irregular quality, a kind of dusty brittleness, that very old veneer sometimes assumes. Pieces of the fancy wood had been worked symmetrically in wide bands along the entire length of the curve, and the seams were spaced regularly every foot or so in order to show off the wood's pattern. The keyboard end of the piano was towards me, and the most distinctive feature was a second small curve which reversed the concave swoop of the long side and continued around to enclose the right side of the keyboard with a baroque flourish. As we eased our precious load down the single step and on to the sidewalk, I stood up and started to admire what was now revealed, but Luc hurriedly admonished me to keep pulling as he bent low to the task of pushing. 'Later, later!' he cried. 'You can spend all the time you like looking at it once we get it into the atelier.'

While his manner was not furtive, I saw that he was anxious to get this piano indoors, as if he were concerned that we would not be noticed. The top and legs were removed, more than half of the strings were missing, the ivory of the keyboard was deeply yellowed and many of the keys were broken. Surely only a connoisseur could imagine the significance of this instrument, not an ignorant passer-by.

Luc moved the wooden ramp from the door we had just exited to the door of the atelier, directing me to hold the dolly steady as he hurried around me. With the ramp in place, he again took up his position at the piano's narrow tail, giving it a sudden push without warning me. The dolly lurched forward and the piano pivoted and nearly fell, narrowly missing a metal pole holding up a 'No Parking' sign. I grabbed my end of the piano frantically and managed to keep the fragile cabinet from striking the pole. Luc grimaced wildly as he saw what he had done, but he could do nothing to help. I was frozen with the wide end of the piano in my hands, its strings still resonating with a hollow, metallic tone caused by the sudden jolt. Luc and I looked at each other and our relief was palpable as I relaxed my grasp and we centered the piano once again on the dolly. 'Du calme,' I whispered, flinching at the realization of how close we had come to disaster and Luc nodded as he exhaled. 'Oui, c'est ça. Du calme.'

Once we were inside and dusting off our clothes and hands, Luc stood back and admired his latest acquisition. 'Le voilà: le piano de Beethoven!' I crouched down to examine this beautiful creation of eighteenth-century Vienna. A small oval disc in a delicate cream-colored ceramic graced the panel above the keyboard; I read the words painted across it in fine black script: 'Johann GOTTING in Wien'. The surface of the sumptuous wood was lightly blistered in a few spots, patches where the veneer had slightly separated from the underlying structure. What strings remained all ran straight back from the pin block − this was built before the innovation of diagonal overstringing or even the partial metal frame − so that the cabinet was particularly long and narrow on its straight left side where the bass strings were extended to their full length. The absence of a cast-iron frame is what had made it feel comparatively light when Luc and I lifted it, but I now saw more clearly the thick wooden struts that gave it a rigidity that pre-dated the machine age. The whole thing was more like a big harpsichord in its hand-crafted detailing, but the mechanism was nevertheless that of a true piano.

'How do you know this was really Beethoven's?'

Luc laughed softly at my too-literal understanding of his words. There was no proof, he told me, just the accretion of details that made it 'possible' that Beethoven had played this piano: from Vienna, built by a reputable maker, dating from the late eighteenth century, incorporating the latest developments in grand pianos. 'What matters is that this is the *kind* of piano he would have played and composed on before he was famous. Think of those hands smashing down on this keyboard!'

I peered again at the instrument that sat in front of us, so delicate-looking now, like a big fruit crate on its side. Imagining the power that would have descended on the thin strips of wood that lay exposed, I better appreciated how excited Beethoven – or any of his contemporaries – would have been as metal bracing strengthened the frame and allowed a fuller, louder tone to come forth.

I asked Luc who would be the likely buyer for a rare piano like this in such evident need of restoration. He said that he had already found someone: a Belgian collector with whom he had traded it for a Steinway Model O from the twenties with superb art deco detailing.

'What about the Charles X Erard? Do you have any takers?'

He smiled and said no, and then he described a scene that had revolved around that very piano just recently. It seems that the young man who had sold it to him had been in the back of the atelier looking at other pianos when a potential customer for the Erard arrived at the front. Luc didn't want the two of them to meet, so he closed the door to the back to keep them separated. *'J'ai fais la petite porte pour apparaître devant.'*

I hadn't known that there existed a little hidden door that led from the atelier to the storage space next door, the same space from which we had just moved the Viennese treasure. By passing through that space, on to the sidewalk, and back through the front door of the shop, Luc was able to carry on two discussions without either person suspecting the presence of the other. But there had been some anxious moments as he kept having to excuse himself from the front to 'check something next door', and from the back to 'consult a document in the office'. And when the man in the back had wanted to leave, he had had to interest him in some other detail until he could get rid of the visitor in the front. '*C'était du Molière!*' he said, chuckling to himself.

As we were talking the bell rang and Mathilde, the dark-haired woman I had met at the atelier some while before, joined us in the back. Luc's expression brightened considerably as she entered. He introduced us again and explained that Mathilde had become, like me, a frequent visitor to the back room.

'Ah, these beautiful old pianos, they're like a drug,' she sighed. 'I can't stay away. Has Luc showed you his collection of ancients?'

'He just helped me move the Viennese,' Luc said.

'I'll be sorry to see that one leave,' Mathilde stated. 'Did you hear its tone?'

'It made some noise when we moved it,' I answered, 'but we didn't play it, no.'

'Ah, listen to a few notes at least. For me it's more like a carillon of bells than a piano.'

Luc explained that he had carefully tightened certain of the strings from among those that remained and Mathilde now squeezed between the pianos on either side to gain access to the Gotting's wrecked keyboard. She delicately played a chord with her right hand, then one in the bass registers with her left, and the effect was indeed distinctive. A soft ringing, very much like bells with slight metallic overtones, lingered in the air. There was nothing loud or sharp about the tone; it had the same dynamic range as a harpsichord without the clipped quality of that instrument's attack.

Mathilde then played a scale on one octave, but many of the notes were missing and the result was strangely distorted and incomplete. She abandoned her place at the keyboard with a look of good-natured frustration. 'I even brought in my little tape recorder to try to capture some of this wonderful softness!' she exclaimed, gesturing up to the skylight as she played one final note on the piano that so captivated her with its soft sound. 'But it's like trying to capture moonlight in a net.'

I told them how much it had impressed me when I had helped Luc move it to consider that this piano was more than two centuries old and that it had been made almost entirely by hand.

'Remember, too, that the trees for the wood that was used to build this piano were most likely planted in the late sixteenth century.'

Mathilde and I looked at Luc dumbfounded, unwilling to believe that he could know so arcane a fact, and at the same time trying to calculate just how old that would make the materials that had been used. Luc explained that the woodworking tradition was firmly established in Germany from the Middle Ages, and that guilds and families regularly replanted trees in order to provide the right kind of wood for their descendants. It wouldn't be unusual for someone's ancestor to have planted a grove of trees two hundred and fifty years before they were to be cut down, say in 1520. After being harvested, the wood would then have been allowed to cure for anywhere from ten to forty years. And that would bring us to the late eighteenth century and to the instrument that Luc now referred to as 'this little marvel'.

In French he said 'cette petite merveille', running his hand lightly along the curved edge that stuck out from the clutter. There was a deep respect in the gesture, almost a tenderness, and his voice revealed just how impressive he found the series of human machinations that had prepared the way for this masterpiece of the woodworker's art.

'What kind of wood is it?' I asked.

'Some kind of fruit wood. The man in Belgium who is going to restore it says the veneer is most likely plum or pear.' The wood's appearance was extraordinary, unlike anything I had seen on any of the nineteenth-century instruments that I had watched pass through the atelier, even the most grand. Wood of that age, he said, chosen so carefully and worked with painstaking skill, was incomparable. 'It simply isn't available any more. Even by the nineteenth century it was rare, but now it's a substance that has gone out of the world we live in.'

This pronouncement was categorical without being harsh. Instead, it was almost elegiac, as if the world were poorer in ways we didn't even suspect now that the entire human undertaking of planting, cultivating, and harvesting trees that would yield precious woods after hundreds of years of care had passed from the scene.

Luc noticed Mathilde's dreamy look. 'What are you thinking about?'

'I'm thinking about that grove during all those hundreds of years. If only we could know what happened under those trees!'

Mathilde's look suggested amorous trysts of lovers, meetings in the leafy shade of low-hanging fruit trees. Luc cut through the atmosphere of revery as with a knife. 'Ah, you musn't suppose that it was all hearts and flowers!' he declared. 'Martin Luther might have pissed on those trees. Now that would be something worth knowing!'

20

MASTER CLASSES

Re-entering the world of the piano as an adult gradually brought me a series of revelations about the practice of self-discipline, none more telling than when I witnessed the methods of two acknowledged masters in the field. During the first several months of my lessons with Anna I rediscovered the simple joy of having a teacher. There are people in this world who are true autodidacts at the keyboard but they are rare, and I knew that I was not one of them. With the exceptions of composition and improvisation, playing music is a strange mixture of a given structure – the score – and one's creativity in its interpretation. Being able to play all of the notes is just the beginning; the real work is in adding your own self transparently to the composer's intentions. To return to this discipline as a grownup was deeply humbling but strangely exciting, too. Only a teacher can provide the push that allows the infinite perfectibility of music to take flight.

In my first few months of lessons Anna was both reassuring and demanding, focusing on fundamentals before worrying about the challenges of interpretation. My sight-reading was terrible and my knowledge of the relationship of the major and minor keys virtually nonexistent. Still, my hands seemed to have a memory of their own, so that I played certain exercises and passages with an assurance that I didn't realize I possessed. It was a strange, disquieting experience to be unable to recall skills I had mastered long years before while other elements reappeared with a facility that surprised me.

From the outset Anna had me practice a series of exercises that aimed to relax my shoulders, arms, and hands, and that depended on my having what she called a 'natural posture' when seated at the keyboard. These she referred to as 'Peter's exercises' and soon I learned that they had been developed by Peter Feuchtwanger, a well-known teacher in London whom Anna revered. The exercises had principally to do with consciously relaxing the arms and hands, and then, as Anna put it, 'throwing' the fingers at the desired note.

Superficially they were simple – the notes were easy enough to play – but everything had to do with the quality of the movement: a sudden explosion of energy, the launching of the hand, and an immediate return to a centered repose. Seen this way, they were extraordinarily difficult for me to master. I would anticipate the movement and tense my arm for it; Anna would stop me each time, grasp my arm, and shake it lightly until the muscle relaxed. 'Rest, throw, rest!' she would chant, but reaching the initial rest was tough going. As I performed the exercises regularly, however, I began to understand how they were designed to undermine the kind of strained anticipation that so often accompanies us to the keyboard, and I came to appreciate their value in changing a habit that must have established itself in me as early as Miss Pemberton's.

At the close of one of my lessons Anna told me that Peter would be coming to Paris the following month to conduct a workshop for three days. In the music world this is called a master class, a special form of teaching where an acknowledged expert gives lessons back-to-back over several days and the sessions are open to all of the students and, less frequently, to the public. She said that it was premature for me to take part as a student but that I would be welcome to sit in as an auditor. Over the next several weeks she occasionally asked for help with translating from the English various faxes that she received from him, and so it was that I learned the biographical outline of this teacher whom Anna only half jokingly referred to as her guru.

He was discovered as a self-taught prodigy in his adolescence and studied with some of the greatest pianists of the day – Fischer, Gieseking, Haskil – before going on to a short and brilliant career of concerts. Since then he had devoted his life to teaching and was highly regarded as an original mentor for many concert pianists. He'd written, 'There are many ways of doing things, but there is always one way that is natural', and this seemed a perfect summary of the philosophy Anna was trying to instill in me.

The workshop was held on a long weekend – Friday, Saturday, and Sunday – and fifteen of us assembled at Anna's small apartment for the day-long sessions around the venerable Bechstein grand. Peter was a tall, slender man with the mien of a sage: his features were lined, almost severe, but their angularity was relieved by enormously expressive eyes that danced behind thick glasses and a half-smile that flitted periodically across his face in a mixture of bemusement, curiosity, and fun.

His perfectly straight spine gave him an air of great dignity, but when he moved his arms a fluid quality to his gestures surprised and delighted me, as if a tree trunk had sprouted wings. His age was impossible to determine (I guessed sixty): sometimes he looked old and even wizened, but the next moment he would assume the energetic movements of someone twenty years younger and his features become pliant and youthful-looking.

The master class began at nine and we found seats on the couches and chairs drawn up around the room facing the piano. My friend Claire went first – she played several preludes and fugues from Johann Sebastian Bach's *The Well-Tempered Clavier* – and we listened attentively as she interpreted the score with Peter seated to one side following on his own sheet music. She hesitated or missed notes in a few rough spots, but overall it sounded convincing and conveyed real beauty. When she finished we applauded enthusiastically and Peter rose silently from his chair and placed his score on the adjacent pile of sheet music.

He began by asking Claire a few questions about how long she had been working on the piece, why she had chosen it, and the like. He told her to take several deep breaths and once she had relaxed a bit he asked her to repeat one of the sections. Now he stood behind her and before she had gone very far he stopped her and said, 'We must work on your arms.' He talked about the need for elliptical, relaxed movements of the hand, a natural fluidity with no preparation. Conservatories too often teach preparation, he said, so as not to hit the wrong note; ironically, preparation causes tension and we miss the note. 'Natural movement is riskier,' he acknowledged, 'but life is risky and music is an element of life, so it is risky, too!'

Peter asked Claire to play some *forte* chords from the score, giving her specific advice about how to move her arms and hands to achieve the desired tone. 'The faster you open the hand, the more *forte* the sound. You see? You want quick, relaxed movements with absolutely no preparation. It should be like a chameleon catching a fly.' He then took Claire's arm in his hands and shook it lightly, much as Anna had shaken mine.

Next he flattened Claire's hand gently, uncurling and lengthening the fingers so that they extended well on to the keyboard. 'We must all forget those old, ridiculous rules, such as "Use your fingers pretending they are little hammers" or "Play the piano as if you were holding an apple in the palm of your hand"!' You don't want to lift the fingers to hit the keys from above, he said. Rather, the fingers are like extensions of the keys, elongated and fluid in their movements. He instructed Claire to play a passage with these ideas in mind and there was immediately a different quality to the tone she produced.

Peter worked closely with Claire on trills and embellishments ('Add ornament, then take it away: a room full of people can also be very pleasing when they leave'); alternative fingerings ('The most dangerous thing is "finger memory"; if you really know a piece harmonically, it doesn't matter what finger you use, but if finger memory fails you, it falls apart utterly'); and avoiding accents at the bar measure ('Call me "Professor No Accent"! As Schnabel said, bar lines – like children – should be seen and not heard').

After she played a final page of the score with an entirely new nuanced phrasing, Peter thanked her for the 'lovely reading' and complimented her on the progress. Collectively we breathed out after the intense focus of the preceding ninety minutes. Anna's small living room was now transformed from a classroom into a party venue and a half-dozen conversations erupted loudly as drinks and refreshments were passed around. Those who had yet to play worried out loud about their level of preparation, while Claire herself radiated relief, satisfaction, and joy.

I wondered at how easily Anna's unremarkable apartment in this modest suburb had been transformed. The mere presence of her Bechstein changed the level of the proceedings, for it corresponded perfectly to the caliber of Peter's teaching. A lesser piano would have altered the mood, as if some part of a player's problems could be ascribed to the instrument's limitations, but the Bechstein forestalled that logic. It was as good as a piano could be; the rest was up to the player.

Four participants played each day, two in the morning and two in the afternoon. The level of playing ran from gifted amateur to concert artist, but Peter's approach was uniformly serious without being rigid and he adapted his comments to the person at the keyboard. He spent considerable time on each student's individual issues and his methods varied according to the particular needs of the moment. 'What was the composer trying to say with this piece?' was a frequent refrain, and he used every kind of insight to get closer to the answer. Sometimes it was an extraordinarily specific historical development that governed the style and for a few minutes Peter would hold forth on the composer's influences. 'You must know Carl Philipp Emanuel Bach's work to approach Haydn properly. In his sonatas, Haydn combines the northern German school of counterpoint with an Italian singing line and gradually the two styles become indistinguishable. You should try to hear that.'

On other points his comments, although steeped in history, were more prosaic, reminding us that composers were people, not gods. Chopin played very little in public, he told us, and he always played very softly. Rather than because of any inability to produce loud tones, as it has become popular to believe, this was clearly a choice. He preferred his Pleyel to the pianos of Erard since for him the Pleyel was beautiful only when played softly and with subtlety. Of Erard, Chopin said, 'Everything always sounds beautiful, so you don't have to pay as close attention to producing a beautiful tone.'

Humor frequently cut through an over-serious atmosphere, as when Peter told the story of Ravel's impatient comment to a pianist practicing his *Pavane pour une infante défunte*: '*Madame, c'est l'infante qui est défunte, pas vous!*'

Tolerant, even indulgent, he still objected with good-natured irony when someone made the mistake of not taking the music seriously. One of the students played through a Granados suite and suddenly stopped, rather than continue with the repeats. '*Le reste, c'est pareil,*' she announced offhandedly. There was a moment of absolute silence in the room as Peter feigned horror before he pounced. 'The same? The SAME? Do you think this is just a case of a VCR on fast forward? If Granados wanted a repeat, he did so for a reason, a reason that makes musical sense. A repeat is NEVER "the same". Let's look at the score, shall we?'

Another student played several wrong notes in a reading of a Schubert dance and moaned, '*Chez moi je ne fais pas d'erreurs!*' Peter at once responded, 'I'd like to see this magic piano where no one plays wrong notes! Actually, getting all the notes right isn't the point – it's how you express the music that counts. Find me a piano that does that for you and I'll believe in magic.'

Certain of his dislikes inevitably became apparent over the three days, most often mannerisms he attributed to the distorting lens of the modern era. One habit that particularly irked him was the tendency to play things too loud. Playing a passage marked *crescendo* as loudly as possible was for him the great cliché of the last one hundred years. Several times he worked carefully with students on creating a *forte* that had a beautiful tone. In order to produce those nuances of tone, he returned to his fundamental principle of playing with a natural movement. He likened it to the rhythm and variety of speech where timing, intonation, and gestures mean so much and come naturally to us.

During lunch Peter regaled us with anecdotes, as when he heard Rosalyn Tureck, one of the great Bach interpreters, play the clavichord. 'At first it was almost inaudible, a whisper in a loud world. It was like entering a darkroom, we had to give our senses time to adjust.'

This reminded him of the discussion between Wanda Landowska and Rosalyn Tureck as to whether the piano was a suitable instrument for Bach's music or if, as Landowska contended, only the harpsichord was appropriate. 'You play Bach your way,' she announced to Tureck, 'I'll play him *his* way.' An amusing *bon mot*, Peter acknowledged, but he pointed out that Tureck's view has come to prevail.

Over the weekend an intimacy developed among the group that made it hard to let go as the master class wound down on Sunday afternoon. This was very different from the recitals that I had for so long found distasteful and, while I was not yet confident enough in my playing to prepare a piece for others, for the first time I itched to give it a try. I was intrigued later to discover that he uses this same method, particularly his exercises, to coach some of the world's foremost concert pianists.

Everyone at Anna's was motivated to improve his or her playing, and each had chosen this forum and this teacher to move things along.

Peter approached playing physically, almost as if it were a kind of dancing at the keyboard with the upper body, and this demanded the concentration and the suppleness of a gymnast. With this he combined his highly personal philosophy of music, firmly based on what we know about the composer's own intentions, and the result was something astounding.

Not long after Peter's workshop ended I had the opportunity to attend a very different kind of master class given by György Sebök, one of the acknowledged masters of this special form of teaching. Until his death in 1999, Sebök was unusual in that he was also a highly respected concert artist who had continued to perform and to record well into his seventies and yet he had not restricted himself to those more public activities.

I first heard about Sebök's famous master classes from a friend who ran a summer arts festival in Canada where Sebök taught each year. 'The interesting thing is that it's not just pianists or even musicians who attend them. Everyone goes – writers, painters, people from the community – lots of people who don't know anything particular about music. He teaches the piano, yes, but at the same time he manages to teach something profound about life.' When I read that he was giving a master class at the Sweelinck Conservatory in Amsterdam that would be open to the public, I couldn't afford to miss it.

There were about seventy people of all ages in the room, most of them sitting together in groups of twos and threes. Some were clearly students in other disciplines at the conservatory: padded cases for violins, and various brass and woodwind instruments littered the floor and the empty seats. Others were faculty members whose students would play for Sebök and for those of us in the hall. The rest were members of the public, a fairly unusual – and very Dutch – accommodation to the interest of those outside the academy in seeing and hearing how the magic of music-making is transmitted and learned.

191

For a nominal fee, anyone could enter and sit in on the various sessions during the course of the five days scheduled for these annual piano master classes.

Twenty students had been selected for the honor of participating in this class and the competition had been intense. Each successful candidate had prepared his or her piece for months previous to this meeting. An hour and a quarter was allotted to each player. The first piece was played from start to finish, as in a concert, and then Sebök worked with the student on particular issues. The audience witnessed it all.

On the stage sat two Steinway grand pianos: nearest the audience, a Model D, the estimable concert grand of most public recitals; next to it, its keyboard aligned as an extension of its neighbor's, a Model B, slightly smaller than the concert grand. Behind the piano benches stood a small table set against the wall with a chair drawn up beside it.

The first student played an early sonata by Beethoven, Opus 13. To my ear he played it beautifully, without apparent difficulty, fluidly and with a confidence that went beyond his years. There was a hush when he finished and then enthusiastic applause from the hall. Sebök smiled approvingly as he rose from the table where he had been listening motionless. He took his place on the other piano bench beside the young performer and waited for the clapping to subside, focusing his attention entirely on the young pianist at his side. 'Tell me about your plans.'

'For this piece, you mean?' the student responded.

'No, no. For yourself.'

Of each student he asked these general and at the same time very personal questions. 'Tell me about yourself'; 'Where are you from?'; 'How did you start your musical career?'

Each time the students were a bit surprised. Gradually, however, a bond of trust was created as Sebök drew out of them some particulars about their lives as musicians.

'I studied at the conservatory in Madrid before coming to Amsterdam'; 'I entered a national competition in Japan last year, but I was not selected for the finals'; 'I have played this piece several times in concert, but it still confounds me.'

The answers were direct, candid, trusting, and it was as if those of us in the audience – variously friends, strangers, rivals, and teachers – had suddenly disappeared and were not overhearing this frank, almost confessional talk. A more subtle reasoning for this unconventional opening revealed itself. Each student had in effect just given a concert before a public that was likely to be as knowledgeable and as discerning as any he or she would ever face. They had given their all for fifteen or twenty minutes, and when they finished it was with adrenaline pumping through their veins, a potent mixture of relief, exhilaration, and doubt lending their features the look of a world-class athlete who has just completed his event. Sebök had spent his life as a concert artist and clearly he knew how delicate a moment this was, how heady the feeling when one had descended into the world of a Schubert or of a Debussy as completely as a human being can, only to return to the world of analysis, of understanding, of learning. What was needed was a transition and Sebök's method was disarmingly simple. Slowly he inquired about matters other than the music at hand, quietly reassuring the student while the torrent of notes and crescendos in our minds subsided like a silk veil floating down upon our shoulders.

Almost imperceptibly he turned the talk to the music and most often gave some form of praise for the interpretation. 'This is very close to what I would call a finished product.' 'That you are a good musician I knew after four notes; you proposed a tempo, you didn't impose it.' 'I have very little to say: *Chapeau!*'

Then he began to analyze each particular rendering, beginning with the overall conception of the piece. To a young man who had just given a powerful reading of Beethoven's sonata No. 30 in E major, Opus 109, he cautioned: 'Everything Beethoven tells us is important; but if everything is equally important, then we become anesthetized.'

The playing reminded him of a time when he was a young boy in Hungary and his uncle solemnly took him aside. The uncle looked him straight in the eyes and inquired in meaningful, stentorian tones that Sebök now mimicked: 'How ARE you?' The atmosphere was suddenly relaxed and Sebök went on to make the point that mattered for this interpretation: the emotion expressed should not be out of proportion to the particular passage. Beethoven is not always serious and deep, he said; his music is varied and an over-careful solemnity has the paradoxical effect of making it seem two-dimensional.

The student, encouraged by Sebök's support, dared to ask questions about things that were not clear to him. He wanted to know how best to play a passage in the finale. 'When I play it exactly as written, it doesn't sound convincing.'

Sebök told him not to be afraid to vary the rhythm minutely in order to give it meaning. 'Beethoven was a great genius, but even Beethoven couldn't write anything between a thirty-second and a sixteenth note, there is no musical notation for it. So this is an approximation. You can slow down slightly and then speed up slightly.' He played the passage on his own piano to show what he meant and then, with a nod, he invited the student to do the same.

'No, no. You don't pay taxes twice! Don't slow down and also wait at the end of the phrase.' Sebök's tone was admonitory rather than scolding and one sensed that he wanted the student to understand the concept. The student tried again, this time with a more satisfactory result. 'Yes, that's it. You've bought yourself the freedom of having a choice by paying a down payment on the tempo earlier on.'

Often he used jokes to make a point, as when he talked to a participant who had given a disjointed rendition of a Schubert sonata. 'Do you know the *Ecole Polytechnique* in Paris?'

Bewildered, the student shook his head.

'It is one of the most prestigious *grandes écoles* in France; only the smartest are admitted. And do you know what the French say about it? A *polytechnicien* knows everything, but nothing else.' Sebök waited for the titters of laughter from the hall to subside and then he continued with a concerned look on his features: 'You see, it is possible to know too much and I think that might be your problem with this piece. There are some very beautiful parts to your playing, but they come and they go, as if you know something different about each piece of the score. Let's look at it as a whole. What are you trying to convey when you play the first movement?'

At times the questions were disarmingly innocent, but he declined to talk down to the students or to play to the gallery. 'How do you develop that kind of leaping touch?' asked a Japanese pianist who had played a Brahms sonata.

'That's a hard question. You know, Leonardo spent years developing a codex of body parts. He drew ears, he drew elbows, he drew hands, he drew all the parts of the body in as many different aspects as he could. Then he forgot about it and painted what he saw. You must do somewhat the same.'

He reassured one student who was having difficulty with a Debussy passage where the notes were all soft, almost ethereal, by telling her that the instrument was part of the problem. It was important to understand the composer in this sense, too. 'Remember, Debussy's Erard had a very soft touch; you blow on the keys and they sound. Playing the same *pianissimo* on a Steinway is not so easy, it requires more force to move the keys.'

After discussing the piece in some detail and trying out various techniques, Sebök played along with each student. It was never announced but rather came as a gentle surprise, at a moment of Sebök's choosing. The student would be playing the piece at full tempo, when suddenly Sebök was playing it too, sitting alongside the student at his own keyboard, nodding encouragement as they both played identical notes.

This was more than a brief passage, a small sampling of four or eight measures; Sebök often continued for a full minute or two, right through pages of music with pronounced changes in mood and tempo. The students were at first taken unawares. One could see it from the hall in the way they turned their heads suddenly towards Sebök to confirm what their ears had already told them.

This participation was astounding on a number of levels. The students knew their individual pieces inside out; they had lived with and dissected and practiced them for months in preparation for this moment, and so they rarely consulted the scores. Sebök, too, however, seemed to know all of the pieces by heart, and not just the standard Schubert sonatas or Chopin ballades. Even obscure pieces were at his fingertips as soon as the student began to play and, while he had been offered a score, he rarely needed to look at it. This allowed him to devote his full attention to the student and to the nuances of the interpretation.

Suddenly those of us in the hall were so many voyeurs, witnessing something ineffably lovely and remarkable, but that had fundamentally to do with the two people playing their pianos and not with us. It was a kind of rare magic, which most of us never experience, even from a distance, and the sound was strange and wonderful. Not a duet, not music for four hands; what they were creating was a double performance of the score subtly shaped by Sebök's years of experience.

During a coffee break between sessions I asked a few of the students if these moments were as special as they seemed to those of us watching and listening. A young man who had played Schumann's *Kreisleriana* and had been praised by Sebök for his sensitive phrasing said, 'It sounds corny, I know, but when he begins to play with you, there's something funny that happens, almost as if there were a power radiating from his hands to your own.' He laughed at his own description, but then he persisted. 'Those moments are some of the strongest of the whole master class.'

This special moment takes the two pianists – master and student – someplace that no one else can go. The French call this sort of sharing, this meeting of minds, *complicité* and the word captures perfectly the special bond that instantly develops as two pianists explore together the edge of music. If chamber music can be likened to a conversation, with a constant give and take, a joining and separating of the voices, this is all simultaneity, more like a duo of dancers who perform exactly the same figurations. By some remarkable chemistry a momentum builds that puts the two pianists in perfect concurrence.

Sebök later told me that at certain points this practice was very useful in pulling the score together. 'It depends on where the individual student is in his development of the piece he has chosen and in how open he is to this approach. Most welcome it.' When I told him that one of the students had likened it to an energy radiating from his hands into theirs, he laughed and offered his own image: 'I give them a blood transfusion right there on stage! After all, I'm Hungarian.'

The most difficult aspect of a master class, Sebök said, is trying to get the student to an emptiness, to a still point, where he can truly hear what he is doing. 'It's not an absence, it's an emptiness, and that is a sometimes subtle point to grasp for a young person.' For him, music had to flow out of the pianist, and in order for that to happen there had to be a quiet center.

Technique, he felt, was vastly overrated as an isolated element. The best technique is one that doesn't exist, a kind of disappearing act, so the real focus needs to be on where the technique comes from: an inner calm, the emptiness he insisted on so that one could really listen. 'That's not the same as relaxation,' he cautioned. 'I never talk about relaxation. You can't play Chopin relaxed. Instead, I talk about fear, and I contrast that with love and hate and other human emotions.

Music comes out of those, but it is blocked by fear. That is very often the obstacle that we confront in a master class.'

Sebök continually made clear from his own example that there is no perfection, there is only a lifelong process of making music; once technique and commitment have been suitably mastered, you have to decide for yourself on the right interpretation. It is a complex message.

'There is no such thing as music note by note just as there is no such thing as a book word by word. We have to accept that things are ambiguous,' Sebök said to one of the students on the last day of the master class. Is there any more fundamental lesson that we must learn as we mature? As my friend had told me, he might have been talking about all of life, not just music.

21

PLAY IS THE SOUL OF THE MACHINE

Once the *ferrailleur* had completed his job of straightening the stabilizer bar it was time for me to attach it to the piano's pedal housing. I regarded this task with considerable apprehension but Luc insisted there was nothing to it. His only word of caution was to leave some play in the pedal rods, the iron rods that rise vertically from the back of each pedal to the piano's action. I had thought that they were supposed to sit flush and tight, but he repeated that a very small amount of play was desirable. He looked at me with a feigned air of gravity and pronounced with a deep voice, '*Le jeu est l'âme de la mécanique!*' Literally, this translates to 'Play is the soul of the machine' though it has no real equivalent in English. Luc assured me that it was one of his cardinal rules; tightening anything too much was to be avoided, especially on an old piano.

The straightened end of the bar fit smoothly into the hole at the bottom of the lyre, but the other end had a hinged fitting that took two screws. Rather than fitting into the existing hole in the piano's underside, as the original bar had apparently done, it would be necessary to drill two small holes in the piece of wood that spanned the bottom of the piano in order to fasten it at the required angle. I hesitated to take a drill to my piano, even for a small hole, but I remembered that Luc had carefully described how this should be done. Daunting as it seemed, there was no magic to the undertaking.

I pulled the lyre forward as he had directed, positioned the end of the bar on the wooden crosspiece and then carefully drilled two small holes where I would introduce the screws. I felt peculiar, as if I were recklessly brandishing a weapon at a loved one. When I drilled the two small holes, no more than an inch deep, a rich and smoky smell filled the air, like incense. At first I thought it was the friction from the electric drill, but as the noise subsided and the tiny wood shavings drifted down, I realized the wood itself was sending forth this pungent aroma. My wife was across the room and not paying particular attention, but she looked up and noted the strong smell of cedar.

There was a strange moment as I lay there on the floor under my piano, drill in one hand, when my senses were flooded with the exotic, the unknown, the supposed. Was it cedar? Did it matter? The sweetness of the smell gave me an idea of the pleasure that Luc had once told me he found in working with woods that were old and out of the ordinary. I played the piano briefly and tried the pedals: everything seemed to be working fine and I no longer needed to worry about doing damage to its mechanism. My sense of relief was vivid.

Two days later my friend, Claire, stopped by to play the Stingl. She was preparing a suite of Schumann pieces – *Forest Scenes* – for a master class and I had suggested that it might help her to play the score on a piano other than her own before she confronted a different keyboard during the workshop. She readily agreed, and my wife and I settled down to a private concert from an excellent pianist. There are nine separate pieces to this suite and Claire played them straight through, the volume and resonance varying in accordance with the mood of each movement, from the lilting singing line of the 'Entry' to the pastoral melancholy of 'Solitary Flowers' on to the flitting, abrupt arpeggios of the work's best-known piece, 'The Prophet Bird'. I didn't notice anything strange after the first one, but at the end of the second piece, whose finale was louder and more vigorous, I was surprised to hear the piano resonate longer than it should have after

Claire had stopped playing. The same thing happened after a few of the other sections and at the end of the last piece, with soft notes deep in the bass registers, there was a pronounced continuation of the last chords. At first I thought Claire was persistently – and somewhat eccentrically – holding down the damper pedal at the end of each piece. This time, however, she got up from the bench and moved away while the piano continued to resonate. She mimed a lion tamer's crack of the whip – 'Back, Simba!' – and turned to us. 'Well, you didn't warn me I'd be playing an organ!'

I tried the bass notes and found that many of them resonated a bit after the key was released. Two continued to sound indefinitely and when we investigated we discovered that the dampers for those notes were not descending fully. It was as if the damper pedal were being depressed permanently. I realized that it must have had to do with the way I had attached the bracing bar. In the rush of the moment the problem seemed monumental, but Claire reassured me that, except for the two notes we had managed to isolate, it was actually quite subtle. She praised the piano's tone and the touch of the keyboard, and this calmed me down.

But the next morning I played the piano and it sounded immeasurably awful to my ears, some strange, haunted instrument that kept on playing long after the pianist had left the keyboard. Somehow it seemed worse that I had caused this myself. I had to get Luc's opinion.

I found him alone in the atelier tuning the Charles X Erard, told him what I had done, and with what results. He listened as he leaned over the Erard, taking in my story of good intentions gone wrong while he turned the wrench and adjusted the tone of the strings. Finally he put down the wrench and turned to me with an air of exasperation. 'You forgot the most important thing I told you.'

I hesitated before I assured him that I had pulled the lyre well forward before attaching it, but he shook his head evenly, as much as to say that was merely a detail. '*Le jeu est l'âme de la mécanique.*' He said it quietly, as if its lessons were self-evident, but when I continued to look puzzled he gave his simple explanation: 'Look, it sounds to me as if you were a bit excessive in making sure the brace fit tightly. It's supposed to hold the lyre firm, yes, but not rigid. There needs to be play in all the parts that move. Think of your piano as a seventy-year-old person; you wouldn't muscle around someone of that age and not expect to do some harm.'

This last was clearly an admonition, as if I had wilfully neglected this delicate aspect of my piano. Chastened, I wondered how Luc remembered the age of a piano that had passed through the atelier with so many others. I asked how serious the damage was likely to be and he dismissed my concern impatiently. 'Use your head. Symptoms appear after you do something. So you undo what you did and see if the symptoms disappear. It's as simple as that. There's almost certainly no lasting damage, and I'd be surprised if all is not well again once you remove the bar and attach it a bit less rigidly.'

I asked Luc if he would consider coming by and doing the repair himself, assuring him that I would pay him for his time. He looked up from his work once again and shook his head slowly. 'Try attaching it yourself as I've described and see what happens. If that doesn't work, we'll see.' I sensed that he was, uncharacteristically, not in a good mood, and I saw that my fumbled repair, my exaggerated concern, and my repeated questions had not helped matters.

While we talked, Luc asked me to help him move a walnut upright across the atelier. It was inscribed 'Gunther' and no city's name appeared on the fall board. He responded to my inquisitive look with a shrug. 'It's a plain German piano.' His lack of enthusiasm said it all. He pointed to a golden plaque inscribed neatly on the inside of the open top. '*Diplôme d'Honneur*' it said, with no further detail about who had awarded this particular gold star. 'That', he said, 'is the nicest thing on this piano.'

As we reached in back for a handhold, I realized that the entire frame was covered with a fine metal mesh, making it impossible to gain leverage on one of the wooden braces. 'That's typically German, to keep the mice out.'

Mice will as readily make a nest inside a piano as inside any other dark, closed space, and they have been known to eat felts and dampers, and even wooden pieces. But that is when a piano stands unused and unplayed, and for Luc it was almost to be expected if an instrument were abandoned to the elements. The idea of anticipating and guarding against it struck him as excessive. 'We might as well carry life preservers all the time since there might be a flood.'

We shouldered it across the uneven wooden floor with difficulty and took a rest.

'Actually, German pianos are remarkably good; this is an exception. It's the only country left with such variety and a real craftsman tradition in piano building. Think of the brands: Bechstein, Grotrian, Steingraeber, Blüthner, Ibach, Förster, Schimmel, Thürmer, Sauter, Seiler. They're all excellent instruments. And I consider Steinways made in the Hamburg factory to be German.' I knew that this last was a friendly provocation for an American, but I didn't take the bait.

He then told me to come look at '*une merveille, surtout pour un américain*'. He led me across the shop to where an old piano lay on its side. Or, I should say, to where the cabinet and soundboard lay; there were no strings, no legs, no mechanics at all. The iron frame had been removed entirely and was propped up against another piano, its back facing us. 'Can you guess what this is?' I could tell from his voice that it was something special, but I hadn't a clue. 'It's a Chickering from over one hundred years ago. An American Chickering!' At the sound of that brand name I was transported back to my late adolescence: Mrs Palmer was braying at me about playing her BIG piano too softly. The vision passed and I was back in the atelier with Luc.

It had come to him in pieces – how or why he didn't say – and now he proposed to sell it 'as is' to someone with the skill and motivation to assemble it. He squeezed in between the two pianos and struck the Chickering's soundboard a solid blow with the palm of his hand. There was a clean, simple resonance. Again he struck it, this time with his closed fist. Luc smiled at the sound and at the solidity of this piece of carpentry that was over a century old but that could still be the heart of a fine piano.

'This thing is tough! Just listen to that tone! The problem with many Americans is that they only know Steinway and they assume that's it for good American pianos. But there were a lot of very fine pianos built in America at the turn of the century: Chickering, Knabe, Mason & Hamlin, Steck. Why should Steinway be the only name known to so many of your countrymen?'

Luc then showed me four console pianos of light-colored wood, all grouped together, and told me that he had a client who was coming over soon to choose one. We moved two of the pianos so that they could be more easily approached, and he gave pride of place to a beautiful little Gaveau with an intricate sliding mechanism for covering the keyboard in place of the usual pivoting fall board. 'This is a real gem,' he told me, 'and I think that these people may go for it. They've got very good taste.'

He set to removing the piles of spare parts and papers that had quickly accumulated on the backs of these new arrivals, and he threw me a towel and asked me to dust the Gaveau's cabinet. As I did so, he told me that he was going to take care of 'the most important detail of all'. He then got down on his knees and started polishing the pedals of the piano I was dusting, vigorously rubbing the brass until it began to shine.

When I realized what he was doing, I thought he was joking. 'You're not going to tell me seriously that the pedals are the most important detail!'

Luc looked at me with a straight face. 'Absolutely. There's no question.' Then his features softened. 'Does that surprise you?'

I told him that I didn't see the importance of the pedals in selling a piano, but he insisted that it was a crucial detail. The pedals must be shiny and the rest of the brightwork, too, if possible: the brass casters and rings on the legs, the lock, the name on the fall board if it was of inlaid brass. The pedals, though, were the charm.

When I asked Luc how he knew that shiny pedals were significant, he shrugged and said that it was something that Desforges, the previous owner, had told him. Many years before the old man had worked in a dealership in Paris where hundreds of new and used pianos were displayed, and several salesmen divided the stock among themselves. Desforges sold far more pianos than any of his colleagues, and forever after he avowed that it was because he had always taken care to polish the pedals.

'Look, polishing the pedals on a pile of junk isn't going to change much. But it looks somehow more alive and that's what a lot of people respond to without even being aware of it.'

It was a classic salesman's ploy, like blacking the tires on a used car, but it didn't have the element of subterfuge that a huckster would use. 'You don't usually make the sale on first sight, but you can easily lose it in that moment. So you do what's reasonable to maintain interest.'

We returned to the front of the shop where Luc sat down before a pile of paperwork. As I was going, I asked after Jos.

'He's disappeared.' Luc's face showed a combination of exasperation and sadness.

'Disappeared? You mean he hasn't been by the atelier lately?'

'I haven't seen him in over two weeks. And the last time he came by he had big problems.' Some weeks back there had been an incident in one of the trains that Jos was sleeping in outside the Gare de Lyon. A guard with a watchdog had found him and had beaten him up and threatened him. Jos had been shaken up but not badly hurt and he thought it was an isolated incident that would not soon repeat itself.

A few days later, though, the same guard found him in another train and this time he set the dog on him. 'He came by the next day in real pain. His leg was all torn up and his head was swollen so that he looked like the elephant man. The lousy bastard kicked him while the dog was attacking him.'

Luc's voice was thick with anger, but it was also clear that frustration was part of what upset him. He had said many times that Jos was one of the *malheureux*, the 'unfortunates', who couldn't overcome their problems to make their way in the world. Jos's situation was particularly confounding to Luc since he had several times tried to get him to enroll in one of the detox clinics at the public hospitals, but Jos refused to take the first step to solve his drinking problem.

'What's he up to, do you know?'

'He's holed up in a hotel' – Luc paused and exhaled heavily – 'and it's not the Ritz.'

Luc told me that Jos was staying in a dive near one of the train stations: less than a one-star, a place where one went when all of the options were played out.

The best thing to do, perhaps the only thing, was to offer Jos work, but we were powerless to make him take the opportunity in hand, still less to force him to work responsibly and consistently. After the mess of Anna's tuning I was wary of getting involved further, but I was willing to have him tune the Stingl. What had seemed like a carefree, unorthodox way of life – sleeping in trains, taking the risk of ending up in the far reaches of France on your awakening – had taken a sinister turn that made our tolerance look like an irresponsible frivolity. No longer was Jos's living arrangement a kind of in-joke that we shared.

Very little of this was actually spoken between Luc and me, but we both felt the intractability of the situation and it weighed heavily in the air of the atelier. He told me that Jos had refused to see a doctor and that he had only allowed Luc to patch him up superficially – ointment and bandages – before he had left. 'The sad thing was how depressed he was. Jos always astounded me with his good humour, even when things seemed hopeless. He was always a happy drunk, at least. But this time' – he looked away and shook his head – 'things were different.'

There was no more to be said. We agreed that Luc would have Jos call me if he came by the atelier so I could arrange for him to tune the Stingl. The prospect of a tuning was a convenient eventuality that allowed us to act as if things might still be right.

22

FAZIOLI

'This Car Stops for Pianos!' My wife used to threaten to have that bumper sticker made for me since I still couldn't resist looking at any piano we came upon, although in Paris I was usually on foot rather than in the car. One night we were walking back from dinner at a friend's apartment when I spied my prey, a piano store I had not known before with a dazzling grand in the main window. 'This will only take a minute,' I pleaded, hurrying across the street to inspect the dramatically lighted instrument. A simple black cabinet revolved slowly on a pedestal and the fall board lay open. What I saw inscribed as the keyboard lazily came into view, however, was a word I had never before seen on any piano, set forth in a simple, bold typeface reminiscent of art deco lettering: Fazioli.

What was this piano with an Italian-sounding name? The next time I stopped by the atelier I asked Luc if he had heard of this strange brand of piano and he fixed me with a stare as if he were addressing an idiot. 'But of course. Fazioli is one of the best pianos in the world. These instruments are absolutely extraordinary.'

I told him I had never before heard the name and I explained that I had seen one in a dealer's window. How was it that they were not better known? Were they Italian? 'Fazioli is very new,' Luc said. 'It's the brainchild of a guy who decided less than twenty years ago to build the world's best piano from scratch. Basically, they're handmade and the production is very limited.'

That evening I pulled out some of the piano reference books I had accumulated and looked up Fazioli in the indexes. First I looked in Larry Fine's *The Piano Book*, an excellent guide to buying and caring for a piano written by a piano technician with long years of experience. Not given to exaggeration in his evaluation of various brands, Fine comments that 'the pianos combine tremendous power with great expressiveness and clarity'. David Crombie, in his splendid pictorial history, *Piano*, states categorically that Fazioli 'is classed among the top three piano makers'. These descriptions further piqued my interest, especially when I recalled that this was a maker that had been in business for less than twenty years and whose output was very limited.

The Italian connection also intrigued me. The very best pianos had always been German or French or American; a first-rank maker of pianos had not emerged from Italy since Bartolomeo Cristofori invented the piano in the late seventeenth century. I got the chance to find out more when we traveled to Italy to visit my wife's family over the Christmas holidays. After months of absorbing the dusty atmosphere of Luc's atelier, it would be refreshing to see some pianos that had only just been born into the world.

I learned by calling the factory in Sacile, eighty-five miles north of Venice, that the founder of the business was a certain Paolo Fazioli, whom the receptionist referred to as '*Ingeniere Fazioli*' – literally, 'Engineer Fazioli' – using the honorific as is common in Italy. We fixed a date for my visit and a week later a thick packet arrived from *Fazioli Pianoforti*, elaborately stamped and bearing a big red *Espresso* sticker.

I read the shiny brochures on the small train heading north towards the Alps. Gradually the flat and perfectly ordered fields of the coastal plain gave way to gently rolling countryside, and as we headed north-east the silhouette of the mountains became visible on the horizon. Soon the train got close enough for me to see snow on the tallest peaks and the bell towers in the villages we passed through started to have the slightly rounded caps so typical of Austria on the other side of the massive range.

The Fazioli family had for years run a successful office furniture business in Italy. Paolo, the youngest of six brothers, earned a diploma in piano from the conservatory in Pesaro and he had also received a degree in mechanical engineering at the University of Rome. He had grown increasingly dissatisfied with the quality of the instruments he played, including the finest German, American, or Japanese pianos. Armed with both musical and technical knowledge, and the backing of his family, he was determined to create a new piano that was uncompromising in its quality. Was it possible that in the late twentieth century a single person had had the wherewithal to rethink the entire apparatus that turned out superb pianos and had, in fact, succeeded in equalling or surpassing the finest makers in the world?

My train arrived in Sacile shortly after noon and I walked into town along tree-shaded avenues where no cars were stirring and no people were to be seen on the sidewalks: I was in the provinces and it was lunchtime. A small river coursed through the center, full of ice-fringed rapids and waterfalls, descending from the nearby Alps. I found a small trattoria near the water and ate lunch in anticipation of my two-o'clock appointment at the Fazioli factory.

At a quarter before two I asked the woman behind the bar to call me a taxi while I had a coffee. She looked at her watch, hesitated a moment and then said, 'We have only one taxi.'

'Well, could you give him a call and see if he can pick me up?' I wondered why she looked doubtful, but she phoned from behind the counter.

After a few moments she hung up. 'It is as I thought: he is having his lunch. We'll be able to reach him after two thirty.'

I then called the Fazioli office and explained my predicament to the receptionist. She was unfazed. 'Yes, you can't get a taxi at lunchtime. Wait ten minutes and someone will pick you up.'

Ten minutes later a gray sedan pulled up outside the restaurant where I had eaten and a compact man in his fifties got out and greeted me warmly in English. 'I am Paolo Fazioli. I am delighted to be your taxi.'

He looked dapper in a stylish sports coat, a white shirt, tie, and charcoal-gray slacks with a knife-edge crease. The energy in the way he moved made me think of an athlete. I apologized for the inconvenience and he dismissed my concern at once. The factory was only a few kilometers away and, as we drove there, he asked me if I spoke French since I lived in Paris. I told him that I did and he suggested that we conduct our discussion in French as he felt that it was stronger than his English.

When we arrived at the factory, a massive metal building with a suite of offices at the front, he took me into his modest but bright office. The only touch of luxury came from the large desk, a beautiful expanse of exotic wood worked in modern curves, no doubt a sampling of the woodworking from the furniture-making side of the building. I explained that I was interested to know what had made him come to the decision to design and build a piano at the end of the twentieth century. He leaned back in his chair and said that it involved his love of music and the opportunities that came his way because of his family. 'The first piano I saw was at the house of my aunt who was a piano teacher. When I was still quite young, she would have musical gatherings at her house on Sundays and one of my cousins would be made to play for the family after dinner. I remember two things vividly about those gatherings.' Here he paused to take off his glasses and rub his eyes, as if he were actually looking back into the past. 'The first was my wonder at the beautiful music that came out of this strange piece of furniture. The other was the fact that when my cousin, a girl who was not much older than I was, made a mistake, my aunt would give her a little slap, right there in front of all of us.'

Because his aunt was so uncompromising, his fascination with the wonderful sounds became mixed with a kind of fear, a sense that playing the piano could actually be dangerous if you weren't perfect. 'From that time I was determined to play piano and I asked my father for lessons. At first he resisted, but then he saw that I was using scrap wood from the furniture business to draw the notes of a keyboard and to pretend that I was playing. That bit of childhood play made the difference.'

He made a face of mock disgust as he described the piano his father bought, an upright from Naples with a German-sounding name that he called '*un piano horrible*'. It didn't even have a metal frame, he said, so that it was virtually impossible to keep in tune, especially since Rome's changeable weather increased the wood's tendency to expand and contract. Ironically, this frustration led him to open up the piano and to tinker with the insides, and so his first investigations into the mechanics of pianos happened as a result of his trying to fix the unfixable. 'It was a bad design that had been badly built, but I became familiar with how it was put together. It was a good first lesson for a piano builder.'

He entered the conservatory at Pesaro when he was eighteen and there, for the first time, he found excellent teachers who understood all aspects of music, not just a narrow approach to developing technique. After he received his diploma from the conservatory it was unclear what direction he would take. He gave some concerts, but it was already evident to him that he would not be among the first rank of pianists if he continued along that path. He received a degree in mechanical engineering and then joined the family furniture business, rising to manager of the factory in Rome, then of the operation in Turin. But he was always looking for a way to integrate his love of music into the rest of his life.

His youthful tinkering with pianos now joined a more mature impulse: as his piano playing had become more serious over the years, he was continually surprised, and disappointed, to find that the pianos he played – even the finest brands – were not especially well made. He found them neither mechanically nor musically satisfactory and he began to form the conviction that he could do better. What if one were to rethink the piano from top to bottom, with the objective of making the finest instrument possible? Barely in his thirties, he began to form the idea that would become his life's work.

In the late 1970s he consulted experts in acoustics, harmonics, woodworking, metal foundry, musical instruments, and other specialties that related directly to the piano to see if they would participate in designing a new instrument from top to bottom. The initial reaction to his plans was, at best, highly skeptical. One of the people he talked to, a renowned expert in acoustics, voiced a typical reservation. '"You must be crazy!" he told me. "This isn't a trumpet or a drum. Pianos are complicated!" But when he heard that my family had a furniture company, he started to be more positive.'

Step by step, Fazioli did his research, persuaded the doubters, and assembled a team of expert collaborators. His father provided business advice and his brothers agreed to back him financially. For the better part of a year the team systematically studied all that was known about the building of fine pianos. They studied pianos of all sorts, played them, analyzed their acoustics, disassembled them, talked over their makers' philosophy. 'Our point of departure was never to copy. I wanted to use what was there and then add to it to make a better piano. Why just reproduce what others have done?'

In 1978 Fazioli and his team were ready to start production and took over a wing of the modern furniture factory. By 1980 the team produced its first prototype, a grand piano measuring 1.83 meters, and the results were encouraging. 'There were problems, of course, but mostly they were minor. When I heard that piano and the special tone that it produced, I knew that we would succeed.'

The perspective of twenty years had not changed his conviction.

'But remember, aside from that first piano, it hasn't been a case of one big revelation and then everything is clear. It's like building something very large: you progress step by step, but you keep the same idea in your mind.' The same idea that Fazioli kept in mind was to make the best piano in the world. When I asked if he thought he had succeeded in that, he thought for a moment. '*Oui, je pense que les pianos que nous fabriquons sont les meilleurs.*'

He pointed out that they make six different models and they turn out a total of no more than sixty pianos a year. These are the world's most expensive pianos – a plain black Fazioli concert grand costs well over one hundred thousand dollars. There are fewer than one thousand Fazioli pianos in existence, each of them essentially hand-made. With that kind of output, he said, it would take a while before a significant number of pianists experienced his pianos first-hand and could compare them with others.

I wondered if artists sometimes visited the factory and he said that it was becoming more commonplace. He particularly liked watching from close up as accomplished artists played his pianos; it was always a revelation to see how they addressed the keyboard. Some were tense, others relaxed, and the tone they produced varied accordingly, even allowing for wide disparities in technique.

'You know, I can now tell what their approach will be just by watching them sit down on the bench and look at the keyboard. Before they play a single note, they reveal a lot.'

He proposed that we have a look around the factory and we made our way out of the small office and on to the shop floor. We were at one end of the massive steel building, modern and spotless, in which entire rooms had been built to stand free beneath the ceiling soaring some thirty feet above.

My host showed me the various way stations on a piano's progress through the process of fabrication. To one side of the first space, two grand piano rims sat on stands, each of them bristling with more than sixty clamps that pressed the inside and outside edges together. The different laminations had been shaped and then glued to each other, he said, and now they were drying into the distinctive asymmetric curve of the grand piano.

As we stopped at various work stations, he explained the particular process that was under way: sanding the key bed, adjusting the action, applying lacquer, testing the soundboard. Each area had its own focus and no more than one or two of the relevant parts were worked on at a time. This was about as far from a mechanized assembly line as it is possible to get and still turn out a uniform product of such complexity.

In each area one or two technicians in green smocks bearing the Fazioli name on the chest pocket worked in an aura of intense concentration, something like a research laboratory where a team is engaged in precision work of a high order. Tools were carefully arrayed in gleaming holders when not in use, and the entire operation – floor, walls, work tables – was almost spartan in its purposefulness and lack of clutter.

Fazioli motioned me into a small, temperature-controlled room that he referred to as *le patrimoine*, the heritage of the company. Here was stored the precious red spruce from the Val di Fiemme that was used to make the soundboard of every Fazioli piano. He picked up one of the three-inch-wide strips and handed it to me. It felt light for its size. 'Look at how regular the grain is. It's light, but also amazingly strong and supple.'

At the back of the room he pulled forward a large curved sheet fashioned of the same wood, beautifully sanded but otherwise unfinished. I realized that it was a fully assembled soundboard for one of the pianos. He tilted it forward and struck it soundly in the center with his fist, as if it were a bass drum, just as Luc had struck the soundboard of the century-old Chickering at the atelier. The modern soundboard before me let out a low, sonorous report and Fazioli struck it again with evident satisfaction. 'Do you hear that? That's a very special sound.' He attributed it to the unique flexibility of the spruce he used.

I told him that I lacked the discernment to hear what he heard, but I was willing to believe that special wood worked so carefully would vibrate in a distinctive way. As we walked through the factory he ran his fingers across a recently sanded support strut, he squinted and aimed one eye along the edge of a key extension to test for a true line, he condensed his breath on a newly lacquered black cover to test for minute imperfections. I had the sense that, rather than doing this for the benefit of visitors, he was following his ordinary routine which my walk-through had momentarily interrupted.

We came finally to a small room where there were four fully assembled pianos pushed one against the other and covered with heavy drop cloths. These were the finished instruments, awaiting shipment in the days ahead. At the front of the room stood the flagship of the line, a model 308, the world's longest and heaviest (more than three quarters of a ton) concert grand currently in production, arguably the finest piano in the world. This last was being sent the next day to its buyer in Belgium. 'He's a very gifted pianist,' Fazioli said. 'It makes me happy that he will have this instrument.'

Suddenly he turned to me and said, 'You must try the 308; it really is a remarkable piano.'

It was neither a question nor a command, but a spontaneous expression of enthusiasm from this man whose obsession with pianos had culminated in the splendid instrument that lay before us. It was an eventuality I had not even considered, much less hoped for, and it seemed impossible to demur without being rude. I made noises about how I really wasn't a serious pianist, but the combination of panic and curiosity that now seized me made my weak protestations sound like false modesty. He had undoubtedly heard this before, and his own anticipation of offering such a singular pleasure to any kind of pianist now took over.

216

He called over two workmen and had them pivot the massive piano forward, remove the drop cloths, and open the top with the full prop stick. They pulled over one of the padded benches from the side of the room, and Fazioli rolled back the fall board and motioned to me to take my place at the keyboard. 'Play anything at all. I just want you to feel the keyboard and hear the tone.'

I now remembered what he had said only minutes before about being able to decipher the approach to the piano of those who played in front of him, even gifted artists, merely by observing how they looked at the keyboard. By that standard, I reasoned, he had already determined how tense and hesitant I was. The truth is that I was torn between two wildly contradictory impulses – to flee and to play.

The room was extraordinarily quiet, its floor uncarpeted and the walls unadorned. I realized that the workmen who had moved the piano had not left the area; they stood just outside the open door, a look of anticipation on their faces. If it had been the empty stage before a full house at Carnegie Hall it could not have been worse, but it was very definitely too late to change my mind. I was nine years old and back at the keyboard of Miss Pemberton's Mason & Hamlin for my first recital.

My vision tunneled down to the ten-foot expanse of gleaming strings and hardware that stretched out before me, my fingers formed claws as I tried to extend them. My hesitation, I realized, was looking like the torment of profound reflection that many artists need in order to compose themselves before the explosion of virtuoso fireworks: the longer I waited, the worse things would get. I jumped.

I played a series of arpeggio chords, major to minor, from left to right across the keyboard. My first reaction, an instant after I struck the first notes, was to be startled by the volume and the clarity of the sound. This was nothing like playing the Stingl, even with the top fully open, and it was even appreciably different from the six-foot Bechstein that I played for my lessons with Anna. An enormous

217

quantity of sound was coming back at me, like a wave that had caught me by surprise at the beach, and it was hard to credit my puny efforts with the results that were produced.

After this initial and essentially agreeable shock, though, came the realization that everything I played was so clear that any wrong note, even in the simple harmonic progressions that I was playing, jumped out and proclaimed itself. The tone was extraordinarily powerful and satisfying, but I could only hear my mistakes so that I became preternaturally self-conscious. It was like trying to think yourself through a high-wire act with one eye on the ground below. And the bulk of the thing was phenomenal; it stretched out before me like a limousine or a yacht.

I tried a few scales and the touch was consistent and precise across the entire keyboard. I played some *fortissimo* chords with the sustain peddle and it sounded like an orchestra was in the room with us. And then I stopped, bowled over by its tremendous power and embarrassed that my playing was not equal to its might. The chords continued to resonate in the room as I turned to Fazioli. 'Well,' I said, 'it certainly doesn't lack power.' He nodded with enthusiasm and asked me to continue playing, now that I was warmed up.

I felt a sharp sense of frustration for what might have been. If only I could launch into a late Beethoven sonata with style and grace, give a confident and passionate reading of a score worthy of this matchless piano, then discuss its merits intelligently with the man who built it!

I told Fazioli that I was unprepared to play a piece, but that I had loved the feel and the resonance of his concert grand. I would much rather hear a serious musician at the keyboard, I said, and asked him to play. He hesitated for a moment, but when I got up from the bench he took my place and graciously let me off the hook: 'Playing so large a piano definitely takes some getting used to, especially at full volume.'

With that, he struck the keys with both hands in the opening bars of Chopin's polonaise in C-sharp minor. The result was astounding:

the volume was phenomenal and yet the clarity of tone was in no way compromised. In the highly chromatic passages that followed, the shimmering tones hung in the air for what seemed an eternity as he added layer upon layer of resonance without its ever becoming indistinct or muddy. He was obviously a gifted pianist and he well knew what pieces showed his instrument to best advantage; he played part of a Mozart sonata, then some Schumann and a smattering of Liszt. Each sounded different, yet they all shared a purity of tone that was as sharp as faceted stone. I put one hand on the cabinet as he played and the vibrations passed through me like a controlled earthquake.

Next he told me that he wanted to demonstrate one of the distinctive features of Fazioli concert grands, the fourth pedal that brings the hammers closer to the strings. This makes for a *pianissimo* that is amazingly complex since, unlike the conventional soft pedal which shifts the hammer to the side so it strikes only one string, it allows the hammer to hit all three strings per note in the treble range rather than just one. He began Debussy's *Clair de Lune* and the statement of the theme in the upper range was not just soft, but unaccountably limpid and full of harmonics and overtones. This was something I had never heard before, I thought to myself, as if soft tones had an entirely different quality from what I usually associated with subdued passages.

When he finished, Fazioli got up and told me that I must hear a 308 in a concert hall with good acoustics. As he closed the fall board, it squeaked almost imperceptibly. He raised his hand and motioned for quiet, as if we were listening for a mouse, and then he opened and closed the fall board three times in rapid succession. Each time the faintest squeak broke the nervous silence and his features became a study in disappointment. He called over one of the workmen, repeated the offending gesture, and gave him a look of reproof that was more damning than any specific accusation. 'Remember, it's 'shipping tomorrow,' I heard him say agitatedly in Italian and we left the room where four of these rare pianos, almost as many as leave the factory in a month, awaited their squeakless destiny.

Back in his office, I asked him what was the most important aspect of a piano and he answered without hesitation: 'It's the sound you get when it is played, it's as simple as that. Everything else is in service to that ideal. So it's important to know what sort of sound you want to achieve before you go about building a piano.' He wanted a brilliant, clear and consistent tone, but one that could sustain itself without distortion at high volume. From an engineering point of view, the tone you hear is the combination of the fundamental tone and all of the harmonics that resonate sympathetically at higher frequencies. Getting that balance right is the heart of the piano builder's art.

When a note is struck, we all hear harmonics, higher-pitched multiples of the basic note that resonate much more softly. Generally we are unaware of these subtle tones, but they are an important component in giving a particular kind of piano its distinctive sound. I asked Fazioli if he heard very many of the harmonics and he said that after years of listening he had trained his ear to hear what others could not. Much of his work involved getting the balance right. I wondered why he bothered to make distinctions that others couldn't necessarily appreciate. 'Because it's the right thing to do,' he said. 'But aside from the principle, the fact is that we take into account very many sounds that we don't consciously hear when we form a judgment about the tone a piano produces. Those tones are an important part of what makes a Fazioli sound like a Fazioli. It's a bit like an expert on wine who can taste all the subtleties of a great vintage: you and I don't need to know all of that in order to appreciate an excellent wine, but the winemaker does in order to perfect his art.'

I asked Fazioli what sound he was trying to get. What was the essential idea that made Fazioli pianos distinctive? 'Others will have to say. What we hear is such a subjective experience that I wouldn't presume to make the comparison. Let's just say that my pianos aren't meant to sound like Steinways or Bösendorfers or Yamahas; they sound like themselves, and I know what I want to achieve.'

I noticed on his desk a color photo of the Fazioli 308 that had been sold to the Sultan of Brunei, the 'world's most expensive piano' with a fancy cabinet that was in all the music magazines and that was reputed to have cost three quarters of a million dollars. I mentioned that it was certainly distinctive, and with an impassive look on his face he said that it had been an interesting challenge to embellish a cabinet so richly without compromising its qualities as an instrument.

Then Fazioli reached over to one of the shelves and held up a thin piece of blond wood, about one foot long and three inches wide. He told me that it was a section of the red spruce from the Val di Fiemme that was used to make Fazioli soundboards, and he handed it to me across the desk. '*En souvenir de votre visite*,' he said simply.

I took it and turned it over in my hands, the same light yet supple wood that I had seen in stacks on the factory floor. The growth rings were uncommonly minute and evenly spaced: he had explained the science of why its density and regularity were the optimal medium for transmitting the sounds of a piano, and the visual counterpart of his calculations was plain to see. It was the finest wood that this perfectionist could find for the heart of his extraordinary pianos.

I paused and then I handed it back to him as he was putting on his coat. 'I wonder if you would mind signing this for me?'

At first he looked puzzled, then pleased. He took a felt-tip marker and signed the rectangle of wood with a flourish. 'Think of it as the first step towards owning a Fazioli.'

On the train I took the piece of blond wood out of my satchel, 'Paolo Fazioli' scrawled across one side, and I thought about what lay behind this simple stick of spruce. What to my untrained eye looked like a perfectly finished piece of kindling was in fact the end product of a search that had considered every kind of tree that grew in the earth's forest with one point in mind: what will make the finest soundboard for a piano? This question, and thousands of others like it, had been worked and refined and rethought until their collective answers yielded a new combination of parts. The forest gave its wood, the earth its metal, but the rarest ingredient of all was also the hardest to quantify: the particular form of human genius that designed a new piano.

23

MATHILDE

With our trip to Italy for the Christmas holidays followed by a bad case of the flu that kept me out of circulation, I didn't see Luc for some months. On the one occasion I went by the atelier, I found the metal blinds closed and locked, with a small hand-lettered sign attached to the door: '*Réouverture le 3 février.*' This was unusual as it represented ten days of inactivity at the shop, but I resigned myself to seeing Luc only when things had calmed down for both of us.

In the middle of February I happened to be walking by the atelier one morning and I noticed that the blinds were up. I opened the door with difficulty; it swung open a few inches and then jammed. When I managed to open it wide enough to squeeze through, I saw that a rolled-up rag had been stuck into the narrow space between the bottom of the door and the floor, the standard French solution to the much-feared winter drafts. I closed the door and the little bell attached to the door jamb rang out in the quiet interior. There were no lights on at the front of the shop and it was particularly cold, almost as cold as the midwinter chill that prevailed outdoors. Through the glass door at the rear of the shop I saw movement; Luc let himself through the door, careful not to open it wide and shutting it after him. It reminded me of the way the old man, Desforges, had greeted me when I first came to the atelier and I wondered what it was that Luc was keeping from my eyes.

Luc explained that the electricity was out for what he called 'an unknown reason'. I asked if it was the whole *quartier* that was affected, and he told me that he didn't know since he had slept in the atelier and had not yet been out. This surprised me since I had never known Luc to stay there overnight. I offered to go down a few doors to see if the nearest shop was also blacked out. I walked a few meters down the sidewalk and saw that the plumber's shop window was blazing with light against the winter overcast.

At this news Luc said, 'Then it's only us.' He punched the circuit breaker off and on a few times with no result. He didn't seem particularly concerned; I saw that he was in very good spirits. He settled himself on to the housing of a large electric radiator that he used to heat the front of the shop, explaining that there was still a feeble bit of heat left in it after the current had been cut and he intended to take advantage of it *'par les fesses'* ('by the rear end').

We caught up on each other's doings since we had last met a few months before. I told Luc that I had finally repositioned the infamous *barre stabilisatrice* and that, miraculously it seemed, my piano was no longer resonating strangely. The Stingl was fixed – I had not reduced it to kindling – and all was right with the world. I also mentioned my visit to the Fazioli factory, and he told me that he too had recently been on a trip without specifying his destination. While we talked I noticed that there was movement in the back of the atelier; a shadow moved several times across the glass panel in the closed door. Soon there was the sound of someone playing the piano, a simple melody with a light touch, as if it were being sight-read for the first time. It occurred to me that Luc was being discreet if not exactly secretive and I wanted to avoid being intrusive. He had told me that he had spent the night in the atelier and now it was apparent that he had not been alone. I made as if to leave, but he stopped me. 'What's the hurry? You haven't even heard about our trip.'

I wondered who else figured in the 'our' just as the door to the back of the atelier opened. Mathilde, the woman with long black hair whom I had met a couple of times, came out to the front. She wore a heavy wool duffle coat, its horn buttons all fastened, a scarf, knitted woolen gloves, and a wide band on her head that covered her ears and kept the loose hair from her face. She extended her hand to me, apologizing for the glove. 'When I heard you talking I wasn't sure, but then I recognized your laugh. How are you?'

Luc smiled as she then took his hand in her gloved hands and exclaimed how the fire needed to be stoked. He invited her to climb up on to the radiator cover beside him and she did so without hesitation. In one of her hands she clutched some loose pages of sheet music and she brandished these as she talked. 'I've had it with this repeat. The low F-sharp must be a mistake; it sounds bizarre.' She showed us the note in question and pointed out how in the first statement of the melody it appeared two octaves higher. 'More like a Venetian dirge than a gondolier's song!' She laughed and I saw that 'Barcarolle' was printed across the top of the page.

The best way to tell if the note was wrong was to play it and see what it sounded like, Luc told her. We'd listen and give our opinion. She nodded, handing me the sheet music and putting her arm through Luc's. I wondered how long they had been together, remembering how Luc had been protective and reassuring in that moment months before when Mathilde had been so suddenly dispirited in talking about the piano she had lost in England. Before I could look at the notes she changed the subject: 'Did Luc tell you that we went to England?'

The question took me unawares, as if she had suddenly given voice to my memory of our first meeting. She told me they had gone over on the night ferry to Portsmouth and had had a wonderful trip.

Luc disagreed amiably: 'Well, it was wonderful once we got there. But the Channel in winter is no picnic. After dinner a storm came up and most of the passengers were sick.' He paused as he pondered the image.

Mathilde objected, reminding Luc that they had danced in the bar before it got too rough, but he likened their dancing to mountain climbing, miming the pitch of the boat with his torso. It felt strange to see Luc like this with Mathilde, and pleasurable, too. I had come to regard him as sociable, always welcoming in the atelier, but essentially solitary. Their good-natured badinage showed me another side of him. Clearly the *américain du quartier* was being invited to share in the celebration that was in the air and I was flattered to be included in the sweetness of the moment.

I asked Luc if he had seen any interesting pianos in England. There had been quite a few, he told me, particularly in the bed-and-breakfasts where they had stayed. But the good ones never found their way to France, he reminded me, and besides he had been on vacation. 'I've just come across the piano of my dreams, though. Would you like to see it?'

'Oh, you must hear it, too. *C'est une merveille!*' Mathilde was enthusiastic.

With that they both slid off the radiator cover and led the way to the back. I wondered what would be the piano of Luc's dreams, and I thought of great and rare instruments: a Bösendorfer 'Imperial grand', perhaps, with its nine extra notes in the bass register? An Erard or a Blüthner rarity? Or perhaps a vintage Steinway with a one-of-a-kind art case, richly carved and painted?

When they opened the door I was surprised to find the floor cleared and swept, and an openness and a sense of radiance that I had never before seen in the atelier.

There were only a few pianos set up in the back and little remained of the clutter of paper stacked everywhere with the guts of pianos strewn across the floor. A certain order prevailed; most of the documents were piled on the tops of two uprights in one corner and the pieces of pianos were pushed against the walls in a rough semblance of organization. The perimeter was packed, but the entire center of the space was empty and the effect was inviting, almost luxurious in its expanse. The empty floor amplified the beauty of the light streaming through the glass ceiling. I wondered if this was the effect of a woman's sensibility brought to bear on the chaos of a bachelor's lair.

'*Bienvenu à la guinguette!*' ('Welcome to the dance hall!') Mathilde sang. 'Luc and I danced tangos last night by the firelight!' She twirled in front of the stove in her heavy wool coat.

The fire crackled and sparked in the ugly grey stove. I smiled at the thought of the two of them dancing, creating a dance hall that catered to them alone. I murmured that I had never seen the atelier so empty and Luc jumped in as if on cue: 'Ah, I had to sell things at rock-bottom prices in order to make way for the *guinguette*.'

I asked him if he was burning *les combustibles*. 'I no longer have time for that. When there were two of us in the shop, it was possible; one would remove the usable parts, the other would set about dismantling the cabinet. But now . . .' he raised his palms upwards and shrugged as his voice trailed off. He said that an Erard could require up to two days to take apart – 'They were built to last' – and he no longer had the time or the inclination. 'Besides, you then have to chop every piece of wood to a size that can be put through the *télévision*' – he indicated the oblong opening on the front of the stove – 'and that takes some doing. No, now I'm reduced to ordinary packing crates and kindling.'

I couldn't resist asking if some pianos weren't quick work and he nodded as he remembered. There was one, a Bord upright made in France. Once you had removed the action and the strings, you could literally stand in the empty case, brace your hands against opposite sides and, with a supreme effort, collapse all of the vertical faces so that they fell down flat on the floor around you, like a cardboard packing crate. I conjured a vision of Luc liberating himself from a hollowed-out piano, a strange Samson in an even stranger temple.

Luc strode across the dance floor to a grand piano set up at the back. Its top was propped against it on the floor, and scuffs and chips covered the black casework. The keyboard was open, the bench drawn up, and sheet music lay on the music stand: this was apparently the piano we had heard Mathilde playing earlier. '*Venez voir mon enfant trouvé.*' ('Come see my foundling.') Luc beckoned proudly with a sweep of his hand. It was a full-sized Pleyel grand, a fairly rare model from the twenties. The mechanics had been superbly maintained and the tone, he assured me, was without equal. I thought for a moment about what such praise meant for Luc who had heard every variety of piano imaginable. He invited me to play it so that I could see for myself why he was so enthusiastic and Mathilde encouraged me, too: 'Ah, you'll see, it's like honey.'

I made the usual noises about not being good enough. 'Forget Beethoven and Chopin,' Luc insisted. 'Just play some scales; the thing is to feel the action and to hear the tone.' That was reassurance enough and I realized that I was among friends who would neither judge nor dismiss whatever I played. The Pleyel was suddenly an island in a tranquil sea.

I picked out a tentative scale in E minor, eager to feel both the accidentals and the naturals – the black keys and the whites – beneath my fingers. The touch was extraordinarily light, as if merely breathing on the keys would have depressed them and brought forth music. And this lightness was uniform across the entire keyboard, a sensation I had never before encountered. Even more remarkable was the tone produced: from bass to treble a sweetness coupled with power such as I had never heard from an old piano.

'You see?' Luc said softly when I stopped after a descending scale.

I recalled all of the times that Luc had let me try various pianos in the atelier, and I had to admit that nothing had produced this strange combination of power and clarity. The keyboard had such a fine touch that one felt like an artist just playing scales, I told him.

'And there's another element that really makes this a find,' he said.

This, it turned out, had nothing to do with the sound of this piano, nor with the perfectly balanced keys. It happened that the cabinet of this Pleyel was made of ash, a wood that Luc particularly liked. Ash and beech were commonly used in France for the cabinets of fine grand pianos from this era, but they were invariably lacquered black or veneered with mahogany or rosewood to cover the modest wood. Luc wanted to have a grand piano in unfinished ash, a piano that would combine a perfect mechanism and superlative tone with a unique cabinet. Finding pianos made of ash was not difficult, but getting the paint or veneer off was another matter. This was exceedingly difficult, but the ebony veneer of this Pleyel was badly damaged – loose strips of it hung from some parts of the cabinet – and Luc felt that he would be able to remove it entirely and expose the ash beneath, like peeling bark to reveal the solid core.

'Solid ash is extraordinary!' Luc was enthusiastic. This piano's appeal, he told me, lay partly in its novelty, but mostly it was the look of ash that he liked with its fine grain and inherent strength. Pleyel was particularly renowned for the quality of its woodworking in the era during which this piano was built, and so he was confident that he would find beautiful pieces of wood perfectly joined when he lifted the veneer.

He liked the idea of having a first-rate instrument in a piece of furniture that defied and, in a sense, subverted the conventions of what a grand piano should look like. 'Yes, partly it's to shake up the bourgeois, but there's a lot more to it than that for me.' He referred to ash as 'a noble wood', declaring that it was much underrated both for its strength and its inherent beauty. He told me that ash had often been used in the delicate, load-bearing elements of wagons, for instance, and it could be shaped to curves – essential in a grand piano – without losing its great structural integrity.

'Aren't you in danger of falling in love with too many of the instruments you are meant to sell?' I reminded him that this was the second Pleyel grand piano, after the 'little bruiser', that he had decided to keep for himself since we had first met.

'Ah, but others will use this piano besides me,' he responded. He looked towards Mathilde and they exchanged a glance. Then he rubbed his hands together and shivered, moving back to the stove to warm himself; Mathilde and I both wore coats, but Luc had only a light sweater. As he stirred the fire, we heard the front door open and the delicate ringing of the bell as it was closed. Luc went to greet the visitor and he returned in a moment with an older man wearing a ski parka in incongruously bright colors.

'*On n'a plus de jus*' ('We don't have any juice'), Luc announced, explaining the lack of electricity that was responsible for the dark front office and the piercing cold of the atelier.

The old man looked around him in apparent wonder and he cried out in a surprisingly loud voice, '*Et alors, quoi de neuf? Moi j'ai plus de jus non plus!*' ('So what else is new? I don't have any juice either!') He moved towards the stove. 'Cold is good for pianos,' he exclaimed. 'It's too bad we're not as resistant as these beasts. Miserable human beings, we have to crawl through life wrapped in cloth from head to toe.'

'Not in the tropics,' Mathilde responded and he fixed her with a startled look that turned into a hesitant nod of agreement.

'Well, you've got a point there, young lady. But not one that's of much use to us in Paris, wouldn't you say?' He blew her a puff of smoke in the frigid air as if to underscore his point. As he shuffled over to the Pleyel he grumbled over his shoulder, 'Besides, pianos hate the tropics.'

He asked Luc about the Pleyel, and as he listened to Luc's plans he peered and poked at the exposed insides with the inquisitive persistence of a homicide inspector. He circled the piano and when he returned to the front he looked expectantly at Luc. A nod of Luc's head answered his silent question and he sat down on the bench, a slender gray figure drowned in the bold colors of his ski parka. He pulled back each of the sleeves, paused with his chin on his chest for a split second, and then began to play.

He played a sonata by Domenico Scarlatti that I happened to know from a recording. Technique didn't even occur to me since his was so confident, so apparently flawless that it disappeared and the music came forward. Mathilde, Luc, and I were all leaning against the piano's case. With the top removed we could see every movement of the hammers striking the strings, and a deep resonance came through the wood and entered our bones.

In playing, the old man was changed utterly, transformed from a stooped body with a hesitant gait to a vigorous athlete who addressed the keyboard with a boundless urgency. He was not sitting *at* the piano, he was indivisible from it, his hands and feet striking the keys and pedals with a potent, sinuous force. The piano, too, was transformed. No delicate lines now, no strange decorum about the silent object: this was what it was meant to do.

The tempo was very fast – *presto*, I guessed – but his touch was sure and regular, never frantic, never flagging. On the repeats, especially, he managed to contrast tone, volume, and color so that identical passages seemed wholly new. The turns were unexpected yet not abrupt, like watching a large and beautiful leaf fall slowly to the ground from a great height: the destination was never in doubt, but the sudden changes made a dance of the descent. He became part of that endlessly subtle, witty, and insistent conversation that is music.

Just as suddenly as it began, it was over. Motionless, he held the final chord for a long moment and we felt – I could almost say watched – the harmony rise into the light-filled cold of the atelier. Before any of us could say anything the old man rose abruptly from the bench with a pleased look on his face, slapped the side of the piano, and cried out: '*Et alors, celui-ci, il a toujours du jus!*'

Our delight was spontaneous; Mathilde even clapped her gloved hands. The pianist turned his attention back to the piano,

231

congratulating Luc for such a find, and I realized that this was his particular form of modesty, to deflect attention from his playing. I wanted to talk to him about the sonata, I wanted to thank him, I wanted him to play more, but finally I saw that the sincerest form of homage would be to follow his lead and talk about the instrument. He knew that we knew, and the rest was noise.

Luc and the old man made their way to the stove and warmed their hands briefly, then walked towards the front of the shop talking about some strings the old man needed to buy. At the door to the front he turned to us and inclined his head modestly as he said '*Au revoir*'.

'*Au revoir*,' Mathilde replied. '*Et merci infiniment!*'

He gave a nod of his head, before stepping through the open doorway. Luc and he remained talking in the front of the shop for some time – we could hear the murmur of their voices through the closed door – and Mathilde and I were left alone in the atelier with the newly stoked fire crackling in the silence.

I asked if she knew who the old man was, but she said that she had not met him before nor even seen him. 'I've heard some extraordinary pianists here. What I've learned is not to ask too many questions. If Luc wants you to know something, he'll tell you.' I agreed, intrigued by her plain but very acute reading of his temperament, and we moved over to the stove to warm ourselves. I felt closer to Mathilde somehow, as if we had crossed a hidden barrier together and emerged with a shared sense of the exultation that great music can bring.

It turned out that we both loved Scarlatti, but we seldom had an opportunity to hear any of his works played live; his music was prodigiously difficult and not sufficiently in vogue among the finest pianists who had a technique worthy of his sonatas. But their sheer sonic richness appealed to both of us, explosions of chords followed by intricate runs up and down the keyboard, all of it infused with grace, energy, and a robust wit. Each sonata conjured an original vision with a concentrated tone, as if a landscape artist had chosen the miniature as his medium. We felt a kind of intoxication in the air, an unwillingness to let the moment pass since we knew that we could not conjure another.

It was hard to square this apotheosis with the shabby appearance of the Pleyel's cabinet sitting silent before us in the dust of the atelier. I asked Mathilde if she was looking forward to playing it. 'You know, Luc chose it partly because he felt so badly about the piano I lost in England. When I first played it I felt something powerful, and he said that this could be the spiritual successor to the one I left behind.'

I asked how she had come to lose her piano. I sensed that she wanted to talk about it and I was curious to know the turn of events that had so affected her. Twelve years earlier she had been living in England, in Dorset. A sudden illness sent her back to France in great haste and she had left the piano, an old Pleyel upright which she had played as a girl, in the care of an English acquaintance until she could return. Mathilde was gone longer than she had expected and the person to whom she had entrusted the piano had to leave the area after a few months. She in turn left the piano at the village inn, where they assured her that it would be looked after until its French owner came to claim it.

When Mathilde returned some months later, the inn had changed hands and the piano was nowhere to be found. The new owners claimed never to have seen a piano when they bought the premises. 'You're free to have a look around,' they told her and Mathilde now repeated this in her heavily accented English, her voice heavy with remembered frustration. She had searched the surrounding area – nearby villages, antique and music stores, auctions, even farm sales – but nothing had turned up. No one knew of a French upright piano. And so she had to accept the grim fact of its disappearance, although the matter had never been fully resolved in her mind or in her heart. Her piano had just vanished. She liked to think that it was being used by someone who loved music, but she realized that she would never know.

'It was the family piano. I played it almost every day as a girl and my father played, too. When I left home, my parents made me a gift of it and it was really like a part of them that I had with me wherever I went. When my father died I felt its loss all over again because it had been my constant connection to him and to the music that we shared.'

'It must have been difficult to be back in England in some ways. Were you tempted to take up the search again?'

Her voice became softer and indistinct. 'Just ask Luc. Every time we walked into a pub or a hotel or even a church that had a piano, I had to take a look. But of course, it never showed up.'

What about it was so different, I asked, and she shrugged her shoulders. 'I honestly couldn't say. It's just that it gave me a wonderful feeling when I first played it. It's not logical, of course. For me it's something like the premonition that some animals have when they sense that an earthquake is about to happen. One moment the world is just as you knew it, and then your pulse quickens and everything shifts to another register. If it didn't sound so Catholic, I'd say it was a kind of visitation.' She made an exaggerated sign of the cross in the direction of the Pleyel grand. Her gloved hands gave the gesture a mock liturgical air, but the grace of the movement kept it from being farcical.

The fire was burning down, so we added some pieces of wood and poked the coals to bring forth flames. Mathilde excused herself and I was left alone in the quiet atelier. I could see what Luc saw in her. She had a spontaneous sensitivity, a sense of humor that favored the surreal, and – not least – a deeply personal passion for pianos and their music. When Mathilde returned, she drew close to the stove. 'It's Siberia in the provinces!' she said with a shiver. She'd adopted Luc's habit of calling the unheated bathroom at the back of the atelier '*les provinces*'.

We had long since heard the little bell ring and Luc's muffled goodbyes, signalling the departure of the man who had so unexpectedly played Scarlatti for us. We heard Luc's murmurs for a while longer – he must have been making phone calls – and then it was quiet. He opened the glass-paneled door and joined us in the back, one hand tugging distractedly at his short beard. 'The monks are coming,' he announced. His remark had the desired effect: Mathilde and I exchanged glances of studied perplexity, and she uttered a soft and bright '*Ah bon?*', the universal expression of unflappability in France when one is nonplussed.

Luc explained that he had been on the phone with the Cistercian abbey that made sitars and strings that were also suitable for harpsichords. It seemed that one of the monks was working on a hybrid instrument – part sitar, part Western keyboard – and he wanted to visit the atelier the following week to refine some details of his design and to adapt parts for it. 'They're preparing for a big Mass in April,' he said.

'Ah, the atelier will be the antechamber of the Temple!' enthused Mathilde. 'We'll have fifty couples dance the tango to sitars and pianos combined!'

She moved out on to the empty floor of the atelier and did a pantomime of a tango, all slinky legs and stylized profile, twirling dramatically to a Latin tune she loudly hummed for us. She was remarkably graceful in her bulky coat, scarf, and gloves, and the sight of her vamp was at once seductive and hysterical. Luc and I encouraged her one-woman spectacle by shouting ideas from the wings: 'We'll have a couple dance on top of each piano!' 'With a priest at every keyboard!' 'And monks and nuns will all dance the tango in the mezzanine!'

At this last she stopped her pantomime dead in its tracks and reproved us with a look of betrayal. '*Ça alors, non! Le tango, c'est sacré!*' ('Not that! The tango is sacred!') Her unfolding smile told us that she was fooling, but it was clear that the tango – even within the craziness of our mock theatrics – truly was sacred to her. Still, the vision of a monastic order walking unawares into a Latin bacchanal of tangos and pianos captured our fancy and we continued our joke unchecked, adding detail upon detail, like jazz musicians riffing on a theme. Eventually our giddiness subsided and with it the urgency of the moment. The atelier was once again quiet, an empty space with a few pianos around the edges and the single Pleyel set up at one end. For a few minutes our minds and our voices had filled it to overflowing, and now the spirits withdrew.

24

ANOTHER DREAM PIANO

March was wetter than usual and the incessant cold rain prolonged what had already been a severe winter. Snow flurries made an appearance once or twice, and a series of windstorms blew small branches and a few pieces of roofing zinc down to the streets. For weeks the sidewalks in the neighborhood were strangely empty, like the decks of a ship in a storm, and my walks in the *quartier* were infrequent and shorter than usual. Then towards the end of the month, the day before the vernal equinox, the dark skies vanished as if on cue.

I found myself at home alone one sunny afternoon and I took advantage of the quiet to play the Stingl. It was one of those times when things went well, when my hands seemed to have a momentum of their own on the keyboard and the notes sounded purer than I expected. I had managed to practice regularly for the previous month or so and my lesson earlier in the week had been both challenging and satisfying. The Mozart Adagio that I was working on sounded newly profound and suddenly its complexities seemed within my power. Just for fun I opened the top on the Stingl and the resonance came back at me in waves of sound. It felt as if I had climbed right into the cabinet, the vibrations were so all-enveloping.

Press key, hear sound – the multiplicity of sounds and subtleties, even in my unpolished playing, overwhelmed me all over again. I was astounded to consider that, merely glancing at the score, this phenomenal system of abstraction we call sheet music, gave my hands the means to bring Mozart's thoughts alive. All I had to do was to press the right keys – a challenge, to be sure, but possible – and this deft machine allowed me to encompass the composer's ideas and translate them from the kinetic to the infinite orbit of music.

As the last chords hung in the air and slowly receded, I got up from the bench and looked down into the heart of this ever strange instrument that I owned but would never master. The music mattered, of course – Mozart was Mozart – but I was again struck with how deeply satisfying it was to play any kind of music at all on my piano. Emotionally, physically, intellectually, spiritually: its satisfactions were limitless, its impact on my life profound. I looked at it from across the room and tried to remember when the triangular corner had been empty. It seemed like another lifetime.

Later that day on my way back from the market I ran into Luc and Mathilde, an unusual occurrence since our routines in the *quartier* usually took us in different directions. I noticed them before I recognized who they were, two lovers with arms entwined sharing a kiss as they walked, a familiar enough happenstance on Paris sidewalks. When they looked up we startled each other. Luc teased me about being loaded down 'like a donkey' with grocery bags. We talked for a minute or two and he asked me about the Stingl. '*Et le piano, il chante toujours?*' ('Does your piano still sing?')

I thought of the enjoyment of the late afternoon and nodded. '*Ah, oui, il chante toujours.*'

Mathilde encouraged me to come by the atelier again soon. 'Luc has a new love, an English mini-piano. You must see it.'

Luc nodded as he hugged Mathilde. He told me that it had been made by Eavestaff in the thirties, 'completely British, totally quirky'. It looked like a large radiator, he said, and he was rebuilding it from scratch. Now it was my turn to kid him. 'How many dream pianos can you have, anyway?'

I went through the catalog, surprising myself that the litany of his

238

enthusiasms sprang so readily to mind. There had been the magnificent rosewood Steinway, the one that didn't fit in his house, and then the Pleyel shaped like a harpsichord that he had called 'a little bruiser'. He had made much of the Gaveau with the lemonwood cabinet, the Charles X Erard that he had bargained for without seeing, and then the Gotting's dusty hulk, 'Beethoven's piano'. Now it was a shrunken English keyboard.

Luc took it all in, my mock reproach and the wonder that lay behind it. We stood together on the sidewalk for a silent moment. He looked at Mathilde and then at me, and said simply, 'You can never have too many dream pianos.'

SOURCES

While the scope of this book is neither scholarly nor inclusive, I have relied on the works of others for many of the factual underpinnings of my narrative. There are a lot of books out there about pianos and about Paris, and one of my chief delights has been to wander through the rich fields of this literature. The following works served me as sources and, often enough, as diversions from the work at hand.

For sumptuous pictures of pianos of all sorts, from Cristofori's invention to the modern day, David Crombie's *Piano: A Photographic History of the World's Most Celebrated Instrument* (San Francisco: Miller Freeman Books, 1995) offers a comprehensive look at the piano's evolution in a splendid format. In *The Piano: The Complete Illustrated Guide to the World's Most Popular Musical Instrument* (London: Carlton Books Limited, 1996) Jeremy Siepmann gives an overview of the instrument, its composers and great artists with a text that is always clear and illuminating. David Dubal's *The Art of the Piano: Its Performers, Literature, and Recordings* (New York: Harcourt Brace & Company, 2nd edition, 1995) is a useful compendium of pianists and composers with lists of the recordings available. And for the simplest, clearest description of all the parts of a piano, and how they work together, the indispensable book is Larry Fine's *The Piano Book: Buying & Owning a New or Used Piano* (Jamaica Plain, Ma.: Brookside Press, 3rd edition, 1994).

Beyond the many conversations and interviews I had in Paris, I relied on the series of articles assembled in *Le Pianoforte en France: Ses Descendants Jusqu'aux Années Trente* (Paris: Agence Culturelle de Paris, 1995) to understand various aspects of the piano's history in France. Arthur Loesser's *Men, Women and Pianos* (New York: Dover Publications, 1990) is a comprehensive social history, brimful of facts, where improbable observations and anecdotes bring the players alive. The story of the Steinway family and their meteoric rise to the top is fascinating, and no one tells it better or more thoroughly than Richard K. Lieberman in *Steinway & Sons* (New Haven: Yale University Press, 1995).

I used *The New Grove Dictionary of Music and Musicians* (London: Macmillan, 1980, ed. Stanley Sadie) for many of the facts and dates having to do with piano manufacturers, pieces of music, and composers. I also found it useful for discussions of the fine points of musical terminology. For a lucid and highly readable account of how and why a piano is tuned, I depended upon Otto Funke's *Le Piano, son Entretien et son Accord* (Frankfurt: Edition das Musikinstrument, 1961).

Finally, I'd like to mention two books written by pianists whose approach is entirely different from the more conventional histories. *Piano Pieces* by Russell Sherman (New York: Farrar, Straus and Giroux, 1996) is at once a poetic meditation on the piano's challenges and rewards and a work of deep insight into how to think about playing the piano; it is entirely captivating. Laurent de Wilde's *Monk* (Paris: Gallimard, 1997) is a jazz pianist's appreciation of one of the titans of the keyboard. As only another musician can, he makes real the sparks and then the flame that gave us the genius of Thelonius Monk.